Deviant Justice: The American Gulag
by Lawyer X
First Edition 2013
ISBN 9780961549756
Published by Mindglow Media, New York
Designed and typeset by Tau Ceti One, New Zealand
Edited by Tau Ceti One, New Zealand

Library of Congress Control Number 2013949831

Deviant Justice

The American Gulag

Lawyer X

Dedication

To all victims, past, present, and future,
of preventive detention anywhere.

Disclaimer

This publication is designed to provide accurate and authoritative information with regard to the subject matter covered. It is sold with the understanding that neither the author nor the publisher is engaged by way of this book in rendering legal or any other professional advice. If legal advice or other expert assistance is required, the services of a competent professional person should be sought. The author and the publisher specifically disclaim any liability or loss incurred as a consequence, directly or indirectly, of using or applying any of the information in this book.

Table of Contents

Preface

It is with regret that I feel compelled to write this book under a pseudonym. Because of my background at law, the pen-name I chose is a fair self-appellation.

It is a sad fact of modern mass media, including publishing, that if one writes on a controversial topic, and especially if one's theme runs contrary to established interests, not only will cadres of opponents immediately set about devaluing one's book in the media, but additionally they'll try to discredit the author in every way possible.

Historically such discrediting efforts were confined to questioning the author's academic, professional, or experiential qualifications, or criticizing previously published works as either shoddy scholarship or examples of unsupported extremism. Recently, however, such criticisms have become vitriolic *ad hominem* attacks, crossing the line into the 'politics of personal destruction'. One suddenly discovers private investigators sifting through the trash, professional opportunities suddenly withdrawn, associates' doors closed, unwarranted harassment by everyone from government agents to dogmatic special interest groups, and internet-based smear campaigns suggesting everything up to and including bestiality.

In particular, those who dare to 'speak truth to power' quickly find themselves on a short list of enemies, against whom any form of retaliation for their published writings is fair game. In the context of a field typically evoking strong emotional reaction, these underhanded tactics sink to new depths of contemptible villainy and record heights of prevalence. I simply refuse to throw myself to such jackals. I am not the issue; this book addresses the issue. Let's stick to it.

Against this backdrop of win-at-any-cost incivility, I worry for the future of meaningful public discourse in our country, and in the rest of the English-speaking world. Frankly, you should too.

I have labored diligently in the research and writing of this book to ensure its correctness and accuracy. Realizing the urgency of publication while the topic remains in the collective mind of the public, I have worked in great haste. As a result, some aspects of this book's organization have suffered, and instances of technical problems with the writing will be apparent. I ask the reader's forbearance on such superficial defects. It is the facts that count, after all.

And what facts!

Those unfamiliar with sex offenses and sex offenders will find this entire work to be like stepping through the looking glass, only to find that the other side is also part of our reality. But even those with some knowledge will, I'm confident, be stunned by at least some of the revelations herein. Many who read the following pages will come away with a surprising 'everything-you-know-is wrong' epiphany.

So welcome, my friends, to the truth, which, if less than pleasant, will always set you free.

Introduction

This is not a book about sex crimes or atypical sexual attractions or interests. If you seek to be titillated or horrified about such matters, this book is not for you. Nor is it collectively or individually about those who have committed sex crimes, except insofar as necessary to illustrate a point about the topic at hand: 'civil commitment' of sex offenders. I place the term 'civil commitment' in quotes here to emphasize that nothing about commitment of sex offenders shares anything in common with what one normally thinks of as civil commitment of anyone else.

Traditional civil commitment was directed at individuals who suffered episodic loss of contact with reality — delusions so engrossing that their ability to function personally and socially was totally disrupted, including matters as crucial as the ability to safely cross a street; or who suffered from pathological urges to destructive actions, either against themselves, other people, or someone's property (the proverbial 'homicidal maniac', for instance).

Granted, this could include irresistible impulses to commit a sex crime. However, the focus in traditional commitments was not so much on the particular type of act that would be committed, but rather, on the immediacy or imminence of the irresistible act and the powerfully driving urge that made the feared act imminent. Only those who were indisputably under such irresistible impulses were subjected to commitment.

In contrast, in the twenty states that have any kind of current sex offender commitment laws on the books, although words like 'impulse' and 'urge' are used, they mean any motivation, no matter how abstract, attenuated, and strictly confined to fantasy a sexual thought or desire might be. Thus, there is no limitation to immediate or imminent sex crimes and no requirement of true irresistibility of such sexual motivations. Indeed, so-called 'expert' forensic psychological testimony at sex offender commitment trials will often include an assertion (stated with a perfectly straight face) that the individual in question will be somewhat likely to commit a sex crime sometime between ten years into the future and the end of that person's lifespan.

In another contrast, traditional commitments not only require a finding of a specific mental illness, but also focus on its causation of the 'dangerous to others' status (where it exists). But in the case of sex offender commitments, no mental illness is required. In fact, to facilitate such commitments, psychiatrists have invented definitions of mental states called 'disorders'. Some of these merely restate the fact of a sex offender's particular crime, while others lapse into boundless vagueness (such as, 'antisocial personality disorder' — often panned as being nothing more than 'jerk syndrome').

In truth, all of this is simply excuse-making for refusing to release convicted sex offenders once they have reached the end of their prison sentences. This is done, not out of any reasonable fear that any of them will commit another sex offense immediately following prison release, but instead out of fear that, eventually — perhaps many years or even decades later, they might do so.

Contrary to a cultural myth propagated by those with something to gain by spreading fear and hatred, the reality is that, as a class, sex offenders have nearly the very lowest rate of committing new sex crimes after release from prison, as compared to recidivism rates of prison releasees who committed other types of crimes for a later crime of the same type as their conviction. Therefore, in order to justify such commitment of a given sex offender, forensic 'expert' witnesses must come up with all manner of hair-splitting distinctions and exceptions in an attempt to cast the targeted sex offender as 'highly likely' to reoffend, with a 'substantial difficulty' in restraining himself from doing so. The fact that such distinctions and exceptions are either subject to great scientific disagreement, or simply have no basis in science at all, doesn't appear to bother these 'hired character assassins' or the judges who accept their every word as if stone tablets delivered by the hand of God.

All in all, judges and other participants in this judicial system of sex offender commitments know full well that these opinions and prognostications by such 'experts' are merely prostitution of the psychiatry and psychology profession, and that such testimony is merely the plausible rationalization for predetermined judicial will: preventive detention for an indefinite term and, by the numbers, probably for the remainder of that sex offender's life.

One purpose of this book is to expose preventive detention for being just that, despite meaningless claims to the contrary of release-through-treatment. We will closely examine actual sex offender recidivism rates, and take in a quick overview of the history of sex offender commitment. We'll also describe the prison-like conditions of confinement of committed sex offenders, and outline the ways in which civil commitment trials of sex offenders differ from the constitutional protections governing criminal trials, such that one being tried for such commitment may as well be hogtied and gagged. We will point to cases illustrating how utterly outrageous the commitment process is, including the extreme way in which the legal standards for such commitment are applied in practice by courts, leaving the defendant defenseless. We will describe the impossibility of predicting anyone's future with any accuracy whatever. We will cover the approaches that have been advanced by prosecution experts to justify commitment, including the latest method of creating fear of recidivism by the specific defendant, based only on the recidivism of other sex offenders. And we will confront the argument that a person's past is the best prediction of his future, as a 'sounds logical' yet baseless fallacy.

A second aim of this book is to highlight the surreal 'chutes and ladders' process of so-called treatment in sex offender commitment facilities, not serving to actually ready anyone for release, but rather as a means to thwart release. And we will consider the frustration of treatment 'refuseniks' in such facilities who know futility when they behold it. We'll also discuss the bureaucracy and the politics that ensure that commitment for treatment really means permanent detention. And we will discuss the toxic role of anti-sex offender fanatics that have thoroughly infiltrated into such commitment facilities, claiming to hold out treatment as a hope of release, while politically advocating behind the backs of their charges against any release — ever.

A third objective of this book is to point out the utter lack of necessity for such permanent preventive detention, or even for sex offender commitment at all. In this, we will examine the impossibly high bar set to qualify an offender for release from commitment. We will also consider an approach that actually works well to prevent sex offense recidivism before commitments, and look closely at the unfortunate but rare tragedies of violent, recidivistic sex crimes that were seized upon as supposed rationales for commitment, and we will confront the unreality of a 'perfect world' wishful thinking that also has been manipulated to garner support for commitment of sex offenders.

Last, we will consider the future at law, particularly under the U.S. Constitution, of sex offender commitment, as its true, preventive-detention nature emerges more clearly with each passing year. In addition to the possible resurrection of 'as-applied' claims of denial of 'substantive due process' as one means to attack such commitment, we will also discuss a long-overlooked, but more direct means to confront and overturn such preventive detention: its true nature as a 'bill of attainder', something our Founding Fathers thought they had done away with forever some two-and-a-quarter centuries ago.

It is the author's fervent hope that the reader will come away with a realization of the unjust, immoral and wasteful boondoggle (at great public expense) that is sex offender commitment, quietly opening the trapdoor to a steep and very slippery downward slope into a dark abyss of totalitarianism where, like *1984* and *Minority Report*, individuals of any class can be detained indefinitely or forever, not for any crime but just for 'dangerous' thoughts or emotions.

Foreword

There are so many things wrong with 'civilly committing' sex offenders who have served their time and are otherwise about to be released, that it's difficult just to compile a list of unfair, wrongheaded, vengeful and contemptible things about it. Nonetheless, this work will undertake to do just that, and to explore in detail each aspect of this abomination unto American law.

To find out why sex offender commitment laws were a 'feel good' con game perpetrated on the American electorate, and why all such laws should be repealed immediately, read on. Got a particular interest? Just pick from any of the topics listed in the Table of Contents.

Big Lie No 1 —
"Sex Offender Recidivism Is Nearly 100%!"

To borrow a Nicholas Cage line, "No, no, no!". Not only is this hysteria-producing lie false, it is 180° opposite from the truth. In a pithy summary, Prof. Wayne A. Logan, in "Sex Offender Registration and Community Notification: Past, Present and Future", 34 New England Journal on Criminal & Civil Confinement 3, at 15 (Winter, 2008), notes:

> "... [T]he perception repeatedly parroted in legislative findings ... [is] that sex offenders recidivate at a far greater rate than other sub-populations ... [W]e now know this to be untrue."

In fact, as Prof. Logan continues at Footnote 46:

> "[I]t is well established that ... persons convicted of most serious sex offenses do not recidivate at higher rates than those convicted of less serious offenses.".

In fact, studies conducted by the U.S. Dept. of Justice and various states show that, on average, the percentage of sex offenders committing a new sex offense after leaving prison ranges from 5% to 15%. Indeed, large, long-term studies in both California and Minnesota discovered that sex offender recidivism most recently was a mere 3.2% (*Sex Offenders Unlikely to Commit Second Crime*, New Scientist, Vol. 19, Issue 26, p. 6-6 [7/5/2008]) See: Minnesota Department of Corrections, *Sex Offender Recidivism in Minnesota* (April, 2007) — hereinafter, *MN DOC Sex Offender Recidivism Report*).

That Minnesota report on recidivism is worth scrutiny. While the foregoing percentages were for short periods, that study had an 8.4 year average follow-up time period as to released offenders (Id., p. 5).

Contrary to false assertions that recidivism cumulates on a straight-line probability basis over long post-release periods, the Minnesota study found that "... the longer offenders are in the community, the more likely they are to remain crime free" (Id, p. 4). More specifically, study results revealed that "... [o]f the offenders who recidivated sexually, most reoffended within the first five years" (Id., p. 20). Indeed, comparing the 5-year to the 10-year sex re-arrest rates in Table 1 (ibid.), this conclusion is rather conservatively stated. Since only a 2% difference exists between those numbers, it is fair to conclude that, with only statistically insignificant later reoffending, almost all sexual reoffending occurs within the first five years post-prison-release, if at all. This contradicts claims that 20-year or longer extrapolations of chances of recidivism must be considered in sex offender commitments.

Most significantly, the MN DOC Sex Offender Recidivism Report found that a tremendous drop in 3-year post-release sex-crime reconviction rates occurred between sex offenders released in 1990 (16.7%) and those released in 2002 (2.5%). That drop was paralleled across the board by figures for re-arrest and for re-imprisonment for sex crimes.

Noting that both length and the intensity of post-release supervision of sex offenders in Minnesota had greatly increased in that same period, that report concluded that ... "[t]he reduction in sexual recidivism since 1990 is likely due, in part, to the longer and more intense post-release supervision of sex offenders" (Id., p. 3).

Indeed, so intensely and conscientiously is that new close supervision of sex offenders performed that release supervision violations rose from 11% during 1990 to 56% during 2005 (Ibid.). Excluding violations based on instances of recidivism, the net increase in release revocations due to purely 'technical' violations has been enormous. Although some technical violations have nothing to do with tendencies toward recidivism, other types of technical violations do. As that report states:

> "... [W]hen sex offenders are placed on ISR [Intensive Supervised Release], they are continuously supervised by a team of three to five supervision agents, whose caseloads are capped at 15 per state law. During all four phases of ISR, offenders are required to maintain steady employment, comply with random alcohol and drug testing, and are subjected to unannounced face-to-

face contacts with their supervision agents at both their residence and place of work. Further, offenders must remain on ISR until they successfully complete all four phases of the program, or until they reach the expiration of their sentence.

"...[P]rior to committing their crimes, [sex] offenders frequently engage in behaviors such as consuming alcohol or drugs, viewing pornography, associating with minors, 'grooming' their victims, and so on. However, *the increased length and intensity of supervision may not only deter offenders from engaging in this type of pre-offense behavior, but it also increases the likelihood that supervising agents will detect this behavior when it does occur.* The enhanced detection afforded by longer, more intensive supervision has led to a marked increase in supervised release revocations. But *it may also have enabled supervision agents to revoke offenders before they fully relapse and have an opportunity to re-offend sexually.*" (Id., pp. 33-34; emphases added).

Thus, a very persuasive argument exists that release revocations based on those types of technical violations have been an important tool toward averting sex offense recidivism.

This being so, and considering the intensity of round-the-clock monitoring of sex offenders' whereabouts and activities, one may well ask what need exists, beyond all this, for civil commitment of sex offenders.

The only rejoinder to this is the contention that those committed are so obsessed with, and compelled to recidivistic sex offenses that they will succeed at evading all of those restrictions and requirements (including 'house arrest' provisions) and promptly commit another sex offense.

To respond to this rejoinder, let's consider the following.

The Minnesota Sex Offender Program (MSOP), to which all sex offenders civilly committed in Minnesota are relegated, asserted in a report to the state legislature in January, 2011, that only MSOP could give committed offenders sufficient treatment to prevent re-offense, on the implicit premise that otherwise each of those detainees is 100% certain to re-offend sexually (Minnesota Sex Offender Program, *Options for Managing the Growth and Cost of the Minnesota Sex Offender Program: Facility Study* — hereinafter, MSOP Report, Jan. 2011, pp. 15–18). However, psychologists testified at the respective commitment trials of virtually everyone committed to that program to the effect that each of those detainees had far lesser re-offense probabilities.

Still more than this, an examination of who is actually getting committed belies the preposterous nature of that rejoinder. Truly impulsive, obsessed sex offenders are the very rare exception; most of those who have committed a sex crime have little or no desire to repeat that experience, and they are as far removed from notions of 'impulsive' or 'obsessed' about matters of sex as one can imagine.

That Minnesota DOC Sex Offender Recidivism Report also cites three other factors of note that may well have contributed to reduction in sexual recidivism. First, 'Police investigation and prosecuting practices', as greatly enhanced and intensified over the last 20 years as to sex crimes, and particularly as now so easy to connect to anyone with a sex crime(s) record, serve as a powerful deterrent due to the high probability of detection and apprehension.

Second, community notification laws everywhere, including a very thorough provision in Minnesota, rating sex offenders by 'risk level' and applying the most comprehensive community notification measures to the top-risk-level releasees, probably serves, through such `spotlighting', to further deter sex crimes by releasees.

Third, "[e]xisting research has demonstrated ... that cognitive-behavioral treatment in the community significantly reduces the risk of sexual recidivism" (Id., pp. 34-35).

Hence, in light of these deterrent effects, and the successful effect of community-based treatment of sex offenders, in addition to the superb work on the part of supervised release agents (supra), committing sex offenders who otherwise are subject to all of the above is redundant, draconian and overwhelmingly expensive, compared to the surprisingly low cost of even the most intense post-release supervision (more on this comparison, infra). In short, commitment holds no necessity whatsoever.

Concluding this point, that report summarizes: "Finally, due to the dramatic decrease in sexual recidivism since the early 1990s, recent sexual re-offense rates have been very low, thus significantly limiting the extent to which sexual re-offending can be further reduced" (Id., p. 4). Note further that all sex offense recidivism records were included in this study's figures. This excludes the impact of commitment from the recidivism percentages in this report for offenders released and only later committed (as prompted by a recidivistic crime, for instance).

It is not a perfect world, nor is it likely to be so in the foreseeable future. In this connection, it must be borne in mind that commitment is nothing more than an attempt to continue incarcerating those thought most likely to recidivate (but bearing in mind that predicting any individual's future accurately is not within the limits of science). But since sex offender commitment cannot end sexual recidivism, and since that Minnesota DOC Sex Offender Recidivism Report thus concludes that such intensive post-release supervision is already reducing sex crime recidivism to the lowest achievable levels — apart from any impact by commitment of sex offenders, commitment of sex offenders is superfluous, as well as highly dubious crystal-ball-gazing.

This is true even calculating in all sex offenders with more than one sex offense and those who had already committed a sex offense and who had gone to prison for it before later committing their current offense. Even the claim that such former recidivistic sex offenders are more likely than not — i.e., 51% or more — to commit yet another sex crime is a 'fallback lie': a lie resorted to when the first lie proves untenable.

All this lying started when politicians discovered in the 1970s that legislative and other governmental careers could be made by terrorizing the country, by suggesting that lathering sex maniacs were lurking behind every bush, just waiting to pounce on all defenseless women and children. If, after all these years, you still believe that, give yourself the Most Sustained Gullibility Award, and prepare yourself for an epiphany.

The other fact those politicized con men discovered is that, apart from distant academia, no one countered those lies. Certainly, sex offenders did not rise in defense of themselves or their kind. This, of course, becomes understandable when one realizes that many were already imprisoned, and thus were only dimly aware of this campaign to instill paranoia and were without any research resources to refute those lies. Those not imprisoned — understandably — chose to remain silent from a wish to avoid personal attention in the news media.

Once the 'hysteria bandwagon' was under way, the con men also realized that voices of reason and truth from opposing legislators could easily be silenced by suggesting, as electioneering propaganda, that any given legislator seeing and willing to oppose insane measures was 'soft on sex offenders', or worse, was 'the sex offenders' friend'. Opposition to even the most radically extreme, utterly senseless legislation against sex offenders — even against anyone merely accused of a sex crime — dried up overnight.

Thus, this crazed juggernaut of hysteria and loathing has rolled on to this very day, some 35 years later.

Section One

Where We Are

Chapter 1

How Did We Get Here?

In the early part of the 20th Century, many states enacted what were termed 'sexual psychopath' laws. These operated in the same manner as civil commitment laws for those suffering from mental illnesses as serious as paranoid schizophrenia or catatonia. Such laws were applied to those who committed particularly heinous sex crimes (usually those coupled with violence) on a compulsive basis. These criminals were deemed to be 'too sick' to benefit from the supposedly 'rehabilitative', or at least the personally deterrent effect of a prison sentence. Instead, as an alternative to being criminally charged or sentenced to prison, those deemed 'psychopathic' were immediately committed to the same 'security hospitals' as other violent mentally ill persons. However, by the 1980s, most of those sexual psychopath commitment laws had either been repealed as unnecessary or had fallen into disuse, in favor of then more certain and greatly lengthened prison sentences for all sex offenders.

> "But a handful of horrific and highly publicized cases in the 1980s and '90s spurred lawmakers to act again. Washington State adopted the first sex offender civil commitment law in 1990 after men with predatory histories killed a young woman in Seattle and sexually mutilated a boy in Tacoma.
>
> "After state courts upheld Washington's law, Kansas, Minnesota and Wisconsin passed versions in 1994, followed by California in 1996.
>
> "Then, in a 5–4 decision in 1997, the United States Supreme Court found civil commitment to be constitutional in Kansas v. Hendricks"
>
> *Monica Davey & Abby Goodnough,*
> *'Doubts Rise as States Hold Sex Offenders after Prison',*
> *New York Times, March 4, 2007, p. Al.*

In Kansas v. Crane, a case five years later, the U.S. Supreme Court clarified the limit of the Due Process Clause of the U.S. Constitution on who can be committed under such new sex offender commitment laws of broader coverage than the former 'psychopath' laws. In Crane, the high court declared that in order to be committed, not only must one be proved to still be dangerous and likely to sexually reoffend, but he must also show "serious difficulty in controlling behavior".

While this might seem a laudable or at least reasonable limitation, we shall see later that those words have been applied to such an endless array of supposed evidence claimed to support the conclusion of 'serious difficulty' that the meaning and impact of the limitation have been washed away. Following Hendricks, a wave of national legislation followed, ultimately culminating in raising the total to 19 states having sex offender commitment laws. In addition, the federal government enacted its own such law, applicable to federal prisoners. This last law's effect will be examined later

The Current Status

At present, most sex offenders nationwide who are subject to these new commitment laws have completed their prison terms and thereby earned their release. Most of them would have been placed on some form of parole under the continuing supervision of correctional authorities. In an increasing number of states, such as Minnesota, parole supervision of sex offenders has been greatly lengthened and has become far stricter, with close monitoring and even near-constant surveillance by specialized parole agents.

Nonetheless, as of 2008, nearly 4,000 sex offenders had been committed under these laws. Among the states with such laws, their utilization has varied dramatically. Some populous states, such as California (with the most: 703 committed by 2008), resort to such laws more in total. But idiosyncratically, many smaller, less-populous states, such as Minnesota (with over 600 now under commitment), use their versions of such laws with obsessive aggressiveness, with obvious political motivations.

The 'Junk Science' Used to Commit Sex Offenders

Catering to political misuse of sex offender commitment is the fact that the techniques used by forensic psychologists are effectively no more than 'junk science'. This will be examined in much greater detail later, but for the moment let's glance at the only tool for sex offense recidivism prediction beyond subjective impressions, the so-called 'actuarial risk analysis' (ARA) 'instruments'.

This approach uses risk analysis 'instruments' (RAIs), which are simply questionnaire-based worksheets, on which to compile facts deemed relevant to likelihood of sexual reoffense after prison release. Such facts include the offender's age at release, the number of past episodes of sexual offending, degree of violence involved, etc.

Answers to these questions are assigned a numerical score each (usually 0–4), and all such scores are totaled. An accompanying table listing percentages of probability of sexual reoffense over a given future period is provided, ranking increasing percentages for each ascending score range. These percentage ranges were derived from the past experience of a 'control group' of sex offenders released as many as 40 years ago.

Even so, one of the problems with such RAIs is that those control groups are often so small as to be statistically insignificant. Another problem is that, even with some extra weight assigned to certain answers' individual scores, it remains possible to arrive at any given total score in many different ways involving high scores to different questions on the RAI.

This accentuates inaccurate predictions due to inapplicability of the disparate experiences and motivational states of other sex offenders, compared to the one being rated on the RAI. The inaccuracy of each of the current RAIs is truly astounding, rendering their use in a decision on potentially lifetime preventive detention infamous.

> "Scientists who examine the validity of two popular risk assessment tools reported last year in the British Journal of Psychiatry that at best 'professionals should be extremely cautious', and at worst 'should avoid using [such tools] altogether, as the predictive accuracy of these tests may be too low [for] high-stakes decisions about individuals'.
>
> "Dr. Michael Farnsworth, the former forensic psychiatrist [at the Minnesota Security Hospital], designed [its sex offender commitment treatment program]. But he doesn't place much confidence in actuarial tools.
>
> "'They still have a high rate of false positives and a pretty good rate of false negatives', Farnsworth said. 'With the false negatives, there will still be people who offend against the community, and the public will feel betrayed. Conversely, with the false positives, we lock up the wrong people', at a cost of $134,000 each year."
>
> *Larry Oakes, "They're All Close Calls Now," Star Tribune, June 8, 2008, p. Al*

Psychologists such as Rosemary Linderman who testify in support of sex offender commitments often cite public danger as a reason not to be concerned over such inaccuracies, or over the dramatic rise in such commitments in Minnesota from 2003 to date.

> "[However, St. Paul psychologist John] Austin said [that] spike [in such commitments] is troubling. 'I am unaware of any data that indicates that sex offenders

released since 2003 are at a greater risk to reoffend sexually,' said Austin, adding that a 2007 Minnesota Department of Corrections study 'seems to indicate the opposite, in fact'.

" '... The reduction is sexual recidivism since 1990 is likely due, in part, to the longer and more intense post-release supervision of sex offenders,' the study concluded." *Larry Oakes, ibid.*

Who Are We Committing, and Why?

Particularly troubling is who is being committed. One focus of those who wield commitment authority is older sex offenders. Often, they have served long prison terms, resulting in almost all of their friends and their own families forgetting all about them. Hence, these offenders have no supportive advocates, and are thus politically powerless — a truly vulnerable pick, even though statistics uniformly say that age is the most powerful factor for reduction (indeed, extinction) of sex offense recidivism.

Yet in Wisconsin, for instance, one of those committed is 102 years old, and cannot participate in treatment due to memory loss and poor hearing. In another example, the same Leroy Hendricks of that U.S. Supreme Court case was 59 years old when he was committed, and is now 78 — and still not effectively released. He is forced to live on the grounds of the commitment facility, an isolated location.

> "Sex offenders selected for commitment are not always the most violent, some exhibitionists are chosen, for example, while rapists are passed over ...
>
> "More often, these cases come down to contentious duels between psychologists over how best to analyze an offender's history and likelihood of repeating crimes ...
>
> "The results of the screening process are inconsistent. Some offenders are passed up for civil confinement, only to commit vicious crimes again; others' physical ailments alone make them unlikely repeat predators.
>
> *(M. Davey & A. Goodnough, ibid.)*

In the same article, the authors go on to say that prosecutors in Florida sought commitment of a man who had not been arrested for a sex offense for decades. Meanwhile, in Minnesota, prison staff categorized Alfonso Rodriguez, Jr. a rapist, as one of those most likely to commit more crimes. Yet Rodriguez was not committed, instead being released in May, 2003 at the end of his prison term. Later that year, he kidnapped, beat, raped, and killed Dru Sjodin, a college coed.

Davey and Goodnough further point out that in a similar case in 2006, Jerry Buck Inman, having finished up a Florida prison term for rape, but not committed then, went to South Carolina and raped and strangled a coed. Opinions obviously differ among reviewing psychologists.

The authors conclude that emotional reactions and political considerations obviously place heavy thumbs on the scales in deciding who to commit. Commitment verdicts reached by elected local judges or juries are almost always impacted by the emotionally raw details of a given offender's sex-crime history and public furor over media attention to it.

> "A cottage industry of professionals who diagnose sexually violent predators has developed in the last two decades, and several hundred psychologists, often with little or no background treating sex offenders, make a lucrative business of recommending who should be committed ...
>
> "'I don't think, in my personal experience, that the vast majority of the examiners I've come across have sufficient working knowledge of the empirical literature,' said Dr. Prentky of the Justice Research Institute.
>
> "But that literature is still of limited use. Most actuarial tools used to predict someone's risk of recidivism consider only unchanging factors, like their number of past offenses — how much treatment an offender gets, for example, and how old he has grown — should factor heavily into actuarial risk assessment too."
>
> *M. Davey & A. Goodnough, "For Sex Offenders, Dispute on Therapy's Benefits:..." New York Times, March 6, 2007, p. Al*

Thus, overall, it should be very clear: selection of certain sex offenders for commitment, including commitment trials themselves, are rife with political considerations and loaded with below-the-belt blows, and rank appeals to decision by sheer emotional reaction. This is a far cry from the American paradigm of dispassionate justice and due process of law. Indeed, the last section of this book makes the case that sex offender commitment, as actually practised, is something so long not seen in Anglo-American law that it predates the American Revolution: a 'bill of attainder'.

Chapter 2

Treatment — An Endless Series of Unscientific Experiments

'What's to Treat?'

'Treatment' of sex offenders is itself more of a political meaning than a truly therapeutic effect.

> "The American Psychiatric Association, National Association of State Mental Health Program Directors, and other groups have objected to civil commitment of criminals. They argue that most aren't mentally ill and that using mental health systems in this way discredits both psychiatry and the justice system.
>
> "The problem, critics say, is that disorders such as antisocial or narcissistic personality, which have been used under the Sexually Dangerous Persons Act [Minnesota] to justify commitments of offenders, are prevalent in any group of criminals and not unheard of in non-criminals.
>
> "'Using that standard, you could commit a lot of bank robbers,' said Dr. Fred Berlin, founder of the Sexual Disorders Clinic at Johns Hopkins University and a critic of civilly committing sex offenders. 'It can be a slippery slope.' "
>
> *L. Oakes, 'They're All Close Calls Now, supra*

Treatment Problems in General — a Sampler

Indeed, only a small fraction of committed sex offenders have ever completed treatment to the point where they were released to the satisfaction of commitment facility treatment staff.

Davey and Goodnough in their March fourth article point out that treatment of sex offenders in commitment is highly problematic and go on to cite the following problems.

The overarching question that still haunts the field without definitive answer is whether treatment really results in reduced recidivism by sex offenders? The very nature of therapy varies drastically from commitment facility to facility, most often a mix of different 'regimens/modalities' administered concurrently or in sequence. The fact that combinations of these unproven, expensive regimens find little agreement among the commitment facilities shows the uncertainty of what sex offender treatment really is.

Hours of treatment vary greatly among commitment states. Nationwide, the average over all such facilities is less than ten hours per week - less than one third of the 31.5 hours weekly promised in Kansas v. Hendricks to induce the Supreme Court to OK commitment.

The most commonly used and longest-accepted treatment regimen for sex offenders is "relapse prevention." (See discussion concerning Dr. Farnsworth, post.) In relapse prevention, it is deemed therapeutically critical for the offender to admit all previous crimes. However, this includes uncharged crimes, even those previously unknown to police. Consequently, attorneys often advise committed sex-offender clients not to participate in treatment. And indeed, those committed cannot be forced to attend treatment sessions.

Nor does treatment lead reliably to release, and release is the clear exception, rather than the rule. Among all committing states, only 250 offenders have been released. Of these, half achieved release purely on legal or technical grounds rather than treatment success. In Iowa, 9 sex offenders have been released unconditionally, but none through treatment completion or through the facility's recommendation for release.

Thus, it is no wonder that there is no strong motivation to participate in treatment in such facilities. In California, for instance, only ¼ of committed sex offenders participate in treatment. Around the country, those who don't participate in therapy spend their time instead watching TV, playing video games, gardening, and in other pastime activities.

Even so, daily life in sex offender commitment facilities closely resembles that in prisons. Cell doors are often locked overnight, for instance, and all mail is restricted and searched by staff.

The Folly of 'Relapse Prevention'

It is Counterproductive When Applied to Sex Offenders

There is no convincing evidence that the relapse prevention treatment method works with sex offenders or, indeed, that any other method does either.

> "Similar to aspects of Alcoholics Anonymous, relapse prevention has sex offenders own up to wrongdoing and resign themselves to a lifelong day-to-day struggle with temptation. But one of the few authoritative studies

of the method, conducted in California from 1985 to 2001, found that those who entered relapse prevention treatment were slightly *more* likely to reoffend than those who got no therapy at all."

A. Goodnough & M. Davey,
"For Sex Offenders, Dispute on Therapy's Benefits",
New York Times, March 6, 2007, p. Al;

The outcome of that California study corroborated an earlier study that culminated in a 1997 report of the Minnesota Department of Corrections to the state legislature on recidivism, conceding that sex offense recidivism was measured at 11 percent among those who did not have treatment in prison, but at 12 percent among those who did. In those mid-1990s years, sex offender treatment in Minnesota prisons was centered firmly on the relapse prevention method.

When one considers 'relapse prevention' a little more closely, it is no surprise that it was a failure when applied to sex offenders in general.

It is Tied to Anti-Sexuality

An example of the utter poppycock used in 'relapse prevention': a post-release treatment program at Pure Life Ministries in Kentucky, whose website says its goal is "leading Christians to victory over sexual sin" *(A. Goodnough & M. Davey, ibid).* Any so-called treatment program that confuses therapy with anti-sexuality sums up the corrupted folly of its underlying theory.

Sex Is Not an Addiction

Unlike alcoholism or nicotine, the behavior of sex offenders is not an addiction. In the lifetimes of all individuals, some more than others, sex is at times experienced as a powerful emotional attraction, both to certain types of persons and certain desired interactions, or to certain auto-sexual behaviors (masturbation or fetishes). It is only socially collective shame in Anglo-American society in particular, and in the Judeo-Christian and Islamic worlds more generally, that creates the false conceptualization of 'sexual addiction'.

'Irresistible Sexual Impulse' Is a Cultural/Political Myth

Even in this modern age, there remains a strong tendency, arising from individual perception from childhood on, for such collective social shame and taboo about matters of sexuality, especially anything out of the ordinary (the true meaning of 'deviant', incidentally). Arising from this, there is a strong sense of personal privacy, even secrecy, as to matters of sexuality, especially as to experienced desires and actions.

As was once sensed personally by a broader swath of Americans in the days before gay liberation, the more one's orientation and desire depart from the mainstream in society, the more intense that perceived need for secrecy about matters of one's own sexuality. Within such secrecy, there is a natural tendency to focus upon, and thereby to assign a sense of greater strength to, one's sexual desires.

This sense of greater strength is not addiction, nor is it an 'impulse' or internal compulsion. To call it such is actually to make the grave mistake of making a sex offender believe that it is an irresistible force, or one that at best, can only be resisted with great constant struggle. While this is untrue, such suggestions can have an self-fulfilling-prophesy effect, especially when voiced by surrounding treatment staff and other treatment participants — just like any other form of successful suggestion; in this case, by an overbearing brainwashing rather than by overt hypnosis. This is probably the most adverse aspect of the relapse prevention approach.

Dr. Farnsworth's Background as Origin of the 'Relapse Prevention' Misapplication

It is understandable that Dr. Farnsworth, who came from a background at the Minnesota Security Hospital, would have held this preconception. At that facility, for instance, he had occasion to study and to work with, among others, some of Minnesota's most completely addicted alcoholics.

More to the point, the tiny number (never more than 30) of sexual 'psychopaths' committed in Minnesota also wound up in Dr. Farnsworth's care. Let's disregard for the moment the disconnect between legal definitions employed in that commitment process and true indications of actual mental illness; the fact remains that these individuals had engaged in the most horrific sex crimes, had the most intractable views that their inhumanly violent misconduct was acceptable (in some cases, misperceived by them as morally mandatory), and by frank admission were bound to reoffend with equal or perhaps even worse severity, immediately upon release.

In this context, it's little wonder that Dr. Farnsworth came to misconceive that this group of committed psychopaths had mental pathology of an addiction nature, in common with his alcoholic patients. That mistake was greatly compounded when he drew up the relapse prevention treatment mode for sex offenders of a more 'garden variety'.

Sex Crimes Are Contemplated, Often Plotted in Advance.

Farnsworth also failed to consider that most sex offenses (both original and recidivistic) are contemplated in advance, often specifically plotted in a very deliberate manner by the offender. Sometimes (particularly in the case of an offender oriented toward assaults or molestations of stranger victims) an opportunity matching a pre-plotted scenario will suddenly present itself, and such specifically oriented sex offenders will strike seemingly suddenly. However, this appearance only clouds the reality of substantial pre-contemplation and plotting.

This has two ramifications. First, conceptualizations of sex offenders as slavishly subject to momentary and irresistible 'impulse' are utterly misgiven; accordingly, any treatment modality designed to address such falsely assumed impulsiveness is far off target and thus doomed to total ineffectiveness. Hence, even recidivistic sex crimes can be deterred by criminal penalties alone.

Second, because such advance contemplation is involved, standard crime deterrents, notably harsh penalties and a well-publicized ability to promptly detect and investigate such sex crimes and to identify and apprehend the perpetrator, have far more effect at preventing such crimes than had been previously anticipated.

Both such harsh penalties and the certainty of perpetrator identification and apprehension are at their height of effectiveness as to recidivistic sex offenses, as evidenced by the huge drop in sex offense recidivism across the country in recent years (see the discussion of the Minnesota Department of Corrections 2007 report to the state legislature). This alone seriously calls into question the need for the massive sex offender commitment programs in states that have created them.

What's Really Needed or Useful as 'Treatment' of Sex Offenders Can Be Delivered Quickly in Prison

More to the point, this powerful deterrent confirms the uselessness of 'relapse prevention' treatment of sex offenders. It also calls into question the need for the 'behavioral' part of 'cognitive-behavioral' treatment modalities for sex offenders. Given that most if not all sex offenders are rational, deliberate individuals who pre-plan their crimes, it could well be that all that is really needed is an elaborate educational program designed to disabuse sex offenders of some of the faulty notions that lodge in their heads as justifications for their crimes, and to inform them of the catastrophic consequences of their actions. This simple, rapid, yet comprehensive approach, with no need to self-incriminate, could be accomplished in less than a year in a prison-based program.

The Disutility and Needless Interminability of Other 'Treatments'

Likewise, so-called 'aversive conditioning' therapies, including genital electroshock (or elsewhere) or ammonia-sniffing, for instance, and other approaches, such as Freudian psychoanalysis and anti-androgen drugs, have all been shown as utter failures *(A. Goodnough & M Davey, supra)*.

While other more recent treatment approaches exist, all are to some degree experimental and require a very long time to show useful effects. The most common groupings of these are called 'cognitive-behavioral' techniques. These are intended to change broad, destructive patterns of thought and of reaction. These have been used to treat anxiety and some other mental ailments. In sex offender treatment, the goal of cognitive-behavioral techniques is to change deep-rooted traits and behaviors, and to change how the offender automatically functions.

However, at best "It's a slow business," said David Thornton, the treatment director at Wisconsin's civil commitment center. "You're talking about years of work, two steps forward, one step back" (Ibid). This is the heart of the problem with the cognitive-behavioral approach.

Rather than simply seeking to modify one thought or reaction, as treatment progresses, it is inevitably found that all sorts of thoughts and reactions are interrelated, so that many of each require alteration. This Topsy-like growth of issues to work on, stretches the duration of this treatment method exponentially.

"The program has gotten larger, more involved, and progressively longer," said Robert W. Peterson, a lawyer in Wisconsin who has worked on such cases since 1998 and says he has seen the state's program shift repeatedly in design and focus. "Regardless of the structure of the treatment program, the duration of the treatment program, the nature of the treatment program," Mr. Peterson said, "What we basically have is living experiments."

The same conclusions apply to Minnesota's commitment-based sex offender treatment methods.

Commitment Facilities as Prisons

Beyond problems with treatment, living conditions present a problem at sex offender commitment facilities. For starters, just the current burgeoning expansion of many such facilities creates an institutional environment much like a prison. One such facility in Coalinga, CA, is being expanded to house 1,500 committed sex offenders. Traditional mental hospitals hold far less than that. Florida, Minnesota, Nebraska, Virginia, and Wisconsin are also adding beds. Minnesota's sex offender commitment program administration has requested funding to expand from fewer than 700 detainees currently to 2,200 by 2022.

Then there are the prison-like conditions and operation previously described, plus the loud clanking doors, guard stations, fluorescent lighting, cinder-block walls and high razor wire topped fences around the perimeters. Consequently, most committed sex offenders consider their status as simply extended incarceration.

Conditions in one sex offender commitment facility in Florida epitomize such living-conditions problems. One employee described that facility as "basically a free-for-all prison" *(A. Goodnough & M. Davey, "A Record of Failure at a Center for Sex Offenders," New York Times, March 5, 2007, p. Al).* Sex between detainees, although forbidden, is rampant and blatant. Sex between a detainee and staff person also occurs. Assaults and sexual assaults by one detainee upon another are common. Assaults upon staff are also not infrequent. Many detainees hide knives in their rooms, similar to prison life. Inebriation from homemade liquor is an everyday occurrence. Staff almost always turn their backs on such misconduct. "It was like walking into a war zone," recalled Jared Lamantia, one of the visiting workers, in an interview. "The residents in that place ran the whole facility." *(Ibid)*

That same article also cites the death of one detainee after a fight with another — over a bag of chips. It also recounts a sit-in by detainees that ultimately required hundreds of law enforcement officers to suppress. This last episode resulted in guards at that facility being armed, something unheard of in any mental health facility in the country. That protest was precipitated by forced reductions in allowable personal items. In response, detainees moved into a yard. For months, the staff could not persuade them to go back to their rooms, creating a scene one law enforcement officer called 'Woodstock gone amok' *(Ibid).*

Staff also resorted to holding detainees back in treatment as punishment for minor infractions. Policies for punishing troublemakers are vague. Specific staff persons "harass, taunt — try to get you in trouble so you would get kicked out of treatment" *(Ibid).* In at least one of the stabbings by one detainee of another, staff members quickly mopped up the blood, destroying crime-scene evidence before law enforcement arrived. Inter-detainee violence and predation achieve such heights that some 100 detainees signed a letter calling for an end to housing two detainees in a single room. The facility "is supposed to be a mental health facility, not a prison," the residents wrote. "We are to be treated as patients, not state convicts" *(Ibid).*

Non-Release: Illusory Tantalization — Disparity, Docility and Despair Finally — there is the problem of non-release

A point of great disparity concerns releases from such facilities. As of 2008, thirteen states with such laws had released a total of more than 250 sex offenders from such commitment facilities. In contrast, states such as Minnesota have not fully discharged any of them from such commitments, and have 'provisionally discharged' either none, one (Minnesota), or only a handful *(Larry Oakes, "Locked in Limbo,"*

Star Tribune, June 8, 2008, p. Al.). In this regard, Minnesota presents a particularly egregious case: all other states without final discharges and only up to a few provisional releases are far newer programs that have not been treating sex offenders very long *(Ibid).*

Release from sex offender commitment poses problems of its own. Virtually everywhere, communities object to sex offenders released from commitment taking up residence there. In California, these objections are so strong and ubiquitous that some released offenders have been forced to reside in mobile homes just outside of prisons. In one case, California made 269 attempts to locate a residence for a released pedophile. And in Milwaukee, four years of similar efforts failed even though the released offender was 77 years old

This 'release' is not just cost-prohibitive, it is illusory. Equipped with 26 cameras and a booth from which to surveil its residents, a staff of 12 and a 1,700-pound electrically operated door, it most resembles a prison unit *(Ibid).*

Nationwide, about one in every eight sex offenders in commitment facilities is age 60 or older, notwithstanding well-documented drops in recidivism once one crosses that threshold into old age. Of this older group, most have health problems after many years in prison. The costs of keeping these detainees in commitment are especially high, sometimes astronomical, in part due to their physical ailments and special needs *(Ibid).*

Adding It All Up

Whatever its legalities and court endorsements, civil commitment of sex offenders is outrageously unfair to those who have served their time in prison, is based on junk-science predictions of wild inaccuracy, and is a system born of politics, maintained by politics, and barred by politics from reaching the logical end-point of releases. It seizes disproportionately on the aged, and turns not on scientific conclusions but rather on the sensationalism of crimes in one's past, mostly the distant past.

It employs those who call themselves forensic experts, but who obviously approach the subject with biases based on expressed fear and loathing that rival the emotionality of the basest ignorami concerning the topic. It pays these 'experts' to character-assassinate those vulnerable due to their past records, so as to whip those unreasoning fears in the hearts of judges or jurors to the frenzy required to decide to commit. This happens without consideration that such lucrative careers depend on consistently delivering ominously damning pronouncements — whatever the facts and actual science.

It is a system that delivers the committed to the custody of those who are their captors first and foremost, and their 'therapists' in name only. It provides 'treatment' based on false premises and designed to fail. It is tantamount to a never-ending series of experiments with false starts, such that completion of treatment is only a tantalizing illusion, and release out of the question. It is a psychologically therapeutic environment in name only, with facilities from coast to coast that are merely badly operated prisons in thin disguise, vacillating between near anarchy and brutal reactionism. And, worst of all, this system is in reality simply lifetime preventive detention, 'releasing' only a trickle of those committed, and only to such restrictive and unviable environments as to doom them to failure and to forcible re-institutionalization. It is a living nightmare.

Lest you take this as empty oration, read on ...

Chapter 3

Post-Incarceration Sex Offender Commitment

A Blatant Violation Of Basic Human Rights

Let's start with the reality: sex offenders are typically sentenced to extremely long prison terms. In states that provide parole from prison for other convicts, sex offenders are generally barred as a class from such parole eligibility. In the minority of states that have sex offender commitment laws, when sex offenders are finally released at the end of their prison terms, many are selected either by corrections officials or prosecutors to face petitions for their 'civil commitment' to maximum-security pseudo-prisons with names that often include the phrase 'treatment facility'.

Of course, almost all sex offenders have already been subjected to mandatory, intensive and long-term 'treatment' while in prison, in an attempt to reduce the likelihood that they will recidivate. The question of whether such treatment has any impact on recidivism will be addressed in a later section of this book.

For now, simply bear in mind that any given sex offender having already been subjected to extensive treatment in prison and having certainly derived as much benefit from it as possible, such that a point of futility has been reached as to requiring any more of the same. Moreover, there really isn't any more treatment to offer: treatment in commitment facilities merely repeats the very same curriculum.

Thus, the odds that treatment under commitment will actually further reduce recidivism are very low. This introduces a central theme, namely that 'commitment' of sex offenders is not really for the purpose of providing treatment, but instead is simply a disguised means of imprisonment.

Although one might expect that large, densely populated states might have substantial numbers of sex offenders who are thus ultimately committed, in fact two states that are not large or densely populated lead the pack in commitments of sex offenders per capita of state population: Minnesota and Wisconsin.

Although Wisconsin has committed hundreds of sex offenders (as has Minnesota), Wisconsin's population of those committed through this law has stabilized in the last several years as the number of releases has offset its new commitments *(State of Minnesota, Office of the Legislative Auditor, "Civil Commitment of Sex Offenders" [March,*

2011; hereinafter, the "OLA Report"], p. 19). Among other states with commitment laws, some have released very few sex offenders, while others have released more, but only 17% of those committed, at the top end of that range among states *(Ibid).*

Writing in 'A Record of Failure at Center for Sex Offenders' *(N.Y. Times, Mar. 5, 2007)*, such minimal rates of releases caused Monica Davey and Abby Goodnough to bemoan that the New York State commitment facility under scrutiny "failed to meet a central purpose: treating sex offenders so they would be well enough to return to society".

What they may not have fully appreciated five years ago is the extent to which the 'illness' is politically defined as sex-offense recidivism, or the feared propensity for it. Effectively, not only are sex offenders politically incorrect, they are 'politically ill'.

For this reason, and because Minnesota has a political appointee making release decisions and, as one political observer said "Because no one can guarantee an offender won't rape or molest again, the safest course ... has been to keep offenders locked up regardless of how their treatment has progressed", it is not hard to understand how the political path of least resistance was preventive detention under rubric of commitment *(Jenny Roberts, "The Mythical Divide Between Collateral and Direct Consequences of Criminal Convictions: Involuntary Commitment of 'Sexually Violent Predators," Minn. Law Review, Vol. 93, p. 670 at Footnote 191).* The topic of perceived need for a 'guarantee' of non-recidivism will be revisited.

Minnesota deserves special focus as the 'epicenter' of the 'sex offender commitment political movement'; commitment practices of that state will receive that focus below. For now, simply know that, as of this writing, after committing nearly 700 sex offenders whose criminal sentences have long since ended over the last two decades, and notwithstanding an upwardly spiraling rate of new commitments every year, Minnesota currently has only one sex offender released from commitment. For all practical purposes, in Minnesota, commitment of a sex offender is a second life-without-parole sentence.

This has been attributed to effects from: "(1) referral, petition, and court practices; (2) legal standards for commitments; (3) legal requirements for commitment proceedings; and (4) differences in release practices", as compared to other commitment states *(Ibid).* In essence, it is amazingly easy to commit a sex offender in Minnesota, but attaining release is virtually impossible. Again, this bespeaks thinly disguised pure preventive detention at work.

Personal blogosphere rhetoric, you scoff? Let's see what highly respected professionals have to say.

Enter Shawn Sullivan. Although Sullivan has never been committed as a sex offender and has not served a day in prison in the United States, his case in Great Britain speaks volumes about the true, preventive-detention nature of those so-called commitments, and the tyrannical unfairness they represent.

Shawn Sullivan was charged in the early 1990s by prosecutors in Minnesota with illegal sex with three juvenile girls. Sullivan learned of the warrant for his arrest and immediately fled to Europe. He settled in Ireland, where he was convicted for sexual crimes with two girls. He received a suspended sentence, but again fled — this time to continental Europe, living in various countries.

Meanwhile U.S. authorities were hardly inert. At their request Sullivan was placed on Interpol's Most Wanted list. He was arrested in London in June, 2010. While in jail contesting his pending extradition, Sullivan married a British woman. A month later he was released on bail.

His attorneys raised the contention that if Sullivan were extradited to face those Minnesota charges, and were he convicted, he could ultimately find himself in Minnesota's sex offender commitment facility/prison, rather than being released at the end of his projected prison term. One of these attorneys told the British court: "Minnesota commits greater numbers of sex offenders per capita of state population than any other state in the union".

His attorneys were quick to add that under Minnesota law, Sullivan could face such commitment even if not found guilty at his projected criminal trial. They also pointed out to that court that, except for one inmate provisionally released, but re-incarcerated in that commitment facility, Minnesota had only successfully released one committed sex offender in 17 years.

Agreeing that Minnesota's sex offender civil commitment process amounts to a life-in-prison sentence without possibility of release, the British High Court demanded a guarantee from Minnesota prosecutors that, if Sullivan were extradited, he would not be committed to that facility. Those Minnesota prosecutors refused to agree to that proviso. So the British High Court refused their request for extradition, ruling that the prospect of such commitment was a "flagrant denial" of Sullivan's rights under Article 5 of the European Convention on Human Rights.

Professor Eric Janus, president of the William Mitchell School of Law in St. Paul, Minnesota, and a national expert on civil commitment issues, said that Britain's decision in the Sullivan case restated the European position: that Minnesota's program does not recognize basic human rights. The two British judges writing the decision noted that Minnesota commitment law calls for potentially lifetime detention for those ruled to be "sexually dangerous". Those High Court Judges cited a litany of concerns, including that sex offenders don't have to be mentally ill or without self-control, and that their underlying crimes don't have to be recent.

Peter Wold, Sullivan's criminal defense attorney in Minnesota, said that British judges had balked at the prospect of permanent detention. "That offended them, and it should offend a lot of people, to have the prospect of people being committed with no end in sight."

There is no doubt that the United States has, for approximately the last 35 years, been swept away by a tide of public furor over sex crimes. The public has been purveyed an incessant diet of sex-crime horror stories designed to instill hysterical fear and to inculcate intense loathing of those convicted of sex offenses.

At the same time, images of lathering maniacs, reflexively committing rape upon rape and molestation of every child encountered — however out of touch with reality — have brought the public to such panic that many women carry tear gas mini-canisters or even stun guns or seek protective escorts when on their own in public places. Parents everywhere, who previously allowed their children to venture out for errands or amusements unescorted, now quail to let their children out of their sight anywhere in public, and become anxiety-ridden, if not panic-stricken, at every instance of a child's tardy return home.

In the first place, despite all that propaganda, sexual assaults and molestations by strangers have always been so infrequent as to border on the rare. Yet the media — ever hungry for spellbinding sensationalism and the emotionally hypnotic 'gasp factor', have incessantly focused on isolated atrocities.

In one infamous campaign of distortion that even angered federal authorities, news media cited wildly inflated numbers of 'child abductions', with blatant innuendo of stranger-perpetrators with sexually malevolent intent. Instead, corrected the FBI (but with almost no one listening), almost all 'child abductions' in its prodigious statistics were cases of non-custodial parents taking their own child from the custody of the other parent without judicial permission — obviously not a sex crime at all. Again, the public hysteria that this long-running distortion deliberately engendered was completely unjustified by the true reality.

More recently, the false suggestion has been bandied about that sex offenders have extraordinarily high recidivism rates eclipsing those of other types of criminals — perhaps approaching 100%.

In fact, this is exactly opposite of the truth. Recidivism among convicted sex offenders, while the subject of modest professional uncertainty, and modest circumstantial variation such as increasing age of a released sex offender, is almost invariably found to occupy a range of less than 20% of releasees investigated. This is nearly the lowest rate of recidivism for all crimes, which otherwise range as high as 70% (just within the first three years!) for drug-motivated crimes, for instance.

Now enter the DSM-IV-R and DSM-V, the largest monuments of the modern age to the prostitution of an entire profession by its willingness to engage in junk science for pay. DSM stands for Diagnostic and Statistical Manual, a publication of the American Psychiatric Association. It serves as the diagnostic 'bible' for psychiatrists and for clinical and forensic psychologists.

Effective in its most recent editions, the DSM has added an entirely new realm of things other than mental illnesses. These are termed mental (or emotional) 'disorders'. Among these are pedophilia (never before so deemed but rather, until then, simply a socially castigated variant sexual attraction) and anti-social personality disorder, derided because its defining indicia can be summed up unclinically as 'asshole disease'. If someone you know is an asshole, you can accuse them of having 'antisocial personality disorder' and pay some bucks to a forensic psychologist to listen to your tale of woe and offer his written 'professional' opinion backing you up.

Don't believe this? Try it and see!

The overpopulation of the field of psychology has caused many underemployed psychologists to gravitate to the sub-field of forensic psychology, from which prosecutors' offices and courts hire them to malign sex offenders whom, in many cases, they have never even met. This is done by plugging facts of record (including uncharged accusations in some cases) into a matrix of specific recidivism statistics to find ways to elevate a specific sex offender's appearance of likelihood to vastly outstrip the low average recidivism rate applicable to sex offenders generally. This technique is known by the pretentious name, 'actuarial instruments'. However, in reality it is a classic instance of the old complaint about statistics: 'Liars figure'.

The scientific refutation of this crass misapplication of statistical data lies in the fact that such 'actuarial instruments' are designed only to elevate the percentage of likelihood of recidivism. While sometimes wildly asserting that a given sex offender, with specific adverse 'factors', is 100% likely to reoffend, no one is accorded a zero percent probability, and according to these 'instruments' only a sliver of the sex offender population have anything less than average chance of recidivism.

Ponder this a minute: given the tens of thousands of sex offenders in the U.S. Dept. of Justice study of sex offender recidivism, the reliability of its overall average range of percentages of recidivism can be accepted as a given. So, when each of the currently used 'actuarial instruments' claim that far more sex offenders are far higher that the U.S. Dept of Justice average, and that few are at or below it, something is fundamentally wrong with those instruments.

Essentially, a sex offender can be committed on nothing more than this manipulation of statistics through junk science.

One leading actuarial instrument, MnSOST, got around to factoring in age only in its most recent iteration (v. 3.1), and then only by dividing sex offenders into two classes: under or over age 30 — the least statistically significant division the authors of MnSOST could have chosen.

Why? Because it is long-known that, as age increases, especially from age 50 up, the likelihood of sexual recidivism drastically reduces, becoming a diving geometric curve as offenders pass age 60 — an inconvenient truth to someone paid to convince a judge or jury that a 60-year-old sex offender is a `recidivating machine'.

Another actuarial instrument (Static-99) statistically penalizes all gay sex offenders (a blatant act of homophobia and abuse of a powerless minority), and all who have not been married or in a pseudo-marriage for at least two years — this last a surprise, no doubt, to any of the millions who fall into this category, but who have never even contemplated a sex crime.

Armed with all this knowledge, the condemnatory comments of one of forensic psychology's own should come as no surprise. Dr. Karen Franklin, Ph.D., in a web article, *'Civil commitment petition against Butner, NC, prisoner dismissed', http://forensic psychologist. blogspot.com/2012/01/civil-commitment-petition-against (etc.) (Jan. 15, 2012)*, discussing sex offender commitment proceedings, observes:

> "Understandably, it is easy for jurors and even judges to brush aside legal technicalities and burdens of proof in the interest of keeping women and children safe.
>
> "But it is disturbing when forensic psychologists collude in this endeavor, disregarding the limits of science by overstating the accuracy of risk assessment (actuarial] instruments, inventing pretextual disorders to justify preventive detention, and even claiming omniscient truth-telling powers regarding ancient, unprosecuted allegations ..."

With regard to the junk science of 'antisocial personality disorder' as a ground for sex offender commitment, Dr. Franklin aptly quoted Judge Freidman in the case from Butner, NC, involving one Mark Revland:

> "The essence of this disorder is that the patient 'fails to conform to social norms with respect to lawful behaviors as indicated by repeatedly performing acts that are grounds for arrest'. Dr. [Jeffrey] Singer testified that the vast majority of prison inmates have this disorder, as they are in prison for breaking the law and failing to conform to social norms. Dr. [Joseph] Pland testified that there is no documented causal link, in this case or in general, between antisocial personality disorder and sexual dangerousness ..."

Dr. Franklin herself concluded thus:

> "Increasingly, cutting-edge researchers are coming to the consensus that, by and large, with a few exceptions at the extreme end of the continuum, sex offenders are not a distinct group worthy of the level of special attention they are getting these days. Rather, they are garden-variety criminals who violate social norms, take what they want, and eventually burn out as they enter middle age.
>
> "The judge's bold language in cutting through the empty psycho-babble about mental disorder and risk harkens back to the little boy in the Hans Christian Anderson tale, The Emperor's New Clothes', who was not afraid to declare out loud that the emperor was naked."

Incidentally, Reviand and the rest of those against whom commitment was sought at Butner, NC, were those simply caught with child pornography. They had not been convicted of any incident of child molestation.

This leads to a different point about the broadening swath cut by commitment legislation, leading one to ask, in the absence of an original sexual assault, whither the concept of recidivism, ostensibly to be prevented by such preventive detention. At this extreme, it becomes instead a matter of permanent detention for merely being the kind of person presumed to be capable of committing a sexual assault someday. Such commitment laws have dropped all disguise and pretense, and become apparent for the 'pre-crime' preventive detention they are. Minority Report, we have arrived!

Make no mistake: the linguistic façade of supposed care and concern for committed sex offenders is paper-thin. In some jurisdictions, commitment facilities are simply part of prisons. In all states with such commitment laws, whether thus sited or located elsewhere, accommodations and facility operation are essentially a prison clone: "Most of the centers tend to look and feel like prisons, with clanking double doors, guard stations, fluorescent lighting, cinderblock walls, overcrowded conditions, and tall fences with razor wire around the perimeters." *Jenny Roberts, supra, Footnote 201.*

Despite the purely fear-and-hate-based obsession that such sex offender commitment laws comprise, they have been enacted in 20 states and even by the federal government (as to its own prison-releasees). Note, however, that Pennsylvania's law applies only to juveniles, and the law in Texas calls for halfway house-based outpatient treatment, bringing the 'incarceration model' of sex offender commitment down to 18 states. That, however, is one federal government and 18 states too many.

Chapter 4

Federal Sex Offender Commitment

A Sampler Of Surreal '1984' Newspeak In Action and The Horrors Of A 'Minority Report' Tyrannical Future Closing In

Surprisingly, the federal government was slower than states to enact a legal system of civil commitment. The Adam Walsh Child Protection and Safety Act of 2006, in addition to numerous other draconian provisions as to sex offenders, enacted a civil commitment process to allow the federal government to indefinitely detain "sexually dangerous" offenders.

This process starts with certification by the U.S. Dept. of Justice (hereinafter, "DOJ") that a given federal prison inmate is eligible for commitment. Under 18 U.S.C. §4247(a)(5), a "sexually dangerous person" subject to commitment is one who has engaged or attempted to engage in sexually violent conduct or child molestation, and who is "sexually dangerous to others" or who suffers from a serious mental illness, abnormality or disorder, as a result of which he would have "serious difficulty in refraining from sexually violent conduct or child molestation if released."

The DOJ certification serves as a kind of court-pleading and is submitted to a federal district court. The assigned federal judge holds a factual hearing. However, as in some states, no jury is seated; the district judge makes the finding. If they judge finds that the prison inmate fills the definition of a "sexually dangerous" person above, on a prosecution burden of clear and convincing evidence (lower than the "reasonable doubt" standard of proof), the judge orders commitment of that prisoner. As in several states with sex offender commitment laws, the DOJ, in making the foregoing certification, may consider conduct that did not result in an arrest or conviction. Indeed, as startling as it is, a federal prison inmate can be certified for commitment even if they have no prior criminal record of sex offenses.

Interestingly, unlike some states (which often adopt a 'rubber gavel' approval process for sex offender commitments), the federal courts have taken a conservative approach to ruling in favor of these commitments. According to USA Today, (www.usatodsay.com), although the DOJ has certified 136 federal prisoners over the six years that this commitment law has been in place, only 15 of those prisoners have finally been committed by a federal court to date. Forty-four of those against whom such certification was brought managed to get the DOJ to drop the case. Another 17 convinced the judge that prosecutors failed to carry their burden of proof. The other 60 cases remain pending to date.

Among these and among others whose cases reached a final conclusion were some who languished for as long as four years in incarceration after their prison release dates, pending resolution of that commitment request. Notable among these is Graydon Comstock, whose preliminary appeal to the U.S. Supreme Court resulted in a 2010 ruling that such federal sex offender commitments are a valid exercise of federal power. Even so, on remand, a federal district court ruled that Comstock did not meet the foregoing criteria, and he was released in November, 2011.

Of note, the U.S. Supreme Court, acting in United States v. Comstock, 560 U.S. , 176

L.Ed.2d 878 (2010), held that the sex offender commitment provisions of that Act were authorized to the federal government (as opposed to being reserved to the states) by the U.S. Constitution's "necessary and proper clause." (Art. I, Sec. 8, Clause 18). Intriguingly, the High Court's reasoning drew its inference of authorization from the implied power to punish. This reasoning appears to suggest that sex offender commitments either are part of punishment for sex crimes, or are derivative from such punishment. This relationship will figure, infra, in an analysis of whether such commitments, at least as they are judicially arrived at and as they are carried out, are a form of prohibited "bills of attainder." No attainder challenge was raised in Comstock.

Further, the Supreme Court expressly disavowed making any unsolicited ruling on other possible challenges, specifically naming due process (substantive and/or procedural), and equal protection violations as such possibilities. Indeed, this disavowal extended not just to the terms of that federal commitment statute (18 U.S.C. §4248), but also alternatively, to "its application." (Comstock, p. 886) This is an implicit recognition that, even if the statute, "on its face," was constitutional as against these disavowed claims, its application under some circumstances and to particular sets of facts might be in violation of those disavowed constitutional provisions/doctrines "as applied".

Crucially, this means that two earlier Supreme Court cases, Kansas v. Hendricks, 521 U.S. 346 (1997); and Kansas v. Crane, 534 U.S. 407 (2002), cannot be relied upon as across-the-board rulings of constitutionality of the commitment laws of different states — as they are applied.

Implicit, but fairly blatant in the federal legislation in question, is that indefinite commitment is intended to prevent crimes prisoners soon to be released *might* commit in the future (they are ruled "sexually dangerous" because there is a danger they might do so.) This is a very unsettling resemblance to the "pre-crime" arrests in the movie *Minority Report* and an echo from the dystopian vision of a totalitarian future in George Orwell's *1984*.

It is no accident, for instance, that the commitment unit established for those "civilly committed" under that act is located within a federal prison in Butner, NC (hence, the reference to Butner in the immediately preceding section). If nothing else, that location suggests that the federal commitment program, at its heart, is simply preventive detention.

As so often analogously happens in state sex offender commitment trials, a battle of partisan "experts" almost always ensues. In the case of federal commitments of this kind, the Bureau of Prisons (hereinafter, "BOP") maintains its own 'stable' of forensic experts who almost always find that certified prisoners are "sexually dangerous." Conversely, experts retained by the defense (non-government experts in private practice) almost universally find to the contrary that certified prisoners do not require commitment. These private-practice, forensic psychologists give more objective, thorough, and nuanced reports and testimony than BOP experts. Perhaps this is one reason why federal courts agree more often with these defense experts.

But a more basic fact is that modern federal legislation has created a host of new crimes relating to sexual interest, but which do not involve any actual 'hands-on' sexual acts. This includes, most notably, the slew of laws against child pornography, including the comparatively lesser offenses of merely possessing, downloading, or simply knowingly viewing online child pornography (which, despite furious efforts at stamping out through busts in legion numbers, remains ubiquitous on the Internet to date). Even these lesser crimes result in long federal prison sentences. Federal judges appear to be bollixed by prosecutorial claims of "sexual dangerousness" about such prisoners, who typically never committed any `hands-on' crime of molestation, and who have uneventfully passed the last decade or two in prison.

In addition to housing those committed, Federal Correctional Institution ("FCI") Butner also serves as a treatment center for prison inmates who are either sent there for sex offender treatment by BOP decision or who volunteer for it. While those unfamiliar with prison matters may not realize it, in prisons (including those of the BOP), sex offenders are typically subjected to substantial harassment, occasional violence, and even rape/other sexual assault, all due to the nature of their crimes.

To avoid this, federal prisoners often volunteer for such sex offender treatment programs, in which they are relatively much more safe. And consequently, those in such programs strive to remain there with considerable desperation. Yet ironically, participation in such treatment programs puts participating sex offenders at a greater risk of being committed. Moreover, statements that sex offenders make to gain admittance to such treatment programs very often contain false claims of un-prosecuted, further sex crimes, in order to convince staff that the applicant `needs' treatment more than others, so that admittance will not be denied or delayed.

Once in treatment, participants will often falsely claim the existence of certain issues of a more extreme, ominous character, in order not to be `graduated' from treatment and thereby returned to general prison population. Unfortunately, both such initial and later statements are not confidential in the eyes of the law and consequently, they are often used against that sex offender later in a commitment proceeding. In particular, this happens to the sex offenders at FCI-Butner with alarming regularity. See, e.g., United States v. Revland, case No. 5:06-HC-02212 (Eastern Dist., N.C., Decision: Dec. 23, 2011); 2011 WL 6749814). Mr. Revland `admitted' in treatment some 149 supposed incidents of child molestation in order to stay Butner's treatment program in prison. However, none of these were true. Revland was smart enough to date his fictions during periods he was incarcerated. The federal court rejected commitment.

The federal Bureau of Prisons (BOP) lacks psychologists experienced in sex offender commitment proceedings who are willing to back commitment of the number of sex offenders who (after discounting those desperate lies to get into, and to stay in prison treatment) have only average, or less-than-average sex crimes records or who, for other reasons, such as middle-age-or-older status as they near release. To cure this shortage and to increase the numbers committed, BOP maintains a psychology pre-doctoral internship program to attract potential job candidates. By dangling the prospect of a doctorate degree in front of psychology-major grads who might not otherwise qualify, BOP is essentially thus able to create a cadre of sex offender commitment 'hatchet-men" it can depend on to submit suitability condemnatory reports.

Yet, faced with the aforesaid reluctance by federal judges to go along with commitment in cases such as where no `hand-on' sex crime had been committed in decades (if ever), or where the offender has attained an age at which reoffending is far less likely, the DOJ has begun dismissing commitment cases, as noted above. According to Derek Gilna, "Federal Sex Offender Civil Commitment Process Under Fire," Prison Legal News, August 2012, p. 1, at p. 4, "DOJ spokesman

Charles Miller said that the dismissals were due to "the totality of circumstances ... age, health status, change of circumstances, supervised release terms, family support, and the opinions of all of the forensic experts." (emphases supplied; emphasized terms discussed in other sections, infra). In one particularly telling passage, Gilna reports:

> "Although most prisoners certified by the DOJ for civil commitment have been convicted of some form of sex-related crime, the certification process falters in the area of determining their probability of reoffending. Notably, the tests used in the certification process provide data related to the likelihood of recidivism by groups of offenders with similar characteristics, but not necessarily the individual probability of reoffending for the person tested. Further, widely varying scores given by psychologists who administer the same tests indicate that the process is far from an exact science." *Ibid., p. 6*

In one case of attempted commitment by the feds (United States v. Abregana, 574 F.Supp.2d 1145 [D. Hawaii 2008]), the court rejected that certification and released Mr. Abregana. Of note, government psychologists applied three different so-called 'actuarial" 'checklist' tests (specifically, "Static-99," "RRASOR," and "MnSOST-R", described and specifically criticized in sections infra) to arrive at frightening predictions of highly probable future sexual recidivism by Mr. Abregana.

Yet defense experts, using those same tests, came up with radically *lower* scores (with correlated lesser percentages of probability of such recidivism). Noting this, that judge criticized these specific tests and the entire application of psychological concepts. The judge sniped at mere "impressions" and "subjective analysis" inherently involved in the process.

The judge's opinion in Abregana contains this lodestar decision, quite often overlooked in commitment cases:

> "The U.S. Supreme Court precedent makes clear that the 'serious difficulty' language does not require total or complete lack of control, but *does require that it must be difficult, if not impossible* for the person *to control his dangerous behavior.* See Kansas v. Crane, 534 U.S. 407, 411 (2002) (citing Kansas v. Hendricks, 521 U.S. 346, 358 (1997) ...
>
> "These are difficult questions that require clearer and more convincing proof than is available in the circumstances before the Court." *(emphases supplied)*

Clearly then in sum, the fact that federal judges have such grave reservations over federal commitment practice intimates that states with sex offender commitment laws have even greater problems with the so-called evidence advanced to support commitment, with the commitment process altogether, and with the goal and practice of so-called treatment in sex offender commitment facilities (not to mention their prison-substitute architecture and operation). As you will see infra, especially through in-depth examination of one state that clearly has gone further into the intellectual jungle of sex offender commitment, that generalization is, if anything, a gross understatement.

Section Two

Psychobabble 101

Chapter 5

Debunking The Forensic Justifications For Sex Offender Commitment

Beyond the definitional coverage of sex offender commitment laws governed by facts of record (prior and current convictions) and 'facts' regarding uncharged allegations, commitments necessarily must also rest upon a constitutional minimum standard of clear and convincing evidence that the offender under scrutiny is highly likely to perpetrate additional sex crimes unless committed *(Kansas v. Crane, 534 U.S. 407 (2002)*. This, of course, is a prediction. Such predictions by non-experts cannot suffice to meet this standard, and are typically excluded as 'opinion testimony by laymen'. Enter the so-called experts of forensic psychology.

The two types of expert testimony by psychologists in sex offender commitment cases are commonly referred to as "clinical risk assessment" (CRA) and "actuarial risk assessment" (ARA)[1].

Addressing both, Janus & Prentky declare that, even assuming perfectly accurate prediction, preventive detention would remain troubling, both legally and ethically. However, this concern is elevated due to the actual inaccuracy of risk assessment, increasing the probability at non-future recidivists and low-probability persons will suffer long-term detention. Because the future simply cannot be known, and also since human judgment, including that of "experts" has inherent shortcomings, the ability to assess a future risk of sex-crime recidivism is limited[2].

The Problem with Clinical Risk Assessment — how can you assess a guy you've never seen?

As *Janus & Prentky* discuss, CRA is subject to several profound criticisms. First, despite the name, in many clinical assessments, there has been no contact of any kind between the clinical evaluator and the offender. This is particularly true of forensic psychologists hired by the prosecution. In many cases petitioned for commitment, the sex offender in question has never (or at least, not in the last couple of decades or more) undergone a psychological assessment particular to sex offenses

1 *See: Eric S. Janus & Robert A. Prentky, "Forensic Use of Actuarial Risk Assessment with Sex Offenders.', 40 Am. Crim. Law Review 1443 [2004] — hereinafter, "Janus & Prentky"].*

2 *Ibid p. 1448..*

or to sexuality at all. *Janus & Prentky*[1] note in passing that, as part of an evaluation, "the expert *examines the individual ...*" *(emphasis supplied).*

In the absence of any such record of psychological testing and interviewing, a so-called 'clinical' evaluator really does not hold such a position, and hence cannot testify about any clinical matters as to the sex offender. In that circumstance, this kind of an evaluator is instead strictly 'forensic', in the sense that he can only testify as to psychological generalizations made by various researchers in the field or as to his personal impression of the sex offender, judging solely from those non-psychological facts of record, as above.

A so-called CRA is subject in general to severe criticisms of the unscientific (and therefore inexpert) character of the impressions offered as testimony. Such criticism applies with fullest force to any opinion derived without any psychological information at all, such as psychometric testing or skilled interviewing by any psychologist or psychiatrist. Would you, for instance, be satisfied with any so-called forensic psychological report to others about you, based on whether you are married, and if so, third-parties' beliefs as to whether you were married happily or unhappily? Or rumors about your sexual habits, or back-biting comments by displeased neighbors or co-workers?

Therefore, before we go any further, let us start with a modest plea: at a minimum, so-called clinical risk assessment by any psychologist *who has had no personal, recent contact with the sex offender and who has no records of any such recent contact by any other psychologists*, from which to form an expert clinical opinion, should not be allowed to testify as an expert from that capacity.

The Inherent Criticisms of 'Clinical Risk Assessment' of Sex Offenders: The Ipsedixitism of Clinical Impression as a Predictive Tool

Janus & Prentky[2] scathe the "Clinical judgments of dangerousness — judgments that ultimately rest on the ipse dixit of a mental health professional"[3]. Janus & Prentky conclude "Frequently, the liberty deprivation decision boils down to a credibility judgment between the clinical assessments of two competing expert witnesses"[4]. None of this,

1 *Ibid p. 1448.*

2 *p. 1444.*

3 *p. 1443, defined, by the way, as an assertion without proof, to be accepted on the authority of the one making it) (The Oxford Dictionary of Foreign Words and Phrases, Andrew Delahunty, ed. (2nd ed., 2008, Oxford University Press, Oxford, G.B.).*

4 *p. 1448–49.*

of course, has anything to do with truth or science. The inaccuracy of clinical assessments has been abysmal. Janus & Prentky cite two recent meta-analyses of no less than 61 sexual offender recidivism studies covering a total of 23,393 subjects[1].

In this aggregation, correlation between clinical assessments and subsequent actual recidivism was 0.10, which is to say, clinical assessments as predictors of recidivism were incorrect 90% of the time. That is stupendously less successful than sheer random chance or laypersons' guesses. Janus & Prentky[2] explain the causes of such wild inaccuracy in CRA by starting with the observation that CRA is inherently an exercise in judgment, something known to be subject to error. Janus & Prentky cite these seven sources of error in clinical judgments:

(1) incorrect base rates;
(2) incorrectly weighting specific facts;
(3) ignoring the statistical phenomenon of regression toward the mean;
(4) not taking covariation into account;
(5) relying on facts unrelated, or only weakly related to the recidivism question;
(6) not accounting for a reluctance to find anyone not dangerous; and
(7) not accepting feedback on judgment errors.[3]

In the midst of all these sources for errors, the aforesaid egregious inaccuracy of CRA is no surprise at all. In a much earlier study by Paul Miehl[4], in those instances in which the clinician had access to a clinical interview, perversely, the inaccuracy of the predictions made by the clinician was even worse. This indicates a strong subjectivity factor at work, where 'impressions', usually simply just plain wrong, trump any effort to approach risk assessment scientifically. In the sex offender context, clinicians enter an interview of a sex offender like witch-hunters of yore, looking for anything to seize upon to confirm their a priori prejudice that the sex offender is (a) suffering from a 'disorder', and (b) highly likely to re-offend.

Janus & Prentky expand on this by noting that, by reason of the nontransparent nature of CRA, CRA's substantial risks of error are invisible. They cite "confirmatory bias" as one common error in CRA,

---

1 *Ibid, p. 1456.*

2 *Ibid, p. 1457.*

3 *Ibid., p. 1457; emphasis in original. See also: Wm. R. Freudenburg, "Perceived Risk, Real Risk: Social Science and the Art of Problematic Risk Assessment," Science, Oct. 7, 1988, at 44 (spelling out in addition to the above, the impact of external social forces, monetary and political pressures, and overconfidence.*

4 *Cited by Janus & Prentky, at p. 1456.*

that is, a tendency to identify evidence supporting a preconception, but ignoring inconsistent evidence. This also affects how one interprets a given item of data, where either of two competing interpretations is equally possible. Janus & Prentky complain that cross-examination can't effectively reveal such errors, since they occur only in the clinician's head.

Apart from CRA inaccuracies, Janus & Prentky also complain of serious ambiguities in communications by the clinician about CRA, often resorting to mere "categorical" terms, such as "likely to reoffend," or covering up uncertainty with quantitative (but unsupported and imprecise) percentage ranges. To the extent "cut-off scores" are used, they are arbitrarily selected by the clinician, and this is not divulged to the trial fact-finder. This effectively makes the clinician-predictor, rather than judge or jury, the decision maker[1].

Hence, illustratively, the Missouri Court of Appeals ruled[2] that clinical assessment testimony had to be excluded from a sex offender commitment trial because it was not sufficiently grounded in science.

Janus & Prentky conclude:

> "... prevailing wisdom among mental health professionals has, over the years, asserted that the ability to predict violence using clinical methods falls well below a threshold of accuracy that justifies the use of such predictions in legal proceedings. Professor Charles Ewing's unambiguous and often cited conclusion, first asserted in 1983, is that 'The psychiatrist or psychologist who makes a prediction of dangerousness violates his or her ethical obligation to render judgments that rest on a scientific basis'. Again in 1991, Ewing asserted that there 'is good reason to conclude that psychologists and psychiatrists act unethically when they render predictions of dangerousness that provide a legal basis for restricting another person's interests in life or liberty'."[3]

Other states' appellate courts have apparently not yet been asked to exclude CRA testimony in sex offender commitment trials as insufficiently based on science. That challenge should be made soon.

Legally, the question of CRA testimony admissibility arose first in death penalty cases, in which psychologists were enlisted to opine on 'future dangerousness' of the killer, if not executed. Barefoot v. Estelle, 463 U.S. 880, 900 (1983), represents the low point in that

---

1 *Ibid, pp. 1488–89.*

2 *In re Coffel, No. ED79989, 2003 WL 716682, at *12 (Mo. Ct. App. 2003).*

3 *Ibid, p. 1463.*

jurisprudence. Barefoot refused to exclude future dangerousness testimony (although based purely on CRA — without that name). The excuse for allowing that testimony (a classic unwitting self-parody for the ages) was that the defense in that case could not show that "psychiatrists are always wrong with respect to future dangerousness, only most of the time". Fortunately, a mere three years later, the Supreme Court implicitly reversed course in Ford v. Wainwright, 477 U.S. 399, 341 (1986), setting a "heightened standard of reliability" for capital sentencing cases. Even though, technically, sex offender commitment cases are not 'criminal' trials, the argument for application of this "heightened standard of reliability" is that, in all likelihood, indefinite commitment of a sex offender is lifetime detention, and, in light of the severity of that lifetime deprivation of liberty, only testimony and evidence meeting such a higher standard of reliability should be allowed.

Erica Beecher-Monas, 'The Epistemology of Prediction: Future Dangerousness Testimony and Intellectual Due Process", 60 Washington & Lee Law Review 353, at 362-63, notes that CRA predictions have proved highly inaccurate notwithstanding considerable examination. She points out that such experts are entirely as susceptible to stereotypes and prejudices as anyone else. Thus, their predictions are as inaccurate as laypersons' guesses. Moreover, no statistics are compiled of a given expert's own error rate in their predictions in many cases.

The American Psychiatric Association has declared its opposition to future dangerousness testimony because of its *extreme* unreliability. It explained that "no one, including psychiatrists, can predict with any degree of reliability that an individual will commit other crimes in the future"[1].

Fortunately, after Barefoot and Ford, the general standard of evidentiary admissibility was modernized by Daubert v. Merrell Dow Pharms., 509 U.S. 579, 594 (1993). Although Daubert is not of constitutional dimension, it has been adopted into the rules of evidence in almost all states. As Beecher-Monas (at p. 369) explains:

> "The [psychiatry/psychology] profession has overwhelmingly castigated future dangerousness testimony based on clinical judgment alone (and so it fails the peer review, publication, and general acceptance prongs of Daubert). Because such predictions are wrong more often than right, they cannot meet the error rate inquiry ...".

---

1 *Ibid, p. 366; emphases supplied.*

Given everything said in this section, these observations apply with equal vigor to CRA testimony in sex offender commitment trials. Consequently, whether as a deprivation of due process or as a Daubert violation, CRA testimony should never be admitted in a sex offender commitment proceeding.

Chapter 6
Actuarial Risk?

Actuarial risk assessment should be excluded as evidence and testimony at sex offender commitment trials.

Since roughly the year 2000, 'actuarial risk assessment' (ARA) has rapidly become the centerpiece of evidence and testimony trotted out by prosecutors in support of sex offender commitment petitions.

Indeed, part of the reason for that meteoric rise in the use of ARA was a concurrent realization that the only other type of expert testimony in such commitment proceedings, so-called 'clinical risk assessment' (CRA) is merely unscientifically impressionistic. That is to say, CRA is based only on the 'professional judgment' (for which read, biases) of the expert hired by either side in those proceedings. The lack of any true science in this mere 'swearing contest' was embarrassingly apparent and reflected a cheap 'forensic prostitution' on a scale never before seen in American courtrooms[1].

Thus, in later years, most appellate decisions affirming sex offender commitments have focused on the often hysterical-sounding predictions of high percentages of supposed likelihood of sexual reoffense by the committed sex offender. In one case, the ARA-generated "probability *was asserted to be 100%*", that is, a predicted absolute certainty of sexual reoffense within ten years after projected prison release. Any reading of as few as several or as many as hundreds of such appellate decisions confirms that ARA-generated predictions of high probabilities of sexual reoffense if a sex offender is released from prison as scheduled are rank, but terribly effective juggling of statistics, used as a scare tactic.

Overarching Flaws and Problems of ARA and its RAIs Reduce to Junk Science

The terms 'actuarial risk assessment' (ARA) and 'risk assessment instrument' (RAI), refer to stating actuarial percentages derived from statistics to provide a probability prediction of absolute, rather than relative risk.

---

1 See, e.g., E. Janus & R. Prentky, "Forensic Use of Actuarial Risk Assessment..." 40 Am. Crim. L. Rev. 1443, 1453-58 (2003). Accord: Minnesota Office of the Legislative Auditor, 'Civil Commitment of Sex Offenders', March, 2011, p. 38.

RAIs consist of sets of "static" (i.e., history-based) risk "factors," weighted to reflect the relative significance each factor is thought to hold as to sexcrime recidivism probability[1].

> "The most that one can say of any [RAI] is that it can give a probabilistic estimate of the level of risk for people who share characteristics with the person assessed. And the estimate is *subject to a great deal of error.*"
>
> *E. Beecher-Monas, "The Epistemology of Prediction" supra, 600 Wash. & Lee Law Rev. at 410; emphasis supplied.*

No one can predict the future. In particular, attempting to predict what a specific individual may or may not do, based on statistics derived from a group or sub-group into which the individual is jammed by such statisticians, is an inherently anti-scientific act. So what if 50% or even 95% of those in that supposed 'group' (cohort) turned out to recidivate in the past? There is no assurance that the individual in question might not actually turn out to be in the non-recidivating portion of that group. "Even the most accurate of the actuarial instruments made predictions of dangerousness for people that did not, in fact, later commit acts of violence. Of people that the VRAG [RAI] placed in the 'high-risk' category, for example, only 55% actually committed violent acts upon release. In other words, 45% did not. Had the 'high risk' prediction been the basis for a death sentence, nearly half the people sentenced to death would not, in fact, go on to commit any more acts of violence."[2]

Even if any further so-called 'refinements' of these groupings could prove conclusively that one is indeed in a 100%-likely-to-reoffend sub-group, such predictions simply cannot take into account the random inputs of future human experience. Even if one left prison with a definite resolve to sexually reoffend, it is entirely possible that one could have a change of heart. Alternatively, any of myriad unpredictable, post-release, non-criminal experiences or interactions could dissuade one from that intent and set one on a completely different course. Since very few sex offenders have revealed such pre-release intents or such post-release changes, the very theory underlying ARA is flawed.

In order to make all of the following points against ARA use comprehensible, it is necessary to first explain how an RAI is used. As noted, supra, each RAI comprises any number of factors, against each of which known facts about the sex offender under scrutiny or his crimes are compared. As to each of those factors of the RAI in

---

1 *Donna Cropp Bechman, "Sex Offender Civil Commitments: Scientists or Psychics?". 16 Criminal Justice 24 (2001-02), hereinafter, "Bechman.*

2 *Beecher-Monas, supra, at p. 414.*

question deemed to be matched by some such known facts as to that sex offender, a weighted numerical score is assessed against the sex offender *for that factor.* In only certain RAIs, and only as to one or more particular factors, such sex offender-specific facts are not judged purely on a 'yes/no' basis as to that factor. Instead, a varying number of points may be assessed for that factor, depending on specified sub-criteria aimed at distinguishing comparatively less, versus more, impact on probability of recidivism.

Pause for a moment to reflect on the nature of a specific factor, as opposed to the nature of the overall test score and of the percentage of likelihood of recidivism predicted for that total ...

Each of the factors used in an RAI appears in it because someone somewhere named that factor as 'being associated' with recidivism. This association is based on statistical percentages of instances of past recidivism among *some* group of sex offenders, in which instances that named factor was involved in some predecessor way. However, quite probably, that group [sample] has little or nothing otherwise in common with any given sex offender later subjected to that RAI.

This seemingly mechanistic point glosses over something profound that is partly responsible for the inaccuracy of RAIs: a factor is of no significance whatsoever if its description merely comprises a *coincidental happenstance* or an *inherently likely coexisting fact or state* to a previous offense, for instance. Rather, to justify being a factor in an RAI, there must be some *causal link between the factor and later recidivism* or, at the very least, the factor described must itself be linked in lockstep to whatever underlying cause of recidivism the factor represents. This is no small point. Although a statistical percentage (correlation) is derived for that factor (cause or not), this is nothing more than a mathematical notation of the observation of an apparent correlation, without knowledge of the link (if any) to causation.

Example: some RAIs have a 'never married' factor (or the like). However, it is far from clear *what,* about never having been married, causes — or is linked in some way to — the *actual* related cause of sex crime recidivism to which never having married relates.

Further, sex offenders are often not an indistinguishable lump, yet all RAIs are based on samples that *tend* to include a cross-section of all or most types of at least felonious sex offenders. Some RAIs have 'achieved' a better cross-section of all sex offenders in their samples (overall, and for each factor), but in so doing, they have overlooked whether a given factor (such as 'no marriage') may have a particular relation to recidivism for one type of sex offender or type of sex crime pattern, but not to any other.

Thus, for the type of offender/crime dynamic *truly* within the causal link penumbra that resulted in the correlative association, the points assigned for that particular factor may understate his tendency toward recidivism. However, on the contrary, a type of offender with crime dynamic *unrelated* to that causal link finds his tendency toward recidivism substantially overstated by the points he also was assessed for that factor.

Next, many factors in RAIs allow a degree of subjectivity on the part of the rater to enter into whether to assess points (or, where allowed, how many points to assess) for a given factor. This will be addressed more formally later.

In the next step, all scores for the RAI's various factors are added up. These total numerical scores are ordered by ranges (or 'bins') from highest to lowest (e.g., 9 'bins'), both for each offender in the historical sample (statistically, the 'experience table') and for any given sex offender under scrutiny later. Based on how offenders in that historical sample did as to recidivism, per score-range (bin), a percentage of probability of recidivism is derived for each bin, with descending percentages for lower score-range bins. The score of a given scrutinized sex offender is matched to its range-bin, and that percentage of likelihood of recidivism is announced for that sex offender.

Nota bene, however, that this overarching percentage, based on the whole instrument score, has *nothing to do with* the percentage of likelihood of recidivism for *any* particular factor, as to which the sex offender under scrutiny is assessed points. The only connection is that *those* points (as points from *any other* factor) contribute to a total score from which the overarching percentage of likelihood of recidivism is derived.

For instance, using the ten factors of the Static-99 RAI, it might be possible for a sex offender under scrutiny to amass a high total score by being assessed points in these factors: (a) current non-sexual violent offense; (b) prior non-sexual violent offense; (c) four or more prior (distinct) sentencing occasions; and (d) age at risk less than 25.

Yet, in this example, this sex offender shares little in common with a sex offender somewhere within the historical statistical sample for the Static-99 who scored *as high (same 'bin')* on the instrument overall, but due instead to points assessed for these disparate factors: (1) prior sex offense; (2) male victims; (3) never married; and (4) convictions for non-contact sex offenses. This latter sample-participant, however, and all like him in terms of these last four factors, who contributed by their subsequent recidivistic histories to the recidivistic probability for that same total bin, have *utterly different offense dynamics* from the first sex offender described, supra, and hence, each of those factors for the second sex offender has *utterly different causes* of the elevated percentage for *each* of *those* factors.

The point-weighting system used in the RAI to total scores is unscientific for four reasons.

1 It is a subjective judgment of the relative impact(s) of each of the factors upon recidivism tendency. Where certain factors merely get one point for the existence of the factor, that single-point assignment is simply an *arbitrary assumption* that each of those factors has an *equal* impact on recidivism. Where the number of points *varies* between factors found to be present, an *equally arbitrary assumption* is at work to the contrary, i.e., that one (or some) factor(s) have more impact than others. However, no data analysis backs up this implicit claim; these assumptions appear to be merely impressionistic in origin.

2 Even if some statistical analyses do support these points-weightings, their integer (whole number) weights, especially shared in common with other factors, or else a point different from some other factors, implies a very coarse-grained rounding. In other words, where one factor is found to be 1.49 times more impactful than a different factor, presumably both are weighted at one point each. On the other hand, if Factor One is 1.51 times more impactful, then it is assigned two points in weight. This means that an actual difference of as little as 0.02 in impact between factors can result in a *doubling* of the weight points of the 1.51X Factor One, relative to Factor Two. Such a coarse rounding is itself a source of inaccuracy in the totaled points, and hence in the overall predicted percentage of likelihood of recidivism.

3 Most fundamentally, the very concept of *adding* probabilities is unscientific. Because each factor was identified in the first place by its elevation of recidivism probabilities, adding the points for each factor present amounts to adding those individual factor-probabilities. However, it is only *assumed* that probabilities can be added in this way. Perhaps instead, it may prove to be the case that the recidivism-heightening properties of respective factors *overlap* each other to some degree in individual instances of factors coexisting in the case of given sex offenders. Further, the degree of such overlap very probably differs dramatically, both from one pair of matched factors to the next, and between different types of sex offender populations. Finally (and most significantly), it would seem likely that there could well be a 'point of diminishing returns' to addition, such that, particularly in certain populations of different types of sex offenders, once one has two factors, say, a third no longer carries the incremental

recidivism-increasing level it would have if it were in addition to only one other factor — and so on for a fourth, fifth, etc., factor. None of this, apparently, has been rigorously studied scientifically to date. And none of it is taken into account in the score-adding process.

4 Lastly, the bins themselves are heterogeneous; that is, if one has, say, five factors that place one in Bin 5 on a given RAI, the RAI pays no attention to *which* five they were. This is on the *assumption* that *any* combination of *particular* factors is the *equivalent* of *any other* combination, including, or perhaps, composed completely of *different* factors. This indistinguished 'strikes' approach has no scientific foundation, since the bins were constructed from sheer *numbers* of factors (and their respective weights). Moreover, because of this last fact, any causal link between specific factors and recidivism, and between any combinations of specific factors and recidivism is ignored and thereby lost by mere relegation to such bins of overall score ranges.

Generally, other issues detracting from the scientific character of ARA and from the ability of such RAIs to accurately predict future sexual recidivism include: lack of peer review; reliance on 'instruments' which aren't actual psychological tests; relying on statistics as to a group to assess an individual; trusting that relations in one sample apply to another sample; and lack of or inadequate cross-validation. Additional criticisms include statistical inaccuracy, insufficient sensitivity, specificity, validity, and reliability, accuracy-reducing low base rates, and high rates of both false positive and false negative predictions. All of these problems show that RAIs are insufficiently reliable to be used as evidence in court cases.[1]

Taking on RAIs on their own terms, an incisive article by Richard Wollert, "Low Base Rates Limit Expert Certainty When Current Actuarials Are Used to Identify Sexually Violent Predators"[2], found startling inaccuracy in various RAIs sufficient to question their use at all, particularly in the 'natural life incarceration' context of sex offender commitments.

For instance, in the case of the Static-99 RAI, Wollert discovered that, when applied to a 1,086 sex-offender historical sample, that RAI was correct in identifying 67 of those who had turned out to be

1 *Berlin, Galbreath, Geary & McGlone, 2003; Campbell, 2004; Gottfredson & Moriarty, 2006)" John M Fabian, "A Literature Review of the Utility of Selected Violence and Sexual Violence Risk Assessment Instruments", Jour. Of Psychiatry & Law, Vol. 34, pp. 307, at 312 (2006).*

2 *12 Psychology, Public Policy & Law 56 (2006).*

recidivists, but it also mis-identified another 62 non-recidivists as supposed recidivists (known as a 'false positive')[1]. Had this been through actual application to sex offenders in commitment trials, those 62 non-recidivists could have been committed based on such undetected, 'false-positive' testimony. This is more shocking when one realizes that, in the non-historical context of such commitment, there is *no way to tell* the accurate from the false-positive predictions offered in testimony by an ARA 'expert' witness. Even more disheartening: Wollert proved that, in lesser overall recidivism samples, the percentage of false positive identifications of supposed recidivists *increased* in the Static-99.[2]

Plugging this into real life, Wollert pointed out that older sex offenders have reduced recidivism (see second subsection, infra). Previewing that aging effect on recidivism, Wollert[3], points out that, in that population of reduced recidivism, RAIs produce much higher percentages of false positives. One wonders how many senior citizen sex offenders have been committed based on this flatly incorrect prediction of elevated recidivism.

Thus, ARA-based expert testimony is junk science for many reasons overall. It is therefore appalling that, in some sex offender commitment states, laws even mandate ARA/RAI use, and in all other such states, ARA-based testimony has been routinely (and often without legal challenge) admitted in such commitment proceedings.[4] However, "not even the best science can predict with an acceptable degree of accuracy what an individual will or will not do in the future. Perhaps even more importantly, there is increasing support for the position that, not only are RAIs not the 'best science', *they are not science at all.*"[5]. A number of reasons that this is true are covered immediately.

Let's start with two recently emerging reasons that deserve special attention ... first because they are so basic, yet (so far) so surprisingly overlooked.

1 — ARA Recidivism Statistics Fail to Account for Recent Huge Drops in Sex Offender Recidivism

All of the most well-known ARA 'instruments', including VRAG (1993), SORAG (1998), RRASOR (1997), Static-99 (2000), and MnSOST-R (1999), are based on recidivism statistics compiled before *the respective 'instrument'* was designed. Because the period of study of those statistics preceding such design was extensive, those recidivism

---

1 *Ibid p. 59*

2 *Ibid.*

3 *Ibid, p. 61.*

4 *Bechman, p. 26.*

5 *Ibid.*

statistics pre-date publication of the respective 'instrument' by at least several years.

Moreover, those statistics compiled at that time were crude, were usually based on comparatively small samples of sex offenders (e.g., only from one state, as for MnSOST-R), and were not constructed in a way intended to answer the questions posed by the research leading to each such `instrument'. In short, an expression descriptive of a pervasive problem of data analysis aptly applies to the foundation for each of these so-called 'instruments' — "garbage in, garbage out".

Since then, something wonderful has happened: around the country, rates of sex-offense recidivism have been plummeting drastically. This has been attributed to various causes, including everything from education about sex offenses (which has both put people on alert and also had some quantum of 'conscience pricking' effect on sex offenders themselves) to far more intensive monitoring and supervision of sex offenders released from prison. Illustratively, as an in-depth study, "Sex Offender Recidivism in Minnesota"[1], reveals that, for that state, average sex offense recidivism by released sex offenders has fallen from 17%, as calculated by a 1990 study, to 3% for sex offenders released between 1990 and 2002.[2] Moreover, contrary to the 'straight-line' extrapolation assumptions behind those earlier 'instruments', this Minnesota study on sex offense recidivism expressly found that "...the longer offenders are in the community, the more likely they are to remain crime-free".[3] During this same period, Minnesota implemented intensified 'supervised release' (parole) for sex offenders, and changes in sentencing laws in that state greatly lengthened the period of such intense supervision.[4] Therefore, that report concluded tentatively that this had some contributory role in such a drastic reduction in recidivism. Similar sex offense recidivism reductions have been observed in other states and on the federal level in that same period.[5]

Now let's see how that reduction in recidivism alters an ARA statistical analysis. Let's suppose that a given individual is in a 'cohort' to whom a 50% probability of recidivism was assigned, based on the aforementioned out-of-date compiled statistics. Using the Minnesota example, one can match that 50% specific-group figure to that former, overall average recidivism figure of 17%. Noting that the new average figure (3%) is 17.6%

---

1 *Minn. Dept. of Corrections, 2007.*

2 *Ibid, p. 3.*

3 *Ibid, p. 4.*

4 *Ibid, p. 3.*

5 *See: Wollert, id., p. 72; U.S. Justice Dept. study of 10,000 sex offenders in 15 states: 5% recidivism in 3 years; similar results in three other one-state studies.*

of 17%, it stands to reason that the corrected, current specific-group recidivism figure for our hypothetical individual is only 8.8%. No court in the land is known to have committed any sex offender with an ARA-predicted probability of sexual reoffense of only 8.8%.

None of these ARA 'instruments' has been updated to take into account these new figures of greatly reduced sex offense recidivism. Instead, they all continue to proceed to draw predictions of probabilities of recidivism from old, far greater overall pools of former recidivism. Because of this, they are now so inaccurate as to not be science at all. Without doubt, they vastly overstate any probability of sexual reoffense for any sex offender to whom they are applied. As a result, they are directly responsible for the completely unnecessary commitment of thousands of sex offenders nationwide.

If ARA is to be retained at all as a technique of analyzing a probability that any given offender is likely to recidivate, at the very least, each of these (and any other ARA) instruments would have to be completely revised to reflect the impact of these changes in the average base-rates of sex-offense recidivism reflected by the new statistics. It should be noted that, in the five years since the Minnesota study, even further reductions in sex-offence recidivism have been noted nationwide.[1] Wollert demonstrates mathematically that, quite apart from lack of correction for lower base rates of recidivism, RAIs inherently are more inaccurate at such lower base-rates, in particular *overstating* predictions of recidivism for subject offenders compared against that low base-rate sample. Therefore, it is not a matter of correction; RAIs *cannot* accurately predict recidivism probabilities, now that recidivism base-rates have fallen so dramatically. For this, and for many other reasons, ARA should simply be abandoned as the folly it is: attempting to predict an individual's future actions by the past actions of any group or sub-group.

2 — ARA Recidivism Statistics Fail to Account for Known Aging-Based Sex Offender Recidivism Reduction

Whether due to 'male menopause' or other causes, "... it is undisputed among sex offender experts that age is an important factor in determining risk of reoffense". In re Young[2], more particularly, "recidivism rates for [sex] offenders decline as offenders get older[3]. Wollert, ibid, reports that one researcher (Hanson) calculated that "recidivism risk declined almost *4% per year* as a function of age"

---

1 *Wollert, p. 59.*

2 *86 P.3d 810 (Wash. 2004).*

3 *R. Wollert, "Low Base Rates Limit Expert Certainty When Current Actuarials Are Used....," Psychology, Public Policy, and Law, Vol. 12, p. 56 et seq., at 61).*

on average, from young to old. Hanson more recently found that "offenders older than age 50 at release" reoffended 'at half the rate of younger offenders'.[1]

Examining Hanson's data more closely, Wollert found that the decline in sex-offense recidivism from age 50 on is even more startling than Hanson portrayed it. While recidivism peaked for *rapists* released from ages 25–29, recidivism for *molesters* peaked in the next five-year bracket (30–34). Recidivism reductions were *equal* in *both groups*, however, in age bracket 35–39. *Steeper reductions* were found among *molesters* thereafter (from age 40 on) until age 60, when both groups (rapists and molesters) 'bottomed out' at negligible figures.

More specifically, among *rapists* released between ages 60 and 69 (inclusive), only 7% recidivated sexually. *Only 4% of molesters* recidivated in that age range. In Hanson's study, no sex offender released at age 70 or beyond recidivated (intuitively, a sensible result). In fact, among *incest* offenders, *no recidivism whatsoever* occurred in those released from age 60 on. This last bursts one 'cultural myth' about supposedly recidivistic grandfathers in incest cases.

Overall, Wollert's meta-analysis of Hanson's data showed that average sexual recidivism rates among released sex offenders declined precipitously past age 40, thus:

Ages	**Recidivism**
40-44	12.0%
45-49	10.9%
50-59	7.6%
60-69	3.2%
70+	0%

Despite these drastic reductions, none of the ARA instruments in use today, except the Static-99, has any age-adjustment factor. The age-adjustment factor added to the Static-99 has been criticized as too conservative. Consequently, *none of the current RAIs are accurate for subjects over 24 years old*, and each of them is *grossly inaccurate to the point of meaninglessness for sex offenders released at age 50 on up* (a '90%' error rate for those in the 60–69 age range).[2] Indeed, "These results also indicate that experts who rely on actuarial tests for predicting likely recidivists for all but the youngest age group [18–24] will be wrong most of the time".[3]

1 *Ibid.*

2 *Wollert, p. 71.*

3 *Ibid.*

Compounding this *average* error rate, Wollert also reports that for those found by ARA use to be in elevated risk groups (with higher stated probabilities of sexual reoffense), the *reductions in advancing age groups were far steeper with each upward step in age*, such that, regardless of such supposedly elevated risk as calculated by any RAI, *the actual recidivism risk for sexual offense from age 60 on up was the same negligible to nil values cited above.*[1] Clearly shocked at the implications from his findings, Wollert concluded:

> "Because the effects of age on recidivism have apparently been overlooked when many older sex offenders have been committed, it would be *in the interests of justice to seek new trials for those individuals* to determine whether they actually qualify as SVPs. A corollary of this position is that *end-of-sentence review committees* that refer prisoners for commitment consideration could 'do a more thorough job of screening potential SVP cases'[2] by *focusing their attention primarily on young adults* who were fully competent at the time they offended and *reducing the number of older offenders who are identified as possible SVPs.*"[3]

The latter suggestion, however, may be much more difficult to achieve than simply owning up to the truth of this age-related recidivism reduction.

Case in point: in absolute number of committed sex offenders, Minnesota is third only to New York and Florida, and in sex offender commitments per capita, Minnesota is first (by 10 times any other state). Minnesota is not plagued by any epidemic of sex offenses compared to any other states. Hence, clearly, something singular is going on in the collective consciousness/zeitgeist and political realm in Minnesota not shared elsewhere.

All of the sex offenders now under commitment in Minnesota were committed upon their respective releases from prison, and almost all of them were committed by instigation (referral) by its Department of Corrections. Not coincidentally, Minnesota's Department of Corrections designed the MnSOST (later: MnSOST-R and MnSOST-3) RAI. That RAI remains in use to date to identify those who presumptively will be referred for commitment consideration. Yet to date, even the current version of MnSOST does not account for advancing age.

A 2007 examination of recidivism rates in Minnesota among released sex offenders curiously *omitted to report any findings about*

---

1 *Wollert, p. 62.*

2 *LaFond, 2003, p. 296.*

3 *Wollert, p. 79, emphases supplied.*

age other than a single, meaningless comparison of all under age 30 versus all age 30 and up. Uncannily, it is as if Minnesota *willfully refuses to acknowledge that the issue of impact of advancing age even exists.*

Thus, for instance, in re Young, 86 P.3d 810[1], Mr. Young, by then under commitment for 13 years, sought release by claiming, inter alia, that "having reached the age of 61, his risk of reoffending is reduced to zero".[2] Prosecutors objected, citing Young's lack of completion of treatment (not a pre-condition for release under Washington law) and the fact that "the Static-99 table indicated that Young posed a 52% likelihood of sexually reoffending within 15 years".[3]

However, the defense expert "indicated that the actuarial tables distort risk assessments for older offenders because they do not adequately account for the aging process, citing several studies that he and other experts conducted. The report included a table with suggested age adjustments to the Static-99 actuarial table. Based on the age-adjustment table, the likelihood of recidivism falls below 50% at age 35. By age 60, the recidivism rate falls to zero percent". Based on this prima facie showing, the Washington Court of Appeals ruled that Young had presented a prima facie case that his condition had changed, and that he was entitled to release.

Note that the 'VRAG' RAI likewise "does not provide mechanisms for adjusting risk due to effects of aging ..."[4].

In this context especially, the intransigence of RAI designers to re-work their instruments to effectively and fully take advancing age into account is another reason that RAIs must be abandoned.

It has long been contended — on fairly convincing evidence — that the real, unstated purpose of sex offender commitment laws is to serve as a *surreptitious weapon of further retribution*, rather than as a means of treatment. *Committing those over 50 — even senior citizens, not just in isolated cases, but in highly disproportionate numbers — all largely on inflated predictions of probability of recidivism generated by ARA use, strongly tends to confirm this contention.*

Any doubts as to this are dissipated by Minnesota's recent commitment of an 84-year-old. It takes no advanced degree in forensic psychology to conclude that someone of such an age is no sexual threat to anyone. In Minnesota, it would seem, vengeance reigns supreme and knows no limits against aging sex offenders.

---

1 *Wash. App. 2004.*

2 *Ibid, p. 811.*

3 *Ibid., p. 813.*

4 *Fabian, "A Literature Review ..." [supra], at 322.*

Such readily apparent, added retribution through commitment also implicates those who designed, and now refuse to downwardly adjust such recidivism predictions applied to the elderly, as *intentionally willing partners* in this *vendetta against supposedly 'dirty old men'* (yet another cultural myth). Any claim to scientific legitimacy or to probative actuarially based expertise, suitable for judicial reliance, is completely forfeit under this circumstance. The only effective 'global' solution is clear: eliminate ARA use altogether.

Now let's consider some additional major problems with ARA use.

RAIs Fail to Account for Any 'Dynamic' Factors Impacting Risk of Re-Offense

One RAI is known as the Static-99, so-named because it was created in 1999 and as an acknowledgement that it — and other RAIs — can consider only historical facts that have already happened or are otherwise not deemed as ever subject to change.

In some case, such as Subsection 2 in this section, supra, matters as basic and crucial to statistical risk calculation as base rates — assumed to be constant forever — in fact have drastically shrunk over the last 20 years. This renders any RAI based on former, higher average reoffense rates an enormous overestimate of any given individual's present risk of reoffense. Scientifically speaking, such incorrect determination of *static* character to what actually is a *dynamic* factor deprives all calculations based upon such erroneous assumption of static character as being science at all.

In other cases, such as Subsection 3, immediately supra, 'dynamic' refers to characteristics of the individual in question that either automatically vary over time (such as age), or which are subject to variance, whether through voluntary action by the individual or through external events or happenstance, or through internal 'change-of-heart', either by whatever perceptible means or merely apparently spontaneously. We have already seen that age-at-prison-release profoundly governs risk of reoffense; yet no RAI (except the Static-99, and in that case, far too conservatively) reckons that fact into its rate calculation.

Another profound factor classed as dynamic is whether an offender expresses or exhibits an unequivocal intention to commit another sex offense at the earliest opportunity. Call this the 'Rodriguez factor', after the Minnesota failure-to-supervise disaster involving prison releasee Alfonso Rodriguez, who made just such declarations of intent that went ignored. Even though it is self-evident that such individuals can be accurately deemed to be at high risk to reoffend, not one of the RAIs in current use include an offender's expressed intention as a factor.[1]

Conversely, none of the five RAIs in most common use give any weight to factors considered as 'protective' (i.e., which reduce risk of reoffense). Being placed in a supervised setting, participating in sex offender treatment, abstaining from drugs and alcohol, involvement in a healthy relationship with sexually appropriate partners, having support from families, friends, etc., and even adverse events, such as developing a debilitating illness, all have known 'protective' effects that substantially reduce risk of reoffense.

However, because none of these factors can be determined from a review of historical data for large statistical sample populations, and in general, are likely to be unknown or even unknowable as to the individual in question on the date of the RAI, they are not taken into consideration using an RAI.[2]

In other words, once one is committed based on ARA scores, *nothing* one does matters; that score can never change, since ARA factors are static. Hence, e.g., regardless of participation in, and success at years of sex offender treatment (whether outside or in commitment), no sex offender can ever reduce his actuarial risk of reoffense. Hence, once in commitment, one is doomed to remain detained for life.

The result is that, using the 'static' risk-*aggravating* factors that RAIs only include, and ignoring the entire realm of ignored 'protective' factors, RAIs inevitably overstate risk of reoffense.

Worse, by that very 'static'-only approach, RAIs treat an individual under scrutiny as a 'reoffending machine', without any will or resolve not to reoffend, and acting only reflexively, automatically, and helplessly. No prediction based on assumptions so contrary to all of human experience should be given any credence whatsoever, let alone bestowed the mantle of supposed 'scientific' status.

Where *Are* You Getting Your Data and Your Feedback from?

Bechman[3] criticizes RAIs as insufficiently supported by published, peer-reviewed academic articles describing in detail the development of any given RAI.

Bechman explains that these articles report "construction studies," which, generally throughout psychology, set forth copious information

1 *Bechman, ibid.*

2 *Ibid., p. 27; accord: Janus & Prentky, pp. 1479-1481.*

3 *Page 28.*

about the background of any new test, the experimental procedures used, and the data derived, in relation to any scientific theory or technique that is thus confirmed[1].

But in the case of RAIs, their creators and their advocates instead rely on "fugitive literature" to claim validity and reliability of the RAI in question. Fugitive literature includes information or assertions appearing only via websites or other forms of Internet circulation, unpublished materials merely submitted at conferences and data informally reported at such conferences. None of these forms of claims or data have been subjected to the peer review process; hence, neither the underlying data nor the methodology used to create a given RAI are held up to scientific scrutiny. Unscientifically, the claimed developmental integrity of such instruments is simply to be taken on faith.

This type of data (known as 'fugitive literature') is subject to academic criticism as not having been subjected to the peer review process. Lack of such review means that the underlying data, and the very methodology employed to create as RAI have never been held up to the appropriate level of scientific scrutiny.

Hence, the validity, reliability, and generalizability (among other crucial questions) of any RAI have never been adequately resolved, depriving RAIs of scientific status.

The Appalling Case of the MnSOST: — Not an RAI at All!

MnSOST-Series Instruments Were Not Designed for Actuarial Use. The MnSOST-3.1 is the latest descendent of the MnSOST 'tool' (which begat MnSOST-R, which begat MnSOST-3, and now 3.1). Having a format very much like a formal RAI, MnSOST, however, was designed purely for the in-house use of the Minnesota Department of Corrections in assigning a 'risk level' (1,2, or 3) to its sex offenders just before their release, for the purpose of determining what conditions of supervision should be imposed upon a prison-releasee who will then be on 'supervised release' (parole), including, notably, the 'package' of conditions known as 'Intensive Supervised Release' (ISR).

For instance, Fabian, "A Literature Review ..."[2], notes that, apart from factors applied by the various RAIs, MnSOST also considers "dynamic factors that focus on treatment amenability and institutional misconduct ... Inclusion of institutional items, namely treatment

---

1 *Ibid.*

2 *Page 328.*

success, may diminish the instrument's predictive validity ... These treatment programs that the MnSOST-R scoring system is based on may be quite different in nature than the treatment programs of a particular offender an examiner is evaluating ...".

First, therefore, because it was not designed as a formal RAI, it should not be confused for one, and it should never be encountered in the context of a civil commitment proceeding. At best, it can only be categorized in that context as a unique kind of guide for *clinical* (not actuarial) risk assessment (CRA). CRA has been shown to be approximately 70–90% incorrect, rendering that whole approach at predicting likelihood of sexual reoffense useless and unscientific to the point of failing the longstanding 'Frye test' of expert evidence or testimony admissibility.

State-Specificity and Small Samples Prevent the MnSOST from Gaining Generalizability

Second, the pool of released sex offenders which MnSOST and its progeny drew upon to derive calculations of probability of sexual reoffense were all Minnesota releasees. This fact strongly suggests that factors specific to *Minnesota* correctional practices, as well as regional idiosyncrasies as to sex offenses in general and sexual recidivism in particular, probably play a dominant role in the figures relied upon as input to those MnSOST calculations. Accordingly, none of the MnSOST sequence of 'tools' can be deemed to have generalized validity.

Distinctly, because the MnSOST series is thus limited to Minnesota sex offenders, the entire statistical sample is extremely small by comparison to the RAIs derived from large, nationwide, or even cross-national pools. This means that almost all of the subsets within that Minnesota-only pool used to set elevated rates of recidivism are tiny (often less than 100 offenders each), and hence, utterly statistically insignificant.

Undisclosed Data Blocks Peer Review

This probably partly accounts for why the Minnesota Department of Corrections and its employees who devised MnSOST have never released its underlying numerical data, which would become a source of professional derision. Of course, however, undisclosed data means that no peer review process of study and publication, as by meta-analysis, is possible. Without that peer review process, MnSOST could not be deemed to pass the 'Frye test' of acceptance by the appropriate scientific community.

The Magnified Error Rates of the MnSOST-Series

Fabian, ibid, also notes criticism of the MnSOST-R due to its lack of cross-validation by outsiders, and also because that instrument itself inflates its predictive accuracy, particularly through base rates suspected of being unrealistically inflated. Unlike other RAIs, which use charges and convictions to calculate recidivism, MnSOST-R uses arrests. The lack of cross validation partly occurs because study samples used for such validation do not include arrest data. Fabian concludes that, while the MnSOST-R can predict general recidivism, it lacks significant predictive validity for both violent and sexual recidivism[1].

We must return to the Wollert (supra) proof that small base rates of recidivism magnify error margins so much that predictions based on divergent 'factors' are reduced in accuracy to the level of pure chance. Statistics derived from Minnesota itself show a huge drop in the sex offense recidivism base rate occurred between those released in 1990 and those released in 2002. As an initial observation, this immediately renders obsolete and unusable at least all but (potentially the latest edition) MnSoST-3.1, as based on overly pessimistic recidivism numbers that no longer apply.

But even more fundamentally, the latest base rate, 3.2% recidivism, is itself *far lower* than the base rates shown by Wollert to be *too low* to derive any prediction above chance accuracy as to recidivism probability. MnSOST-3.1 employs that 3.2% base rate of sexual reoffense, as is shown by its array of 'cut scores' bracketing that figure (2.3% for Level 2; 5.8% for Level 3)[2]. Therefore, the predictive probability percentages derived for each of its 'bins' (increasingly elevated levels of probable recidivism) *must* mathematically carry with them such magnified error levels as to be equally useless as an RAI.

MnSOST-Series Coding Rules Depart from Actuarial Science

All of the foregoing points, taken alone and especially collectively, rule out MNSOST-3.1 as an RAI. However, as if that were not enough, an examination of the coding rules employed as to the MnSOST-3.1 drive it altogether from the temple of science. According to the Minnesota Sex Offender Screening Tool-3.1 (MnSOST-3.1) Coding Rules, a publication of the Minnesota Department of Corrections (revised: Feb. 10, 2012), each of the following determinants, albeit distinctions without difference, and highly counterintuitive in most

1 *Barbaree, Seto, Langton & Peacock, 2007)." Fabian, ibid.*

2 *MnSOST-3.1 Coding Rules.*

cases, are used to ascertain the applicability of factors which elevate the raw score of the MnSOST-3.1 (and hence, potentially radically alter its final 'percentage prognostication' of the probability of sexual reoffense in the case of any given sex offender under scrutiny.

Coding of Sentences

First, in an apparent attempt to eliminate multiple-count scenarios as a source of confusion about prior recidivism, rather than using the number of prior incarcerations or successful probationary terms (as it should), coding rules for the MNSOST-3.1 use number of prior sex-offense *sentences* a given sex offender has. This erroneously assumes that all multiple-count convictions are merged into a single aggregate sentence. In point of fact, at least in *Minnesota* criminal cases, this has not been universally true.

In many cases of multiple sex-offense counts, especially (but not always) with multiple victims in one prosecution, a sentencing judge may sentence each count independently (whether concurrently or consecutively) to arrive at a total, but not 'aggregated', single sentence, while a different judge (or even the same one in a different, but comparable case) will combine all counts and levy an 'aggregate' sentence. Given frequent prosecutorial 'multiple-billing' charging practices, this can have drastically divergent impacts on the MnSOST raw score. For instance, a sex offender *separately* sentenced in the same case on each of six counts would carry a component MnSOST-3.1 score of six from that case alone, while a different offender with a comparable sex offense case (also six counts, we will assume), but who received an aggregate sentence instead, will carry only a component score of one from that case.

This MnSOST-3.1 practice also ignores the less-frequent scenario where a single course of criminal sexual conduct proceeded across county lines over time, thus allowing each of two (or perhaps more) counties to charge the defendant for multiple counts that all relate to that single, ongoing course of criminality. This can occur with greater frequency in molestation cases. Thus, even in cases concerning just one victim, if both counties ultimately sentence this defendant separately for each count, the total number of sentences could easily reach or top a dozen.

Problems in Coding of Crimes

Second, the convictions tallied are for 'predatory offenses', without numerical weighting. These include many sex offenses from First Degree Criminal Sexual Conduct and First Degree Murder committed during commission or attempted commission of a sex crime (1st or 2nd degree) with force or violence, on the extreme end, to possession of child pornography and indecent exposure and misdemeanor sexual misconduct, on the other end.[1] Even kidnapping, false imprisonment, and corruption of a minor are tallied, "regardless of whether the offending behavior was sex or sex-related".[2] Sentences for harassment, stalking, and for violation of court orders — for protection, imposing restraining orders, and barring contact — are tallied even if no sexual conduct or sexual motivation is involved.[3] Disorderly conduct sentences in the last three years are counted — again, regardless of lack of sexual connection.[4] This calls into earnest question exactly what the MnSOST-3.1 is looking for recidivism with respect to.

Conversely, regardless whether sexually motivated, other crimes, such as burglary and assault, are not deemed 'predatory', and hence are not tallied at all.[5]

Inconsistency as to treatment of an offense or conduct that comprises an offense abounds in Mn-SOST-3.1. For instance, counts which are dismissed are not tallied, but a count that is dismissed following a probationary sentence is counted. Self-reported offenses not resulting in a sentence are not tallied, but if such a non-charged, self-reported offense appears in a psychological evaluation, it is deemed 'credible' and is counted.[6] Even though disorderly conduct offenses count (regardless of motivation), a prison disciplinary offense (not resulting in a new criminal sentence) will not count, even if for egregious sexual misconduct of a viciously predatory type.[7]

Coding Problems as to Parole Supervision

Third, in fairness, the MnSOST-3.1 deserves some credit, in any event, for pioneering a factor recognizing the recidivism risk difference resulting from whether or not post-release supervision (e.g., supervised release or intensive supervised release, or condition of release) will be involved.[8] However, rather than correctly recognizing supervision as the salutary, recidivism-reducing circumstance that it is by employing a *subtractive* score for its involvement in a given case, MnSOST-3.1 *adds* a point for its absence (as, e.g., where a releasee is leaving prison upon discharge of his sentence, with no conditional release remaining).

1 *Ibid., pp. 6–7.*

2 *Ibid pp. 8–9.*

3 *Ibid p. 12.*

4 *Ibid. p. 13.*

5 *Ibid.*

6 *Ibid., pp. 9–10.*

7 *Ibid., pp. 10, 13.*

8 *Ibid. p. 15.*

Further, whether additive or subtractive, a single, 'nominal' point drastically understates the difference in recidivism likelihood that supervision, especially of the 'intensive' sort, can make. Particularly in the context of the relatively short (four-year) post-release period that MnSOST-3.1 considers for recidivism, supervision, where it is imposed, will likely extend through that whole period, and will likely be of the intensive kind. Hence, understating this 'supervision impact' on recidivism is inexcusable.

Problems in Coding For Treatment

Fourth, MnSOST does not award a subtractive point for treatment completion while incarcerated on the current (index) sentence or sentence cluster. However, to receive this subtractive point, an offender must complete *both* sex offender treatment and chemical dependency treatment. This applies regardless whether a given offender has any problem whatsoever with chemical dependency.[1] Many sex offenses have no connection to drug or alcohol use or dependency. Nor are most sex offenses a product of any 'sex addiction' — itself a highly controversial term that, at least when over-applied to sex offenses universally, is sheer junk science.

Moreover, MnSOST-3.1 does not grant this subtractive point for community-based treatment programs completed, whether before or after incarceration. It would be understandable to deny credit for a *pre*-offense treatment completion, but to limit *post*-offense treatment completions to those in prison is arbitrary and highly questionable. Finally on this point, no lesser type of programming, such as psycho-educational or self-help programming, is granted any partial credit; only full, residential, intensive treatment programming is recognized. It is dubious that such lesser programming can have no salutary effect in terms of reducing recidivism. The failure of MnSOST-3.1 to at least thoroughly investigate this and to award a partial score where merited, adds to the arbitrary absolutism of this treatment aspect to MnSOST-3.1 scoring.

Coding Problems as to Male Victims

Last, MnSOST-3.1 includes a multiple-point factor for male victims. This factor itself is open to strenuous question and criticism. Its origin was in a Canadian study of all kinds of violence, not just sexual violence. The particular connection to sexual recidivism arose from sexual assaults — often in prison or commitment facilities — upon co-residents, all of whom were adult males. Yet such rapes of adult males in a non-incarcerated setting border on the rare.

---

1 *Ibid., p. 17.*

They are far outnumbered by molestations of male children, for instance. Not as science, but as mere ipse dixit categorization, the unusually high recidivism statistics for the former type of crime have been applied to the latter, even though, by far, most molestations, whether of boys or girls, do not involve rape[1] or any violence or use of force. Between molestations of the respective genders, rapes of girls are far more common than rapes of boys. Recidivistic tendencies for sex crimes are generally higher where rape or other violence is involved in an offender's prior and current crimes. Hence, it would stand to reason that recidivism would be higher for heterosexual molestations than homosexual ones (i.e., upon boys).

In light of this, the authors of MNSOST-3.1 should conduct a study of male-victim molestations and announce their methodology and conclusions. However, those authors have declined to do so for the MnSOST or any of its progeny to date. This deprives the MNSOST-3.1 of any claim to 'forensic' status as a matter of science.

Even assuming a correlation between molestation of boys and increased recidivism, MnSOST-3.1's scoring approach to this factor is exorbitantly high and without rational connection to any increase. This factor *doubles* the points assessed adversely for each sentence involving a male victim. This is disproportionate to any increased recidivism probability. Moreover, prosecutors (presumably through personal rage and political posturing) are far more likely to 'multiple bill' several or more counts in a criminal complaint when the victim is male. To the extent that such multiple counts lead to separate sentencing, this disproportionate doubling of such counts' impact on an MNSOST 3.1 score could easily get extreme.

MnSOST-Series Is Neither Scientific Nor Forensic for the Sex Offender Commitment Context

In sum, MnSOST-3.1 is not scientific, and thus cannot claim the 'mantle' of being meaningfully forensic. It does not limit its focus to antecedent offenses of a sexual type or with sexual intent. It appears to be a tool for assaying *aggregate* likelihood of recidivism by any of a general 'laundry list' of crimes deemed particularly troubling or angering. However, since sex offenses are only some of these, it cannot be said that MnSOST-3.1 offers a prediction of a probability of sex offense recidivism in particular.

Therefore, it is simply not an RAI, and should not be used as one. Finally, the various 'coding' (scoring) rules above show an

1 *Here, the term is used in its limited, traditional definition: involuntary coitus or rectal penetration.*

utter disregard for science in the MnSOST-3.1 scoring practices. Most items are scored with arbitrary absolutism, and many involve inexplicable, idiosyncratic inconsistencies apparently based more on coder convenience than on a fair approximation of the relevant, true circumstances of any given sex offender.

For all of these reasons, a predictive probability (expressed as a percentage) of recidivism derived from application of the MnSOST-3.1 to a given sex offender stands no greater odds than pure chance of being even fairly accurate.

Even just the decisions of the Minnesota Department of Corrections based upon this score (including public notification ramifications and extreme restrictions on a releasee, making even getting or holding a job, and other basics of life impossible or nearly so) have grave consequences, and unwittingly amount to a self-fulfilling prophecy in terms of forcing absconding by releasees from supervision, as well as other non-sex-crime causes for re-incarceration. Because MnSOST-3.1 amounts to nothing more than a framework for guesswork, making such vital decisions based upon it unconscionable, it should be abandoned.

The Leading RAI Is Useless

The Leading RAI, Static-99R/Static-2002R, is unscientific and statistically useless for predictive probability derivation for future sex offense recidivism.

Control Sample Problems

Sample sizes are too small to be statistically significant. Note that all data and other facts herein were extracted from the Static-99R and Static-2002R Evaluators' Workbook, by A. Phenix, L. Helmes, & R.K. Hanson [2012], hereinafter 'Evaluators' Handbook'.

> "The Static-99 may be the most frequently used sexual recidivism actuarial instrument in North America. It incorporates the RRASOR ... and the Structured Actuarial Clinical Judgment-Minimum (SACJ-Min) ...".
>
> *Fabian, "A Literature Review...", supra, at p. 326.*

This fact becomes startling when considering its many profound flaws. For starters, explaining samples used to construct percentile ranks, the Evaluator's Workbook, p. 12, asserts that, "Ideally, the percentiles calculated in the Evaluator's Workbook would consider all Canadian adults convicted of a sexual offense as the reference category". For purposes of use in post-prison sentence commitment of sex offenders, that statement is incorrect. The reference category should *include only those who did in fact serve a prison sentence.*

The Static-99R and Static-2002R RAIs were constructed based in part on a sampling called 'Dynamic Supervision Project', reflecting the recidivism experience of groups totaling 595 offenders, convicted of a sexual offense in Canada[1]. This is an extremely small control sample, falling within the range of statistical insignificance for deriving base rates of recidivism.

The remaining samples used to construct percentile ranks (more on this infra) for both the -99R and -2002R versions were in the same small range: (a) "Federal: BC": 296; (b) "Federal: 1995 WED": 663; and (c) "Federal: Quebec": 457. Each of these figures is statistically insignificant. Even their total (with the 595 added, supra) is only 2,011 sex offenders, a figure barely into the statistically significant range.

However, the fallacy is that merely adding different samples together is not a valid method of achieving statistical significance. Significance is to be judged against the individual sample (e.g., one sample comprising 2,011 individuals). The Static-series of RAIs instead use an *aggregation* of samples.

Unrepresentative Sample

The varying constituency of the respective sub-samples adding up to that overall 'Dynamic Supervision Project' sample makes the overall aggregation unrepresentative, for purposes of comparison to sex offenders at prison release in the United States.

A number of problems are subsumed within this point. First, one sub-sample of the 'Dynamic Supervision Project' sample comprised offenders who had a "non-sexual violent index [current] offense"[2]. Because the dynamics of crime perpetration in general and recidivism in particular differ for those convicted, respectively, of sex offenses on one hand, or of violent offenses on the other, inclusion of violent, non-sexual offenders is a corruption of the overall statistical control sample. Another subset (n=31) was excluded from Static-series calculation because none of those offenders recidivated.[3] Doing this artificially drove up all predicted percentages.

Another similar point: one 'risk factor' in the Static-99R RAI is "convictions for non-contact sex offenses"[4]. Yet at least one sample (Boer, 2003) *excludes* such reoffenses from calculation of reference percentages of probability of recidivism.[5] Again, this increases all

1 *Evaluator's Workbook, p. 12.*

2 *Ibid., p. 12.*

3 *Ibid, pp. 17-18.*

4 *Ibid., p. 30.*

5 *Ibid., p. 20.*

recidivism percentages for specific sex offenders compared against that reference group.

Second, Static-series RAIs are based on varying studies (samples). "Recidivism was defined as charges in about half of these studies and as convictions in the other half."[1] Anyone can, of course, be falsely accused of a crime or misidentified as a perpetrator of one. This includes those with prior records of sex offenses as well as anyone else. Indeed, having such a record makes one a target of suspicion whenever a new sex crime with no known perpetrator is announced. Accordingly, recidivism should be judged only by subsequent convictions, not charges. But even more muddled, this quote indicated that both mere charges and convictions are muddled together, making any accurate calculation of actual recidivism impossible, in turn making the Static-series RAIs meaningless and improper to rely upon.

Third, slightly over half of the offenders in that sample received a probationary-type sentence, and thus never went to prison. This was also true of the other samples used by the Static-series, such as the 'Craissati', et al., study (299 subjects, all of whom were on probation), and the 'Epperson' study (undisclosed portion on probation). This inclusion in Static-series 'routine' samples means that the percentile rankings, as well as the probability percentages themselves, were skewed by adding in such probationers.[2] At a minimum, the problem with this inclusion is that offenders thus sentenced probably either committed *less severe* sex crimes (or with any various *mitigating* circumstance(s) of the offense itself), or personally presented with *favorable*, perhaps even *exemplary* personal backgrounds, such that probation was deemed appropriate.

In contrast, by definition, anyone under scrutiny for sex offender commitment has just *served a prison sentence*. The fact of that prison sentence implies, conversely, that something about the offense, the offender, or both, made probation impossible or inadvisable. Thus, a comparison of any prison-releasee sex offender to the Static-series aggregate sample is unfair, and will *always* overstate recidivistic tendency of anyone rated on a Static-series RAI for purposes of a civil commitment decision, simply on this uneven comparison, largely based against those excepted from prison.

Fourth, in the Static-series 'Dynamic Supervision' sample, even among the roughly half who were sent to prison, another unfair comparison arises. One subgroup (approximately 85% of this half) had been sent to *provincial* prisons, while the remaining 15% had

---

1 *Ibid., p. 31.*

2 *Evaluator's Workbook, p. 28.*

been sent to Canadian federal prison.[1] The Workbook explains that in Canada only those with sentences *less than two years* are sent to provincial prisons. Sentences of two years or more result in placement in a federal prison.

Once again, the higher the sentence, either the more severe the crime, or the worse the background of the offender, or both. More importantly, in this context, a sentence of less than two years for a sex offense implies a comparatively less severe crime or set of specific facts of the offense, or some truly redeeming personal attributes of the offender, or perhaps both, as compared to federal-level (longer) sentences.

Because this portion amounts to 85% of those in this sample who were sent to prison, even that prison sentence half is not a fair comparison to those sent to prison for sex offenses in the United States, where virtually all prison sentences for sex crimes now greatly exceed two years in length. More to the point, the correct base rate for prisoners with longer sentences would be derived from a base sample that had *equally* long sentences.

One can argue that those with longer sentences should be compared to all prisoners with sex offense sentences (i.e., to a sample representative of that average). Indeed, that Evaluators' Workbook declares that the mix of samples is "roughly representative of all adjudicated sex offenders."[2] But comparison to a sample including an 85% portion of *relatively short* sentences once again 'stacks the deck' against those with longer sentences that already imply some judicial assessment of a higher likelihood of recidivism, inter alia. To compare these against those with lighter sentences not reflecting such a judicial assessment is to automatically increase the relative probability of reoffense simply because of one's sentence — a form of a `secret additional factor' in Static-series RAIs.

'Re-Weighting' Percentiles Derived from Samples Destroys the Actual Science Supporting the Static-Series RAIs

At p. 28, the Evaluators' Workbook states, in passing: "These percentiles are from 2,011 cases from 4 samples of Canadian sex offenders, which were re-weighted to approximate the distribution of all convicted sex offenders in Canada." (repeated at p. 41).

Really?!

---

1 *Ibid., p. 12.*

2 *Ibid., p. 32.*

The question that immediately arises is: How would the Static-series authors have the information necessary to do that, without also possessing a sample comprised of "all convicted sex offenders in Canada"? Other comments made elsewhere in that workbook make it clear that no such comprehensive sample was in their possession. Therefore, this 're-weight[ing]' is scientifically baseless and contrary to all sampling regimes of actuarial science.

"What Are We Testing for, Again?"

In the aforesaid Evaluators' Workbook, at p.37, the authors of the Static-2002R declare it to be "designed to assist in the prediction of sexual *and violent* recidivism for sex offenders". Farther down the same page, they trumpet that the "Static-2002R demonstrated moderate to large accuracy in the prediction of sexual, violent, and general recidivism". Yet nothing in this work suggests any different methods of using the Static-2002R RAI to tease out some differing percentages of predicted probabilities of each of those three different kinds of recidivism questions.

On the contrary, administering any of the Static-series RAIs generates a single percentage-based expression of probability of recidivism. This apparent 'one size fits all' percentage would therefore seem to state a general prediction for *any* kind of recidivism (i.e., *any kind* of subsequent crime), rather than confining the prediction to projected sex offenses. Of course, in the context of civil commitment of sex offenders, only the probability of such future sex offenses is under inquiry. Because the Static-2002R conflates the probabilities of all three types of recidivism, the percentage derived, even were it accurate to its own methodology, does not answer the question of what is the probability of just future sex offenses by the sex offender in question? Worse, by aggregating all three types of recidivism into one percentage figure, it necessarily follows that such figure, if mistakenly taken as representing *only* sex offense recidivism, substantially overstates that probability.

Inherent Lack of Accuracy

The low recidivism base rates and wide confidence intervals (CIs) of the Static-series RAIs confirm their inherent lack of accuracy and their disutility in sex offender commitment trials.

The Static-99R 'routine sample' table of 'Estimated 5-years sexual recidivism rates' reveals a bottom-end 1.2%, a median 5%, and a *top* recidivism rate of 29.5% (this last within a 95% confidence interval

(CI) of 22.8 to 37.2%).[1] We shall have considerable separate concerns about the respective 'nonroutine' samples of the Static-series RAIs and their usage in a subsection infra. Even lower are the bottom end 0.7%, the median 2.8%, and the top recidivism rates on the Static-2002R routine sample: 12.5% (this last within a 95% CI of 5.4-26.4%).[2]

First, as Wollert, "Low Base Rates Limit Expert Certainty When Current Actuarials Are Used ..."[3] pointed out, at lower base rates than 50%, RAIs inherently inaccurately overstate predictions of recidivism for subject offenders compared against that low base-rate sample, with the degree of percentage overstatement increasing dramatically the greater the base rate figures depart downward from 50%.

Wollert also determined that wide CIs, particularly matched to such low base rates, reflect a compounding inaccuracy in such particularized prediction for any such subject sex offender. Both low base rates and wide CIs are present in the Static-series RAIs. Wollert's illustrative calculations using the Static-99R show its dramatic inaccuracy as to such particularized predictions, from just these two inherent problems. Hence, even just the Static-99R is too inaccurate to be used in sex offender commitment trials. Comparatively, the even-lower recidivism rates expressed by the Static-2002R, supra, are, a fortiori, burdened with even greater inaccuracy as to such particularized predictions. In sum, therefore, neither current Static-series RAI possesses the necessary accuracy of recidivism-prediction percentage to be employed in a sex offender commitment trial.

The Static-series 'non-routine' sample-based tables of predicted recidivism rates are rife with unscientific methodology, such that they are unusable in sex offender commitment trials.

The Non-Routine Samples Method Explained

Presumably because the predicted percentages of probability of recidivism were not high enough to be pleasing to prosecutors, both the Static-99R and the Static-2002R contain alternative tables of higher percentages of such predicted probability. In the Static-99R, three such alternative tables were constructed: the 'Non-routine sample', the 'Preselected for treatment need', and the 'High-risk/need group' tables. In the Static-2002R, the two alternative tables are, respectively, a 'Non-routine sample' table (with different percentages

---

1 *Ibid, p. 5.*

2 *Ibid., p. 9. Note that these lower rates obtained from the most recent samples of the Static-99R to compile the Static-2002R percentages, reflect the across-the-board reduction of sex offender recidivism within the last 20 years. See Workbook, pp. 17-18.*

3 *12 Psychology, Public Policy, and Law, pp. 56 at 59.*

from the identically named table in the Static-99R) and the 'High risk/need group'. Note that in the case of the 'Routine sample' tables in both the Static-99R and the Static-2002R, only a *single* set of predicted recidivism rates exist, viz., for a 5-year post-prison release projected period. However, in both of those same Static-series RAIs, the alternative tables identified, supra, have two projected periods: a 10-year projected period, as well as that same 5-year period.

In each of these RAIs, the 5-year predicted probability percentages are much higher in the alternative tables than in the 'Routine' table. How much higher? Consider these examples. In the Static-99R 'Routine table', the median (score=2) predicted 5-year probability is 5.0%, and the high-end prediction is 29.5%. In contrast, in the Static-99R's 'Non-routine sample' table, the corresponding 5-year figures are: 9.1% (median) and 51.6% (high-end), and its 'High risk/need group' table's 5-year corresponding figures are 12.2% (median) and 59.7% (high-end). In the Static-2002R 'Routine' table, the median (score=3) 5-year prediction is 2.8% and the high-end prediction is 12.5%. Recall that these reductions from the Static-99R are due to sex offense recidivism reductions. However, in the Static-2002R's 'Non-routine sample' table, the corresponding 5-year figures are: 10.3% (median) and 49.9% (high-end) and its 'High risk/need group' table's 5-year figures are: 12.3% (median) and 55% (high-end).

Notably, notwithstanding the general trend of reduced sex offense recidivism, in both the Static-99R and the Static-2002R, the median-score percentage figures were higher for the non-standard samples than for the 'Routine sample' and, while the Static-2002R's non-standard samples had *slightly* lower high-end percentage figures than the corresponding high-end figures for the Static-99R, the ratio of disparity (the *multiple*) between the Routine sample's median figure and the median figure for the non-standard tables and between the high-end figures of those respective tables *increased* from the Static-99R to the Static-2002R, thus —

	Static-99R			**Static-2002R**		
	Routine	Non Routine	Ratio	Routine	Non Routine	Ratio
Median	50%	91%	1 : 1.82	2.8%	10.3%	1 : 3.68
High End	29.5%	51.6%	1 : 1.74	12.5%	49.9%	1 : 4 **Higher!**

This is no accident. The whole reason for the popularization of the actuarial approach to sex offender recidivism was the prosecutorial 'demand' for expert-testimony justifications for sex offender commitment. The downturn in recidivism statistics for sex offenders in general doubtlessly was greeted with great dismay by prosecutors. Invention of such non-routine probability tables, nearly wiping out the effect of that actual reduction in recidivism, filled that demand for condemnatory testimony exactly.

Let's turn to the fallacies employed in service of that aim.

Cherry-Picked Samples

The samples used for the Non-routine statistical cohort are unrepresentative and are 'cherry-picked' for their extremely adverse attributes.

It appears that samples comprising the comparison set for both the Static-2002R and the Static-99R were picked for their high percentages of recidivism, contrary to the recent, general trend of reduced sex offender recidivism. However, this is partly explained by the long sentences served by those in such samples, meaning that their recidivistic crimes occurred long ago, before that reduction began. Effectively, in this way, any sex offender under scrutiny for commitment can be penalized, not just for his own past, but also for the more distant past of groups of other sex offenders. It is also explained by the extreme attributes of the samples used to make up these non-routine probability tables.

Let's look at the Static-2002R first. Its 'Preselected High-risk/Need' table comprises three small samples (totaling 931 for 5-year data): 'Bengtson', 'Haag', and 'Knight & Thornton', respectively (after authors of studies about each sample). 'Bengtson' is a true classic, comprising a jumble of obviously high-risk categories:

> "The study sample consists of sex offenders who received a *pre-trial forensic psychiatric evaluation* in Denmark. Such evaluations were typically conducted for offenders *suspected of a mental disorder or mental retardation*, offenders *deemed high risk by the courts*, those *accused of serious offenses*, and those for whom *an indefinite sentence was being considered.*"[1]

Obviously, extreme risk factors were considered in each of those determinations, making this an extreme sample.

The Haag sample is noted by the central fact that, unlike imprisoned sex offenders in Canada generally (who are normally released 2/3 of the way through their sentences), all sex offenders in the Haag sample were detained until sentence expiration. This

1 *Evaluator's Workbook, p. 22; emphases supplied.*

happens only when "the parole board is satisfied that, if released, the offender poses a significant risk of committing a serious offense before their sentence expires".[1] This is an individually-based decision upon factors specific to that offender. This makes this parole denial rather like a commitment decision, and this sample akin to a group of those already committed, and hence, strongly suggestive of higher risk factors.

The third sample, 'Knight & Thornton', is overtly just the latter:

"This study followed offenders who were either assessed or treated at the Massachusetts Treatment Center (MTC; a treatment center for sexually dangerous persons) between 1959 an 1984."[2] This overtly samples those who were either tentatively or finally committed — a determination of high recidivism status. Separately, the years of release covered by this sample reflect higher recidivism rates centered on the 1970s — long before the aforementioned 'watershed' reduction in sex offender recidivism. Something else about methodology deserves mention concerning this particularly dubious sample: "If one rater's score did not make sense ..., the other rater's score was used. When consensus ratings could not be generated, the rating was determined by flipping a coin."[3]

In the High Risk/Needs class, similar problems of unrepresentativeness and extremely adverse aspects also beset the samples used by Static-99R to comprise that same table. The three samples above were also used in that RAI, and the following sample as well. The 'Bonta & Yessine' study, using offenders flagged as potential "Dangerous Offenders", those already officially so designated, and those "who committed a violent offense after being detained until [sentence expiration]".[4] These sub-groupings included those with a non-sexual current offense of violence. The 'Nicolaichuk' sample comprised sex offenders detained in "a federal [Canada] maximum security forensic mental health facility".[5] And last, the 'Wilson' sample comprised "high-risk sex offenders who were detained in prison until [sentence expiration]". These problems of unrepresentative and extreme nature of the respective samples should be obvious.

Similar problems impact the non-routine classes in the Static-99R RAI as well. Examples: 'Brouillette-Alarie & Proulx': inmates at a "maximum security psychiatric facility"[6]; 'Hill, Haberman,

---

1 *Ibid.*

2 *Ibid., p. 23.*

3 *Ibid.*

4 *Ibid., p. 22.*

5 *Ibid., p. 23.*

6 *Ibid., p. 21.*

Klusmann, et al': offenders "who committed a sexual homicide". Conversely, samples such as 'Saum' were *excluded* from these non-routine classes as a "statistical outlier" (presumably, close-to-normal recidivism numbers). If that's not 'cherry picking', you tell me what it is.

The Static-Series Rationale for Non-Routine Sample Sets Condemns the Inaccuracy of Static Series RAIs

The inaccuracy of the Static-series RAIs has been conceded and condemned by the pens of their authors themselves. At. page 34 of that Evaluator's Workbook, those authors explain thus:

> "There have been a large number of studies examining the absolute sexual recidivism rates associated with Static-99 scores ...
>
> "The observed recidivism base rates varied considerably across samples *based on factors not measured by Static-99R*. Samples that were preselected to be high risk/high needs ... show the highest recidivism rates, samples preselected based on treatment need ... had intermediate recidivism rates, and routine (unselected) correctional samples had recidivism rates substantially lower than the preselected groups ..."[1]

But then at page 35 that passage turns a corner into a nonsequitur:

> "Consequently in order to evaluate [the sex offender in question], we need to consider the extent to which he resembles the typical member of the routine samples, or if he is more representative of the samples preselected for treatment or the high-risk/high needs samples."

Stop right there! What happened to the self-professed ideal of an RAI based on "all Canadian adults convicted of a sexual offense as the reference category"[2]? As a self-imposed solution to the practicalities of amassing sample data, the authors of the Static-series RAIs constructed the Static-99R 'routine' set of samples that included, inter alia, Canadian federal offenders (longer sentences), and even included one ('Haag') sample used in the Static-2002R *non*-routine sample sets. *So the problem isn't one of non-inclusiveness or under-inclusiveness; it is simply an issue of inaccuracy and failure to account for omitted (and probably uninvestigated) factors.*

---

1 *Emphasis supplied.*

2 *Ibid., p. 12.*

An Example of the Unfairness of Application of the 'Non-Routine' Tables

Ponder this example: Mr. Xxxx is rated on the Static-2002R and is unequivocally, consistently assigned a score of 9. Judged against the 'Routine Sample' set, Mr. Xxxx will be declared to have a 12.5% probability of sexual reoffense within 5 years. While that is substantially above the 'median' recidivism rate, according to that test, it is not excessive compared to traditional average sex offense rates. Yet, based not just on the *same score,* but in fact also based identically on the very same particular factors (and their individual weights), if judged against the 'Non-Routine Sample' of that same RAI, Mr. Xxxx will be declared to have a 49.9% probability of sexual reoffense within 5 years. Indeed, (even though the '*Routine*' sample set does not project 10-year reoffense rate, that 'Non-Routine' projection includes an extension to 60.7% probability of sexual reoffense over a total of 10 years. Should Mr. Xxxx be so unfortunate as to be 55–59 years of age on his prison release date, these 5- and 10-year heightened percentages won't even be reduced due to the fact that most of that 10-year period will transpire after he turns age 60.

In sum, at a minimum, Mr. Xxxx will be assessed a probability *four times* the estimate he would have if judged against the general ('routine') sample set and, in the context of a sex offender commitment trial, will very likely be committed (whereas otherwise he would not), all irrespective of the identical factors and score he was rated on, but instead solely due to which sample set he was judged against. Something is seriously amiss here.

Obviously, both 'non-routine' sample sets of the Static-2002R have higher rates of recidivism. That is so expressly because they were cherry-picked for that purpose. That very fact makes the use of those non-routine percentage tables unfair. Everyone in the non-routine samples would also have been a part of the routine sample sets — and some actually were. The non-routine sample sets are thus subsets of the routine. Every individual should therefore be compared to the overarching routine sample table. Doing otherwise makes the Static-series RAIs unfair as to anyone compared against a non-routine table.

The Decision to Use a Non-Standard Table in a Static-Series RAI Is Unscientific, Involving Rate-Supplied Non-Actuarial Factors

Apart from this, the use of non-routine sample sets is not based on any scientifically validated criteria by which to select the table to use, and it amounts to a disguised extra set of unspecified factors not scored or weighted in the Static-series RAIs at all. As the Evaluator Workbook shows, that decision of which table to use is left up to the rater ('evaluator') on *whatever criteria the rater deemed important.* At best, this amounts to surreptitious importation of clinical considerations (CRA) into what is held out to be a purely scientific, actuarial procedure. This corrupts and invalidates that scientific character.

The woeful, less-than-pure-chance inaccuracy of the impressionistic, anecdotal and highly subjective CRA approach to sex offender recidivism risk assessment has been long documented and utterly debunked. Because Static-series RAIs *invite it back into ARA prediction through this 'back door'*, all Static-series tests based on non-routine probability tables must be rejected as unscientific and inherently invalid and worthless as predictive tools.

Lest you suspect this to be empty oratory, consider this mere 'guidance' offered to raters using the Static-99R RAI:

> "The best method of determining which sample type is the most *appropriate* match to an individual *is not fully known*. The *position of the test developers* is that the *variability across samples* can best be explained by *differences* in the density of *individual risk factors not already included in the scale*. Consequently, determining the *appropriate* sample type reference group should be based on *consideration of psychologically meaningful risk factors* (e.g., a *dynamic assessment scale*). As a *general guideline*, the routine norms should be used for offenders low on external *psychologically meaningful risk factors*. The preselected for treatment norms should be used for offenders with moderate needs on *external risk factors*. The preselected high risk/need norms should be reserved for offenders with pronounced *external psychologically meaningful risk factors* (e.g., reserved for no more than *the top 10-20% highest risk*).
>
> "In the absence of information about external psychologically meaningful risk factors, evaluators can also consider the features of the three samples, which are described in further detail below."
>
> *Evaluators' Workbook, p. 35*[1]

This quote is loaded with 'waffle words and phrases', e.g., 'appropriate', 'variability', 'factors not already included', 'consideration of psychologically meaningful risk factors', and 'general guideline'.

1 *Emphases supplied.*

This alone conveys *the unscientific nature of the decision process the authors are suggesting to raters.*

Further, the admission that "the best method of deciding on an apt sample-set table is not fully known" (a gross understatement) telegraphs the open-ended, subjective, impressionistic, and anecdotally-based nature of that unscientific, virtually visceral decision. The reference to '*individual* risk factors' not rated in the Static-series scales opens the door widely to all of that unscientific, emotionally reactive decision-making.

Although this passage cites as an example of such personal 'psychologically meaningful risk factors' a 'dynamic risk assessment scale', there still is no, and probably never will be any, validated, peer-reviewed, generalizable, and reliable scale of such personal factors, partly because of the long-run unpredictable chaos of individual experience in the day-to-day over time (see Subsection V.D., infra) and partly because personal reaction to stimuli varies dramatically and unpredictably from one individual to another.

Worst of all are the overlaid concepts of psychology which are often misgiven in theory or misapplied. For instance, one item constantly pressed by some as a 'factor' in so-called 'dynamic' risk assessment is lack of treatment as to an individual sex offender. However, by 'grading' or 'scoring' the specific individual about this, it is being misapplied as a 'trait' (as in 'trait-based psychology'), rather than merely being a condition.

This has a profound impact on the utility of such personal factors. As to treatment, the effect or lack of effect of lack of treatment on a specific individual is deeply tied to a plethora of internal psychological aspects of that individual himself. For some, such lack may have significant impact on various aspects of their thoughts and emotions, and ultimately, on recidivism itself. For others, however, such impact may be negligible, as ultimately evinced by a lack of recidivism.

Were there any generalizability and reliability to that particular 'dynamic' factor, it would (like age-at-release) have been adopted as a factor by the Static-series RAIs. The fact that it has not been so adopted speaks volumes about its unreliability in general. Thus, to find the Static-series developers *inviting* raters to themselves import such unscientific decision factors on a matter of table-choice *that alone can quadruple the reported recidivism probability percentage* from a Static-series RAI is the most preposterous, unethical and deeply disturbing tactic imaginable for those supposedly presenting the reliability of actuarial science. How many individuals have been baselessly committed purely because of this *single, unscientific choice* by a Static-series RAI rater?

The Suggestion That Raters Compare a Rated Sex Offender to Various Alternative Attributes in Specific Samples Is the Most Unscientific Aspect of All

The appalling nature of the 'fallback suggestion' in the foregoing quote to compare the rated individual against the non-routine samples is best understood from the differing characteristics of those samples. Because of such differences, they are not homogeneous, and thus, they defy statistical study. Hence they, and use of Static-series RAIs involving their application, are scientifically invalid. To confirm the speciousness of use of such attributes of the respective non-routine sample sets, let's examine the description offered by pages 35 and 36 of the Evaluators' Workbook.

As to the category, 'Preselected for treatment needs', that text explains: "This group consisted of six samples of offenders referred for sex offender specific treatment during their current incarceration". However, currently (in the United States, at least), all prison systems insist on sex offender treatment for all sex offenders. Therefore, *any* sex offender under scrutiny for commitment would qualify for this non-routine category. Of course, because of the universality of this prison-based directive for treatment, each sex offender remains in the 'routine' group as well.

As to the 'High-risk/high-needs' category, the explanation states: "Offenders in this group were referred for services at forensic psychiatric facilities ... It would also include offenders referred to intensive treatment programs reserved for the highest risk offenders ... Offenders identified ... by examining a range of risk-relevant characteristics such as sentence extensions for dangerousness ... would also be in this group". Again, of course, such offenders were also included in the samples comparing the 'routine' group. Distinctly, in many jurisdictions, examination of 'forensic psychiatric facilities' is routine before sentencing, especially where a sentencing judge is pondering probation as an option. Yet the fact that such option is being considered is not mentioned as a countervailing consideration for not using a non-routine table.

As to referral to intensive treatment programs, what is deemed to comprise an 'intensive' treatment program varies vastly among jurisdictions and corrections agencies. Moreover, there has been an 'inflation' of standards of what is deemed sufficient 'treatment' of sex offenders over the last thirty years. When some of the non-routine samples of the Static-series RAIs were being populated (by offenders who received treatment back then), only a small minority received what would be deemed 'intensive' treatment today. Conversely, most (if not nearly all) sex offender treatment programs in American prisons today would have been referred to back then as 'intensive'. Indeed, because current standards of prison treatment call for special inpatient units with programs ranging from 1½ to 3 years in length, with as many, or more, hours of therapy per week than is the case in sex offender commitment facilities themselves, any rater could perfectly reasonably deem any rated sex offender as having been referred for 'intensive' treatment.

Even as to uniquely intensive treatment programs (by current comparisons) to which prisons may refer only a small minority of sex offenders, various questions arise with widely varying answers, depending on the particular state or other jurisdiction: (a) Who is assigned to make the decision to refer, and what are their particular credentials in sex offender treatment? (b) What are the statutory or administrative-rule-based elements/requirements that govern such referrals, and what is their forensic relationship to the question of uniquely high likelihood of recidivism? (c) What was the personal basis for that referral in the case of the sex offender in question?

Because the answers to these questions vary among jurisdictions, have varied over time, and probably even vary substantially from one referred sex offender to another in the same correctional agency, such a comparison of a sex offender being rated against unknown (and simply imagined) criteria for referrals in such non-routine samples, at best, amounts only to an unscientific comparison of the proverbial apples to oranges.

Moreover, in the larger picture, it is unscientific that a sheer referral to such treatment is regarded as sufficient to elevate one into this quadruple-percentage-of-recidivism group. What this effectively means is that one's Static-series percentage-prediction of recidivism is affected merely by whether someone at some time has *deemed* one to be a higher-risk offender. Anyone can so deem for any reason subjectively thought to be sufficient. This is not actuarial science.

Alternatively, use of 'sentence extensions for dangerousness', at least in the United States in the last 30 years, has had a political aspect. Some states have long had indeterminate (life) sentences for sex offenders (as to certain sex crimes) categorically. However, other states (at least initially) passed such longer sentences into law only for recidivist sex offenders. Typically, these were *labeled* as being in response to 'dangerousness', but the statutory formulations turned purely on the second-or-subsequent instance of a sex crime. In some cases with two or more *simultaneous* convictions, one of them was designated a 'second', simply to justify that extended sentence, otherwise unavailable to the judge in the absence of indeterminate sentencing. Even otherwise, however, application of a non-routine Static-series table to one due to such recidivism-based 'dangerousness' sentences is unfair and unscientific, particularly because the Static-series scored scales *already* increase one's score for recidivistic sex crimes. Using a non-routine table for the same reason effectively doubly penalizes one actuarially.

Most intolerably of all, the 'Non-Routine Correctional Sample' table simply serves as a 'catch-all' of sex offenders 'preselected in different ways', some overlapping the first two other non-routine tables, and some simply unspecified. Thus, there really isn't anything to compare the rated sex offender to. The real purpose of this table is merely to give an appearance of justification to assigning such quadrupled estimates of recidivism risk, based only on the fact that the "evaluator believes that the offender being assessed is not typical".[1] This is a bald invitation to the rankest visceral subjectivity and bias, disguised as science. Even if a given rater takes great pains to confine his judgment on this to common 'clinical' considerations, it still is a corruption of the actuarial science supposedly underlying ARA by the unscientific, highly inaccurate guesswork of CRA.

The foregoing are classic examples of corrupting the actuarial-science method by subjective or arbitrary *clinical* decisions. Because of the *huge* disparity in percentages of recidivism probabilities applied to the *same scores* on the Static-series scales, based only on this arbitrary categorization by a rater of a given sex offender being rated, this corruption utterly destroys any science behind Static-series predictions in all three categories of 'non-routine' samples.

Because the Static-series RAIs literally invite such corrupting influx of 'clinical' notions into assignment of what is *supposed to be* an actuarially derived predictive percentage of likelihood of sexual recidivism, it has abdicated its scientific responsibility and status. Any Static-series RAI applying such 'non-routine' tables to a given sex offender must therefore be rejected flatly.

RAIs Have an Unknown Margin of Error

It has been said that "risk assessment has been aptly referred to as 'the mother of all uncertainties'".[2] No one, not even RAI developers themselves, claims 100% accuracy in the risk predictions ARA generates. "Even Dr. R. Karl Hanson, affiliated with the development of the RRASOR and the Static-99, asserts that the instruments are believed to be of only 'modest' accuracy."[3] Thus, beyond dispute, there is some error built

---

1 Ibid., pp. 36,44.

2 *Bailar & Bailar, 1999, p. 273. R.Prentky, E. Janus, et al., Sexually Violent Predators in the Courtroom: Science on Trial," Psychology, Public Policy, and Law, Vol. 12, p. 357, at 371 (2006).*

3 *Bechman, ibid.*

into each ARA-based prediction of probability of reoffense. The question reduces to: what is that margin of error, and is it an acceptably low one? Simply from the foregoing points, intuitively, the answer would appear to be: too high, and unacceptable. However, technically, the question of margin of error probably can never be scientifically answered at all. This, once again, deprives ARA use of scientific status.

The reason for error-margin unascertainability partly concerns the concept of 'base rates'. A 'base rate' indicates the frequency with which an event occurs in a given population. Obviously then, the accuracy of any predictive assessment of probability (such as ARA) depends on the base rate for the predicted event. Now, read this sentence closely: All published studies on which RAIs are constructed contain base rates *for the population studied*. But the recidivism base rate among the *actual* population that includes the individual offender under commitment consideration — that is, a population with *exactly* the complete, true set of all relevant attributes of that offender — is unknown and unknowable. Therefore, the error rate is also unknowable. Thus, RAIs are said to be 'postdictive' rather than predictive, because they can only look back at past, actual incidents or recidivism, among a former group of offenders (this base obviously not including the later, specific offender in question), and yet they attempt to make an estimate of future risk as to him based on observations made with regard to that historical sample.

Creators of RAIs and others aware of this inherent flaw have sometimes attempted to establish error rates by calculating *different* estimated base rates. These calculations involve inclusion of various 'fudge factors' in an effort to account for individual variability. However, RAI opponents refer to these attempts as mere educated guesses (clearly an unscientific procedure). Such estimates (or guesses) may have a place in non-quantitative assessments of *relative* risk, but are criticized as having no place in ascertaining accuracy of tests such as RAIs, avowed to make *absolute*, quantitative risk predictions.[1]

As Bechman concludes, there is serious doubt among scientists and mental health professionals that statistics, inherently derived from large groupings, can predict individual future behavior. Sex offender commitment statutes try to determine the likelihood that a given sex offender will commit another sex crime, a goal "not reached with statistical profile evidence." Such "postdictive group-risk data" do not equate to a prediction as to an individual, leading many to contend that RAI percentage predictions should not be admitted in evidence at all in such commitment trials[2].

---

1 *Ibid., p. 28.*

2 *Ibid., p. 29. Emphasis supplied.*

True Cross-Validation of RAIs Has Not Been Demonstrated

RAI creators often defend their instruments by matching the predictions made to those derived on the same individual offender by using competing RAIs. This is not a significant comparison to the question of accuracy. It harkens back to the old tale of The Emperor's New Clothes, in which the entire populace of a town (save one clear-headed boy) convinced themselves by acclamation that the Emperor was wearing fine new clothes, when in fact he was naked. Unanimity in error does not equal accuracy.

The term 'cross-validation' in statistical science actually refers to the process whereby the result of one study or test can be replicated on a separate, subsequent population. Scientific (peer-reviewed) literature, according to Bechman,[1] "does not demonstrate cross-validation of the RAIs".

Cross-validation is associated with the concept of 'generalizability': that is, if a given RAI, used in different contexts on different populations, replicates its results closely, it can be said to 'generalize' well. However, sex offender populations vary dramatically, including their characteristics. So an RAI constructed on one population may not generalize to a different population. This is where failure to scientifically cross-validate RAIs can be fatal to their accuracy, or indeed, to any useful meaning to their numerical output.

On this, Bechman explains:

> "The instrument known as the VRAG, for example, which contains a weighted consideration of 14 designated risk factors, was developed in 1994 to assess violent recidivism in a population or 'cohort', of mental disorder offenders released from a maximum security psychiatric hospital in northern Ontario in the 1970s. The generalizability of the VRAG to other populations, such as pedophiles in the western United States in the year 2001, has not been empirically established and, in fact, the limited data available suggests that the VRAG has an unacceptable accuracy rate in terms of assessment of sex offense recidivism. The problem presented by population demographics, or cohort characteristics, is vast and potentially insurmountable: Does an RAI derived from a study comprised of a cohort that included convicted rapists generalize to those offenders diagnosed with pedophilia? Is an instrument that excluded from

1 *Bechman, p. 28-29.*

its construction sample non-coercive incest offenders useful in evaluating risk in offenders with a history of non-coercive incest? Elusive as the answers to these questions may be, many scientists and professionals assert that without appropriate, scientifically scrutinized cross-validation, absolute risk predictions based upon RAI scores are meaningless."

Inter-Rater Reliability: Of Coding Rules, Subjectivity, and Home-Brewed `Adjustments'

As noted by Erica Beecher-Monas, in "The Epistemology of Prediction": (etc.), supra, 60 Wash. & Lee Law Rev. 353, at footnote 42, as to RAI problems of interpretation and application:

> "The risk factor descriptions may be vague, decreasing their reliability ... even trained clinicians may differ on what exactly is meant by 'glibness' (a factor on the PCL-R, an actuarial instrument) or 'lack of insight' (a factor on the VRAG and the HCR-20, two other actuarial instruments). Sometimes the factors are not independent, for example, anger and the inability to sustain relationships."

That final sentence points up that what amounts to the *same* observation by a clinician, even if not vague ('anger') can result in the imposition of adverse points on two *cumulative* factors (effectively, a 'double hit') for the same thing (in this instance, inability to sustain relationships due to anger).

However, in the main, vague wording and somewhat nebulous or variably applied concepts (here, 'glibness' and 'lack of insight', respectively) allow for vast disparities in the scoring (coding) of factors on RAI forms, thus drastically affecting the calculations of total score, and hence, of percentage of probability of recidivism predicted.

Separately, some RAIs themselves, such as the 'Sex Offender Risk Appraisal Guide' (SORAG) invite inter-rater coding inconsistency by including reliance on information frequently unavailable. For instance, SORAG, to be complete, requires administration of the PCL-R psychopathy instrument and a phallometric test with the specific sex offender. It also requires information about the offender's elementary school maladjustment. Often, due to omission of those tests and to unavailability of that information, the SORAG is incomplete. Yet the rater will score it nonetheless. "These omissions may damage the predictive validity and reliability of the instrument and some argue that the instrument should not be used when there is insufficient reliable data to score them."[1] Given the high stakes in a sex offender commitment proceeding, that's putting it exceedingly mildly.

See also the 'SVR-20' RAI, requiring component data from clinical conclusions (e.g., mental disorder, social adjustment) and from interviewing the offender and deep investigation of the facts (e.g., attitudes toward treatment and realistic relapse prevention plans), yet is frequently rated upon a bare corrections or court record alone. Note also that the factor, "realistic relapse prevention plans" is merely judged by 'successful' treatment completion, culminating in official approval of such plans. Hence, that factor effectively serves only to doubly weight such treatment completion (Fabian, ibid.). "The SVR-20 has not demonstrated great utility in assessing sexual recidivism for civil commitment populations."[2] Most fundamentally of all, nota bene that the SVR-20 (Sexual Violence Risk-20) is not actually an actuarial instrument at all, but rather a clinical risk assessment (CRA: see discussion supra) guidance tool.[3]

When different raters apply the same RAI to the same individual, in theory the resulting output percentage of recidivism probability should match. This concept is known as 'inter-rater reliability'. Any significant disparity in results between different raters is ground for concern that the RAI itself lacks definiteness necessary to accuracy. Yet little appears in peer reviewed literature to establish that any RAIs have been appropriately examined for inter-rater reliability.

Inter-rater disparities in results fall within the categories of ARA 'measurement error'. As Janus & Pentky, supra, at footnote 121, observes: "The amount and quality of information that is used for rating an ARA scale is undoubtedly the most common and the most obvious potential source of measurement error". In general, the problems of lack of available relevant information, incomplete information, and just plain incorrect information (in some cases, falsified information), coupled with unspoken, unwarranted presumptions and inferences made by a given rater, substantially befoul most ARA analyses, but are typically undiscovered by judges and defense counsel because of their non-record nature. Thus, Janus & Prentky, ibid, said: "... There are many sources of personal bias that enter when it comes to making judgments. These sources of bias also contribute to measurement error".

Although assigning a weighted score to a risk factor, adding all such weighted scores together, and consultation of a table of percentages may seem objective in concept, and hence not easily a venue for

1 *Fabian, supra, p. 331.*

2 *Ibid, p. 332.*

3 *In re Kaelble, 2011 Minn. App. Unpub. LEXIS 394 (Minn. App. 2011).*

inconsistency among raters, the truth in practice could not be more diametrically opposed. Bechman, p. 29, illustrates by noting that, in one RAI , 'offense' includes those not resulting in conviction, while a different RAI includes only convictions. What about mere attempts, or convictions for non-sexual crimes where the intent is sexual? Or as to a conviction reversed on appeal? Not only can RAIs themselves differ on treatment of such issues, but (and less delectably) two given raters using the same RAI with the same evaluated offender may calculate using inconsistent approaches on such issues. Another example is that raters may be unaware that most RAIs do not include any self-reported offenses not resulting in a charge.

Rules to govern application of the appropriate definition to a given risk factors are called 'coding rules'. For some RAIs, these coding rules are found in informally circulated materials, as well as in documents available on the internet (and subject to tampering or other corruption in that medium). However, even assuming a rater possesses and uses a correct, complete set of coding rules, they can be so vague and confusing as to lead to a mostly subjective interpretation. Again, Bechman (pp. 29–30) illustrates by citing the 'gray area' of victim intoxication, noting that this scenario may not be part of an RAI's definition of the factor of 'use of force', but that some raters may simply assume its inclusion in that factor.

Further, whether the victim was actually rendered vulnerable due to intoxication may be subjective, potentially differing from rater to rater assessing the same facts in a given case. Similarly, whether the victim was a "stranger" to the offender may be treated differently between different RAls, or be applied inconsistently among raters using the same RAI. For instance, what about a girl victim living in the same building as the offender, or a nephew of the offender's friend?

Indeed, as these illustrations show, more profound questions lurk in these potential sources of inconsistent interpretation than merely clarity of coding rules. Maybe the motivations that prompt, respectively, a sudden sexual assault on a little girl who lives in the same large apartment building, but who had only previously seen the offender in the building without knowing even his name, on one hand, and a long-groomed relationship between the curious nephew of a friend, comprised solely of fellatio-by-agreement repeatedly preformed by the offender, are so distinct, with radically differing implications for impulse and recidivism, that such incidents, to accurately reflect current forensic knowledge about sex offenders, must be the subject of entirely different attributes, each with their own score, rather than merely being resolved under the under-inclusive question of being a 'stranger' under coding rules.

And, to draw a closer, but still more crucial distinction, what if, on one hand, our stranger-in-the-building offender was driven by a virtually 'M'-like[1] impulse to sadistically inflict maximum pain and emotional trauma, and secretly can't wait to do it again, or what if, on the other hand, his motivation was un-sadistically pedophilic, and his action with that little girl simply reflected abysmal ignorance of the facts of physical and emotional development of little girls, combined with a typical rapist's self-delusion that a forcefully imposed sex act can result in a mutually pleasurable experience, and that our offender now recoils in horror and self-loathing for what he inflicted actually, albeit un-deliberately? Clearly, these two 'what-if" scenarios bespeak two vastly different offenders, with differing probabilities of reoffense.

Thus, for instance, People v. Taylor, 782 N.E.2d 920 (Ill. App. 2002), rejected use in sex offender commitment trials of both the MnSOST-R and the Static-99 RAIs, in part due to issues of inter-rater variability of scoring. "... The MnSOST-R is supposed to be an objective test, [yet] there is a fair amount of subjectivity in scoring. In Dr. Maskel's experience, when multiple examiners have applied the instrument to the same individual, each examiner has arrived at a different score."[2] Likewise as to the Static-99, "... different examiners were reaching different results after evaluating the same individual."[3]

It would thus seem that RAIs comprising as few as four factors, or as many as 21, have no hope of encompassing all relevant aspects of even just one sex crime, let alone potentially several, and all relevant aspects of motivations, and changes in motivation over time (i.e., other than during incarceration or during treatment) of the offender in question.

And what of such motivational changes in either of those milieus? Where are such matters documented at all, much less available as data on large, statistically significant samples of offenders that can then serve to compile relevant 'base rates' for RAI purposes? Without the ability to integrate these examples, and myriad other critical pieces of information about offenders, their motivations, and their crimes, what realistic hope is there that ARA can accurately calculate any offender's actual probability of future offense (over any future period)?

Some users of ARA compound the dangers of the inter-rater reliability problem more yet by applying some 'adjustment' to the score obtained on the RAI. Bechman, (p. 30) explains that this " highly criticized" procedure, "adjusted actuarials," includes using subjective clinical judgment to alter the probability percentages derived from an

---

1 *i.e., the film 'M', with the unforgettably horrifying portrayal of a psychopathic child-killer by the consummate actor, Peter Lorre.*

2 *Taylor, p. 923.*

3 *Ibid, p. 924.*

RAI. Because RAIs are only deemed valid because they are actuarially derived in some scientific fashion, changing the result from an RAI in any given case by reason of such subjective criteria deprives the RAJ of any scientific validity. This 'hybrid' approach is regarded by many scientists with great skepticism, and no evidence exists to support its accuracy.[1]

Prentky, Janus, et al. "Sexually Violent Predators": (etc.)[2], expand on this problem by calling such "adjustment" simply an attempt to "give scientific legitimacy to clinical judgment." They point to some examiners who select only some risk factors from a given RAI, and others who use additional risk-relevant information to adjust RAI results. In their view, "[b]oth methods are highly problematic". The first of these approaches is merely "window dressing for clinical judgment". The latter simply adds some ARA input to what remains a clinical judgment. Both remain as opaque to scrutiny as pure clinical-judgment testimony and both are rife with opportunity for injection of examiner bias.[3]

A special application of such unwarranted adjustment involves attempting to extend risk estimates beyond the study upon which an RAI was based. Prentky, Janus et al. (ibid.) explain this particular fallacy declaring such extension to be impermissible. They observe that an examiner doing so assumes that the shape of the curve will remain the same in later years. However, no data was ever gathered that would support such an assumption, and it is untestable and probably erroneous. In particular, such extension defies the known phenomenon of 'age-mitigated risk reduction'.

RAIs Are Notoriously Inaccurate Overall

In State v. Oberacker, No. 81093, 2003 WL 125277, at *4 (Ohio Ct. App., Jan. 16, 2003), that court reported that:

> "The Static-99 ... was only 37% accurate; so *66% of the predictions of Static-99 would be incorrect* ... The Minnesota Sexual Offender Screening Tool (MnSOST), which Oberacker scored a high relapse quotient on, is a little more accurate, with an accuracy rate of between 45% to 50%, so approximately *one half of the time it is inaccurate* in its predictions."[4]

---

1 *Accord: Janus & Prentky, p. 1480*

2 *12 Psychology, Public Policy, and Law at 379.*

3 *Emphases supplied.*

4 *Emphases supplied.*

Janus & Prentky,[1] discuss the 'VRAG' RAI, which was originally developed to assess *violent (not sexual)* recidivism. At some point thereafter, it was applied to sex offenders. However, the VRAG's correlation with sexual recidivism (i.e., *only* sexual crimes) was a ridiculously unpredictive 20%. Interestingly, both of the particular factors, 'never married' and 'male victim in index offense' were *originally* used in the VRAG original version aimed at detecting *violent*-crime recidivism *(not sex crimes).* These factors, as well as others thought *significant to violence,* not to sex crimes, were simply carried forward in the VRAG's eventual application to sex crime recidivism (i.e., not because of any actual correlation of those two factors to sex crime recidivism). Scientists often copy from each other's work as a means to ensure comparability. Thus, these two factors ('never married' and 'male victim') found their way into other RAIs — not from any true predictive power as to sex-crime recidivism, but simply because 'the other RAIs use it'. Interestingly, the one 'direct descendant' RAI from VRAG, 'SORAG', changed the 'male victim' factor to 'sexual offenses only against girls under 14'.[2] This, together with other changes, brought SORAG to the comparative 'top of the heap' of RAIs in terms of predictive accuracy (still only in the 50% range at theoretical optimum). Yet other RAIs, such as Static-99, also with a 50% correlation to sex-crime recidivism, still use that 'male victim' factor. Another RAI, 'RRASOR' also chose to keep 'male victims' (any age) as a factor.

RRASOR's correlation to sexual recidivism was determined to be only 25%. An Australian retrospective study found that the RRASOR RAI fell significantly below two other RAIs simultaneously tested, and was superior only to an experimental Australian RAI designed exclusively for violent sexual recidivism. Both that experimental RAI and the RRASOR itself performed unusually poorly at predicting non-violent sexual recidivism (Alfred Allan, et al., "Prediction of the Risk of Male Sexual Reoffending in Australia")[3]

Even worse results were reached using the MnSOST-R. Of note: all RAIs have been criticized for use of small sample sizes, thus implying that their conclusions and their rating scales are not *based on statistically meaningful data.*[4] This record of RAI inaccuracy to the question of probability of sex-crime recidivism means that ARA analysis gives results that are only scarcely more valid than pure chance. For this reason, too, ARA use should be abandoned.

---

1 *At 1465-67.*

2 *Id., p. 1468.*

3 *Australian Psychologist, Vol. 41, No. 1, pp. 60-68 (Mar. 2006).*

4 *Janus & Prentky, p. 1471.*

ARA Use Merely Results in a 'Resemblance' to Certain Characteristics of Other Offenders, Not Proof of Personal Tendency Toward Recidivism

Janus & Prentky acknowledge this problem thus[1]:

> "Opponents claim that ARA's group-based information is not relevant to the individual risk assessment required by law. After all, it would hardly be fair to lock a person up merely because he 'looked like' others in his reference group (i.e., others who got the same score).
>
> "As the late Associate Justice Coyne of the Minnesota Supreme Court explained: 'Not only are the statistics concerning the violent behavior of others irrelevant, but it seems to me wrong to confine any person on the basis not of that person's own prior conduct but on the basis of statistical evidence regarding the behavior of other people.'
>
> "The group-based objection has a broad and narrow form. The broad form claims that group probabilities are inherently different from predictions of individual behavior. The narrow form acknowledges that all risk assessment is inherently group-based, but complains that ARA is fixed or immutable, classifying people into predefined bins that are too rigid and fail to account for significant individual differences."

As Janus & Prentky themselves continue, at p. 1478: "In our judgment, *the morality of depriving people of long-term liberty based on predictions of future crimes is questionable*, in significant part because all prediction is ultimately based on group membership."

The Specific Problems of 'Dynamic Risk Factor' RAIs, Including 'SONAR': Unrepresentative Circumstance, the Rapidly Changeable Nature of 'Acute' Dynamic Factors, and Subjective Assessment of Factors

In response to criticism of the various RAIs as comprising 'static' (unchanging) factors judged only by past events, an effort has been made to identify 'dynamic risk factors' which have changed, or may change over time. Some of these are regarded as relatively 'stable' (slow to change), while others are conceded as subject to rapid change

---

1 *p. 1476-77.*

('acute' factors). Only one RAI to date has focused on dynamic risk factors, viz., the 'Sex Offender Need Assessment Rating' (SONAR) RAI.

However, many dynamic factors are judged in highly unrepresentative circumstances of the sex offender in question, typically, imprisonment, or incarceration pending a commitment petition. Even with full cooperation by the offender, it may well prove impossible to accurately gauge matters that turn on how the offender *would* conduct his life, and would react to various stimuli and circumstances, outside of an incarcerated circumstance. Among the factors that are not conducive to accurate assessment during imprisonment or detention are: "poor social support, antisocial peers, antisocial/impulsive lifestyles, anger and hostility, depression and anxiety, poor coping mechanisms ... substance abuse, intimacy deficits, isolation from others ... poor general and sexual self-management ... unemployment ... cooperation with supervision, and poor grooming."[1]

A fortiori, especially without the offender's cooperation, the rater would never be able to garner inferences with any certainty on any of these factors from the record alone in terms of how the offender would feel or act in freedom, if not committed. To attempt to do so is purely a guessing game.

A second problem involves the fact that 'acute' factors, such as mood, anger or hostility, alcohol intoxication or substance abuse, and victim access, are, by their very nature, rapidly changeable.[2] It therefore may be a matter of pure 'roulette wheel' chance whether, on the day of rating a given 'acute' factor is in place. This implies that the outcome of recidivism probability rating can vary drastically on nothing more that such day-to-day, or month-to-month vagaries. This presents a huge problem of the reliability of any given assessment using such 'acute' dynamic risk factors.

Finally, most dynamic risk factors are, by their conceptual nature, open to subjectivity on the part of the rater. This invokes the aforementioned problems of inter-rater reliability and of importation into a purely actuarial process of clinical impression. What exactly, for instance, are 'intimacy deficits', and how are they to be scored? The same challenging question must be addressed to 'negative social influences', 'general self-regulation', 'poor coping mechanisms', 'poor attitudes and cooperation with supervision', and 'poor social support'.

In this connection, James Vess, "Sex Offender Risk Assessment: Consideration of Human Rights in Community Protection Legislation"[3],

---

1 *Fabian, id., p. 332.*

2 *Fabian, ibid.*

3 *Legal and Criminological Psychology, Vol. 13, pp. 24556 (2008), p. 250.*

complains of the "use of incorrect criteria to score dynamic risk factors", explaining:

> "*Idiosyncratic interpretations* of the criteria for items such as negative social influences and attitudes supportive of sexual assault are sometimes applied, resulting in an *erroneous* finding of a high risk that *appears* to be supported by the weight of empirical evidence.
>
> "Estimates of risk based on inappropriate scoring of dynamic risk measures may *substantially mislead* judicial decision makers ...
>
> "When one adds their own 'dash of technical judgment' to the probability estimate of an actuarial instrument, they simply create a new un-normed risk tool (Woodworth & Kadane, 2004) and the efficiency of the actuarial instrument is diminished (Otto & Petrila, 2002)."
>
> *Fabian, id., p. 336*

In light of this, it simply once again proves that psychological forensic testimony is for sale, that the Minnesota Court of Appeals, in Linehan III, supra, at 557 N.W.2d 189, incorrectly stated to the contrary: "According to testimony at the hearing, some research on violence prediction indicates that *combining* actuarial methods with the clinician's experience and knowledge of peculiar circumstances of a given case may enhance accuracy".

What is especially appalling is that judicial reliance on such lies results in drastically adverse decisions about people's lives, and sets precedent for many future cases, all based on antiscientific falsehood.

Because of the open-ended nature of these terms, rating each consistently could easily require a coding manual the thickness of this book. Even with such an aid, the specific facts as to a given sex offender upon which a rating was made for each such factor, to a given sex offender upon which a rating was made for each such factor, would have to be clear, unequivocal, and well documented for such a rating to be scientifically meaningful — a rare combination, it would seem.

Therefore, in sum, although the idea of improving predictive accuracy of the ARA approach by using 'dynamic' factors applicable to the sex offender in question may seem laudable at first glance, the practical problems explained here illustrate the less-than-scientific and certainly un-actuarial nature of these personal dynamic considerations. Hence, SONAR and any other RAIs based on this approach appear doomed to wildly variant and unreliable accuracy.

ARA Evidence and Testimony Should Be Excluded from Sex Offender Commitment Trials

As stated, passim, in this work, the principal theme is that sex offender commitment laws themselves should be abolished, and that other, more effective and cost-efficient means be applied to achieve control and management of sex offenders and to reduce the incidents of sex crimes. However, given that sex offender commitment proceedings are still with us, the purpose of this section has been to demonstrate that the profound problems with RAIs and their use in ARA techniques so gravely call into question their accuracy and their applicable meaning as to any given individual on trial in such a proceeding, that their forensic use in such trials should be abandoned and legally excluded as a matter of admissible evidence and testimony.

Bechman, at pp. 30 and 31, cites several district court-level cases in which exactly that result was judicially reached. Those decisions, although not precedential and not the most recent, are fundamentally persuasive and should be consulted.[1]

In James Francis, the trial court found that neither the RRASOR nor the MnSOST-R RAIs had gained acceptance in the relevant scientific community and did not demonstrate sufficient reliability and relevance under Daubert. Klein ruled to like effect, specifically citing the absence of instruction manuals, concerns over translating group data into predictions about individual behavior, failure to address the concept of base rates, reliance on unproven assumptions, inter-rater reliability problems, cross-validation problems, and a lack of peer-review.

Bechman observes from these cases that some courts strenuously reject the contention that an individual's future behavior can be scientifically predicted. This rejection is endorsed by the American Psychiatric Association and by many psychologists and scientists. Bechman concludes that there may never exist any reliable means of identifying in advance even those who may ultimately prove to be the most serious recidivists.[2]

Confirming this rejection of predictions of dangerousness, Janus & Prentky[3] notes that *both* the American Psychiatric Association and

---

1 *See, e.g., In the Matter of James Francis, No. CV0299-108MH, Circuit Court of Butler County, MO, Division III (Dec. 15, 2000); State v. Klein, No. 05-1999-CF-08148, Cir. Ct. of the 18th Judicial Circuit, Boward County, FL, June 2, 2000; In re the Detention of John Woods, 0-2000-0005, Cochise County, AZ (March, 2001); In re the Commitment of Roberto Valdez, No. 99-000045CI, et al. Cir. Ct. of the Sixth Judicial Circuit, Pasco and Pinellas Counties, FL (Aug. 21, 2000).*

2 *Bechman., p. 32.*

3 *Janus & Prentky, p. 1495.*

the American Psychological Association "have taken formal positions in the past opposing the use of 'dangerousness predictions' in high-stakes legal settings".

In the Roberto Valdez case, that Florida three-judge panel dismissed 14 sex offender commitment cases in a consolidated opinion rejecting admissibility of RAIs, stating in broad principle:

"We note, in passing, that the underlying assumption of these instruments is that human beings do not chance, but are programmed to act in the future in accordance with the manner in which they have acted in the past — an assumption which runs contrary to the basic principles of our legal and penal system and contrary to the premises of clinical psychology and psychiatry ..."

In closing, Bechman adds this ominous warning. Namely, the most immediately apparent worry is that of a '"false positive," i.e., falsely deciding a non-future recidivist as one who will reoffend. However, the converse problem of "false negatives" is just as real, and is aptly illustrated by Jeffrey Dahmer, Wisconsin sex offender and serial killer of 17 known victims. Applying the RRASOR RAI afterward to Dahmer's situation just before that crime spree results in a 37% probability of reoffense over the ensuing ten years – an inadequate level of likelihood to support civil commitment.[1]

In Minnesota, the Dept. of Corrections screened Alfonso Rodriguez and found him not a likely candidate for commitment, presumably applying the same MnSOST-R RAI applied to other sex offenders at the time of his release. And that outcome should not be surprising: Rodriguez' past did not raise red flags according to that RAI. The only warning (unheeded) was his declarations in prison of intent to rape again. In retrospect, it appears clear that Rodriguez was a stewpot of anger in prison, threatening to boil over. But nothing in the MnSOST-R (or any other) instrument is geared to pick up on that.

To be fair, at least one other state failed to identify another ticking time bomb. Joseph Duncan, already a repeat sex offender, was screened by the Washington Dept. of Corrections, using at least an RAI, but was passed over for a possible civil commitment under that state's sex offender commitment law. Duncan absconded from parole, landing in Western Minnesota. There he was charged with molesting a 5-year-old boy. However, the court, then unaware of Duncan's Washington record, released him on bail. Duncan immediately jumped bail and 'headed for the hills' — more specifically those of northern Idaho. There, two young children caught his eye. He broke into their home at night, killing their parents and elder brother and kidnapping that

---

1 p 33.

small boy and girl. Over. the next several days, he repeatedly raped the girl and boy, eventually murdering the boy. Duncan was caught when he later brazenly entered a convenience store with the little girl in tow.

Janus & Prentky[1] have complained about clinicians' conflation of the *probability* of recidivism with the *severity* of any such sex crime in determining 'dangerousness' for commitment purposes. But RAIs don't distinguish between the future Rodriguezes, Duncans, or even 'M's, on one hand, from the 'garden-variety', non-violent, non-threatening, pedophilic oral sex with voluntary victims or from the gropings, or even the 'things got out of hand' date or spousal rapes, on the other hand.

Hence, quite apart from accuracy problems in identifying those with truly high probability of reoffense, RAIs 'homogenize' all offenders, forcing courts to choose who to commit with no information as to what kind of crime — or how severe a crime — any offender will likely commit, if he reoffends at all. A court forced to choose which offender(s) to commit out of any proposed group of 'candidates' either will have to blindly guess — potentially leaving 'Mr. Psycho' free, or will have to opt to commit all, even though knowing that only a small sliver of a percentage have that potential.

Janus & Prentky, supra, give ARA a favorable comparison to the aforementioned CRA technique of non-quantified, impressionistic estimate of (low/medium/high) likelihood of recidivism of a subject sex offender. Yet Janus & Prentky take pains to limit that approval to a prospective, 'wait-and-see' approach, vis-à-vis how ARA turns out (post publication of the Janus & Prentky article in 2003). They warn (at p. 1493): "ARA has a bad influence if it is misused or its limitations are ignored, and it thereby contributes, and lends its veneer of science, to an inherently unreliable process". In footnote 300, Janus & Prentky explain: "Misuse results if application, interpretation, and incorporation into the examiner's finding and conclusions fail to adhere strictly to recommended procedures and guidelines". As will be seen in the review of sample cases from Minnesota, infra, unfortunately, such misuse and transgression of its limits are exactly what is happening in court when ARA evidence and testimony are introduced. Worse, it is going on virtually uniformly in case after case, clearly contributing improperly, but without detection to ill-based commitments.

Janus & Prentky themselves caution: "Although our paper is premised on findings that ARA is superior to clinical assessment methods, we do not take the position that either is sufficient to justify the massive and long-term deprivation of liberty inherent in

---

1 *p. 1449.*

[sex offender commitment] laws".[1] Yet Janus & Prentky[2] unexpectedly stumble through the logical thicket to the sound conclusion that they appear to resist out of emotional attachment to the continued existence of sex offender commitment laws:

> "We wish to make clear that we are not addressing what is a more abstract question: whether the reliability threshold [of commitment courts] is set too low, or, to put it the other way around, whether in the abstract, ARA tools have sufficient reliability to support liberty-deprivation. Were the question posed in the abstract, we might agree with Litwack's conclusion that risk assessment tools are not sufficiently validated 'for use in determining when individuals should be confined on the grounds of their dangerousness' [citing: Thomas R. Litwack, "Actuarial Versus Clinical Assessments of Dangerousness," 7 Psychology, Public Policy & Law, 409, at 409 (2001)]. But if we affirm Litwack's conclusion, we must conclude, a fortiori, that *clinical* judgments of dangerousness *are not sufficiently validated either*, a conclusion *that ought to lead to the abolition of [sex offender commitment] laws.*"

Yes, it most certainly should.

1 *p. 1446.*
2 *at 1459.*

Chapter 7
The Latest Twist

'Cherry Picking' Only Adverse 'Dynamic' Factors ... as a surreptitious return to CRA to make excuses for commitment, not based on high risk of recidivism, but instead only for 'things to work on'

Prentky, Janus, et al., "Sexually Violent Predators ..." (etc.), at 12 Psychology, Public Policy, and Law 378, explain the cherry picking method of risk assessment thus: "The cherry picking method refers to selectively harvesting information that supports and confirms an a priori opinion".

The MSOP Report recounts the transition from reliance in commitment trials upon 'clinical judgment' to actuarial approaches. However, then conceding that such 'static' actuarial approaches had proven inaccurate, the report trumpets a more recent emphasis on 'dynamic risk' assessment techniques. However, it is clear from this discussion that MSOP ignores 'protective factors' that reduce recidivism likelihood, instead accenting 'negative dynamic risk factors' that "are associated with risk for reoffending but, unlike status factors, can be changed through intervention" — redefining such 'dynamic risk factors' as supposedly comprising "psychological vulnerabilities or mechanics" that "significantly increase risk for reoffending" (p. 10). This contravenes the actual forensic literature, which described 'dynamic' risk factors as all things, whether external or internal, or whether deliberately altered by an individual offender or instead simply either spontaneous or inexorable (such as the effects of middle and old age on libido).

As we have seen supra, ARA assessment, using various static factors, has been largely debunked as outrageously inaccurate at predicting sexual recidivism — to the point of pure chance. Further, things at the heart of that actuarial approach, such as sex-offense recidivism rates themselves, once thought to be unchanging (static), have proved to be subject to great aggregate change (downward, as to recidivism). This has thrown the whole basis for such predictions so far off (massive overestimates of probability of individual recidivism) that continued use of such RAIs is mere junk science. This, plus the inherent wild inaccuracy (roughly, 70–90% in error) of so-called 'clinical' assessment of risk (CRAs), has shown the 'scientific' basis for commitment to be worthless guesswork.

It appears that the MSOP Report's emphasis is on this distorted mis-definition of 'dynamic risk factors' as being an individual's purported 'criminogenic needs' (a phrase not encountered outside of MSOP) is a desperate attempt to redefine the overall rationale for commitment, one that effectively merely returns the focus to just such 'clinical impression'.

Having lost the battle for judicial respect for ARA, which garnered so many commitments for MSOP by use of static factors, now MSOP wants to spin dynamic factors as reflecting evils particular to each sex offender, such that something terrible and ominous can be said against each one in commitment proceedings. This is on the overarching implicit proposition that 'all sex offenders need long-term, lock-up treatment, and we [MSOP] are the only game in town'.

Indeed, describing extant DOC sex offender treatment, that report (p.15) describes an initial "psychosexual assessment, which includes psychological testing, a detailed review of the offender's history, and a thorough clinical interview. The assessment identifies the offender's criminogenic needs.

Examples of these need areas include sexual deviancy, antisocial attitudes and beliefs, relationship problems, and problems with self-regulation" *(emphases supplied).* In other words, things that MSOP exclusively calls 'dynamic' risk factors are all adverse claimed 'deficits' that the sex offender must 'work on'— and of course, per the implication of this report, only treatment can allow that, and for some, only MSOP will do. That is to say, these things that MSOP calls 'dynamic' are things that absolutely require treatment to reduce recidivism — in other words, excuses to commit!

Partisanship Of Prosecution And Court-Appointed 'Examiners' And Other Export Witnesses

Partisanship of prosecution and court-appointed 'examiners' and other expert witnesses emphasizes the defendant's need For expert trial consultants and forensic witnesses, rather than 'examiners'.

Sometimes it takes one removed (e.g., geographically) from an ongoing process to fill the role of the young boy who broke the folie à plusieurs about 'The Emperor's New Clothes'. James Vess, an academic psychologist in New Zealand, writing in 'Sex Offender Risk Assessment: Consideration of Human Rights ...' (etc.)[1], fills that role as to this point.

---

1 *supra, at 13 Legal and Criminological Psychology (The British Psychological Society), pp. 250-251.*

Referring to commitment procedure in the United States, he explains the core of the problem thus:

> "Some jurisdictions develop a cadre of risk assessment experts, either within the ranks of staff working for the Department of Mental Health or Department of Corrections or, as in the case of California, a panel of experts who are provided with training and consultation by the state. One result of this approach is that sometimes virtually all of the available expertise is retained by the governmental department that will essentially act as the prosecution in seeking imposition of community protection measures [including civil commitment] against sex offenders.
>
> "This raises the issue of the impartiality of the departmental expert in making recommendations for judicial outcomes like preventive detention, post-sentence civil commitment or extended supervision."[1]

In Minnesota, for instance, special court rules for sex offender commitments urge the state's judicial districts to create lists (cadres) of 'examiners'. Impoverished defendants (after years in prison, almost all are) are compelled as a practical matter to seek expertise from this limited list, as the only experts who will certainly be paid by the court. Only those local psychologists who consistently testify either in favor of commitment, or only weakly in opposition to it (ignoring all of the foregoing avenues of forensic attack on the rationales, procedures, and factual assumptions by prosecution experts, instead saying only that commitment is too 'extreme' under the circumstances) will remain on that court-appointment list.

The court-appointment of these 'examiners' effectively mandates that their role is to 'examine' the defendant, rather than to examine the diagnostic or forensic procedures employed by prosecution 'examiners' or other experts. By refusing to pay such experts for such critiquing services and testimony as beyond that 'examination' assignment by the court, commitment judges effectively bar such testimony.

A momentary explanatory digression is required: like other states with sex offender commitment laws, Minnesota allows clinical impression (CRA) testimony by examiners, as well as actuarial (ARA) testimony. We have already seen that both of these approaches to predicting likelihood of sex offense recidivism have extremely serious flaws and cannot be regarded as comporting with scientific method. Between CRA and ARA approaches, clinical impression is by far the worst offender in this regard, having been determined to be 84–90%

1 *Id., p. 250.*

incorrect in its predictions of recidivism. Basically, the 'institutional bias' of clinical examiners of sex offenders is that everyone is a future recidivist.

The 'witch hunter' simile is not altogether rhetorical. In ancient witch-hunting days, the accused witch was stripped bare, and the witch hunter would examine her skin for any blemish, mole, birthmark, scar, etc., that could be declared to be an identifying 'mark of a witch'. Obviously, any self-proclaimed witch hunter could always find something to seize upon, and any witch hunter who did not do so more often than not would not continue to be consulted for that task

In the same manner, a modern psychologist hired to determine whether one is a future sex-offense recidivist will immediately realize that it is in his interest to so declare, regardless of how flimsy the factual basis for such a conclusion. And the trial judge, eager to have his own bias confirmed, can simply use his discretion to find such a flimsy conclusion 'credible', even over contrary conclusions reached by a defense examiner. Therefore, a sex offender commitment defendant has nothing to gain and everything to lose in this 'battle of examiners'.

Hence, he should flatly, resolutely refuse any such 'examination'—assuming he has not recently been examined already as part of some prison-based sex offender treatment program. The fact that staff from such treatment programs will often be subpoenaed by the prosecution to testify as to such 'witch marks' of likely future recidivism is the strongest reason that no sex offender should ever participate in such prison-based treatment.

In this, as well as other ways, Minnesota postures under the pretense that a sex offender commitment case is not adversarial. On the contrary, it is extremely adversarial, and prosecution experts proceed aggressively as strong partisans to discover anything they can say to staunchly advocate for commitment.

Vess (ibid.) also cites the additional partisanship problem of prosecution experts serving as both trial consultants (inherently a partisan role backing commitment) and also as a testifying 'examiner' or forensic expert. Vess explains that "separating the acceptable bias of the consultant from the necessary objectivity of the examiner is difficult, and maybe not possible" (p. 250). Beyond such partisan consultantship, Vess points out that even a 'pure witness' can be problematic, depending on their motivation: "When the motivation is to contribute as a member of the trial team, sharing its goal to win the case, the psychologist has become an advocate whose opinions should not be offered as objective expertise".[1]

---

1 *p. 251.*

A commitment defendant's counsel would truly have to offer up an extraordinary justification (notwithstanding this collective bias) to gain court appointment of a defense forensic expert (not an 'examiner' from the aforesaid list), particularly if from elsewhere, even though the field of such highly competent, considerably experienced, defense-oriented forensic experts as to such commitments is rarefied. The author, after review of appellate decisions of hundreds of sex offenders in Minnesota in such commitment cases, has not discovered a single instance where such an 'outside' forensic expert was allowed to testify for the defense in a 'non-examination' role.

The foregoing problems illustrate how extremely one-sided a sex offender commitment trial is, as a practical matter. In turn, the only measure that can bring at least some balance to such proceedings is allowing such commitment defendants to retain their own separate experts as trial consultants and forensic witnesses, thoroughly qualified to competently critique the faulty procedures and assumptions employed by prosecution examiners and other forensic expert witnesses.

Unfortunately, as other sex offender commitment states, Minnesota requires that attorneys appointed to defend sex offenders in such commitment cases be limited to a list of attorneys kept by courts for that purpose. This serves to 'keep such attorneys in line', i.e., to refrain from 'bucking the system' by asking for appointment of such 'outside' experts. Also, the total attorney's fees approved on such cases for court payment are so low that such substantial advocacy efforts are effectively prevented.

Due to this low-fee system, attorneys willing to work in this judicial commitment system tend to have lower advocacy skills. In addition, since such appointments are typically a 'last-resort' option for attorneys not attracting sufficient paying clients in other types of cases, their interest in effective defense of such sex offender commitment cases is far less than zealous, and their knowledge of the forensic facts of the field of such recidivism prediction is far less than the mere overview provided by this work.

In light of these further problems, it is very unlikely that appropriate forensic witnesses will be made unavailable for defense use in sex offender commitment cases. Hence, on a practical level in such cases, 'the fix is in'.

Without Science, There Is No Expertise

Prentky, Janus, et al., writing in "Sexually Violent Predators in the Courtroom:" (etc.), at 12 Psychology, Public Policy, and Law at 371-72, observe:

> "We must not ignore ... the natural human proclivity to overvalue vivid or emotionally laden information. Vivid detail, for experts as well as juries, can be misleading and frequently detracts from the objectivity of an opinion ... Emotionally evocative victim statements can bias the professional conducting the forensic evaluation. [This] can lead to an over-attribution of predictive efficacy and erroneous opinions. This form of bias ... appears to be especially common, given the nature of the behaviors (i.e., facts) under scrutiny in SVP evaluations and hearings."

Because this is the case, the importance of strict adherence to the actual science involved cannot be overstated. An opinion, no matter the credentials of the expert uttering it, is worthless if not firmly founded upon valid science, and is even worse than worthless if or when it becomes biased by the influence of emotionally disturbing facts of the crimes of a sex offender under scrutiny for possible commitment.

In Daubert v. Merrell Dow Pharmaceuticals, Inc., 509 U.S. 579, at 590 (1993), the U.S. Supreme Court considered the admissibility of expert testimony and its supporting evidence. Writing for that court, Justice Blackmun wrote:

> "... In order to qualify as 'scientific knowledge', an inference or assertion must be derived by the scientific method. Proposed testimony must be supported by appropriate validation — i.e., 'good grounds,' based on what is known. In short, the requirement that an expert's testimony pertain to 'scientific knowledge' establishes a standard of evidentiary reliability."

Rather than directly concerning due process, Daubert (and the standard it replaced under Frye v. United States, 293 F. 1013, 1014 [D.C. Cir. 1923]) concerned the judicial rules of evidence and particularly, admissibility of expert testimony (including what is known as 'expert opinion', despite being taken as fact) under such rules.

Alexander Scherr, "Daubert & Danger: The 'Fit' of Expert Predictions in Civil Commitments", 55 Hastings Law Jour. 1 (November, 2003), discussing the applicability of Daubert to psychological or psychiatric predictions of future criminal 'dangerousness' (including possible future sex-offense recidivism), starts with this observation:

> "... Over thirty years of commentary, judicial opinion, and scientific review argue that predictions of danger lack scientific rigor. The United States Supreme Court has commented regularly on the uncertainty of predictive science ... Scientific studies indicate that some predictions do little better than chance or lay speculation, and even

the best predictions leave substantial room for error about individual cases ..." (Id., p. 2).

The American Psychiatric Association itself concluded, in its amicus curiae brief in Estelle v. Smith, 451 U.S. 454 (1981), that: "The professional literature uniformly establishes that such predictions are fundamentally of very low reliability ... Psychiatric testimony on the issue of future criminal behavior only distorts the fact-finding process."[1] That passage went on to say that lay witnesses could just as well make such predictions without "the mantle of professional expertise".[2]

Following up on these observations, Scherr (ibid.) comments:

> "Given these critiques, we should expect the rules of evidence, and specifically the reliability standards of Daubert v. Merrell Dow Pharmaceuticals, Inc., to require the exclusion of predictive expertise from the civil commitment process ... Given their notorious unreliability and deep division in the professional community, we might predict that no court would admit predictive opinions either under Daubert or under Frye.
>
> "Yet no appellate court has ever ordered exclusion of expert psychiatric testimony about danger in a civil commitment case, either before or after Daubert. Courts have shown an extraordinary receptiveness to such opinions, admitting and relying on them in their commitment decision-making. Moreover, courts have had their eyes open: judicial opinions regularly refer to, and explicitly accept, the imperfections of predictive testimony. What is going on? How can such unreliable opinions survive Daubert's stress on scientifically valid and reliable expertise?
>
> "The answer is simple ... Even without scientific validation, a court may still use a given opinion if it has a sufficiently strong fit to the demands of the case."

In a footnote to this last paragraph, Scherr concedes that "other explanations exist, most prominently the idea that imperatives of civil commitment justify a waiver of evidentiary rules ...". Whether by judicial interpretation in Daubert and other cases, or by 'waiver' of the expert testimony-limiting rules of evidence, the upshot is the same: so-called experts can opine anything to justify a civil commitment, regardless of how flimsy its basis in science, or even if there is no basis in science at all for their opinions.

---

1 *Brief, p. 8*

2 *Ibid.*

In a later case, Kumho Tire Co. v Carmichael, 526 U.S. 137 (1999), the Supreme Court (per Breyer, J.) wrote that the goal was only "to make certain that an expert, whether basing testimony upon professional studies *or personal experience*, employs in the courtroom the same level of intellectual rigor that characterizes the *practice of* an expert in the relevant field."[1] *(emphases supplied).* Describing this further, Scherr, at 13, adds that this "leaves trial courts free ... to select between methodologies or inferences about which no common consensus exists" (citing Kumho, at p. 153), implicitly approving all expert testimony in "the range where experts might reasonably differ".

Of course, where an entire professional field proceeds on impressions, rather than on 'hard' science (employing rigorous scientific methods), such as the field of forensic psychologists in the singular field of sex offender recidivism risk assessment, experts might, and typically do, differ over almost everything. This leaves the trial court judge or jury in one of two positions as to any point asserted by a so-called sex offender recidivism risk assessment 'expert':

(1) if no opposing expert testimony is offered on the point and no cross-examination seriously impeaches that assertions, the judge or jury must accept that assertion regardless how unscientifically and purely impressionistic it is, or

(2) where such opposing expert testimony is advanced or such impeachment by cross-examination is conducted, the judge or jury must decide the particular issue posed by that assertion only by the *relative credibility* of the witnesses or of the persuasiveness of the opposing points made — *a decision that may well turn upon the sentiment of the judge or jury as to how the commitment case 'should' turn out.*

This last, emotionally driven factor, often motivated by urges to protect 'public safety', as a higher priority than protecting the liberty of the defendant, overrules, as a pragmatic reality, concerns by the judge or jury as to the scientific basis for a testifying expert's opinion. Essentially, because not barred by evidentiary rules, the expert's opinion favoring commitment by reason of claimed 'high likelihood' of recidivism, regardless of how unscientific or even anti-scientific, becomes a sheer excuse for the judge or jury to use as 'support' for actually deciding the case in accord with their own layperson's fears about the unknown and unknowable, i.e., a given sex offender's level of likelihood of sexual reoffense in the future. And of course, that is a powerful fear indeed.

---

1 *Ibid., p. 152.*

Apart from rules of evidence, one would think that the federal Constitution's guarantee (incumbent upon the states via the 14th Amendment) of due process would bar testimony and evidence (albeit cloaked in the mantle of 'expertise' or 'professionalism') that condemned a defendant falsely or inaccurately, contrary to, or simply in the absence of, any basis in the relevant science. Consider, for instance, the furor that erupts in (thankfully, rare) cases in which fraudulent or careless DNA testing procedures result in the wrongful conviction of an innocent defendant. In matters of deprivation of liberty, whether by conviction and sentence for crime or by commitment for 'dangerousness' (fear of high likelihood of future crimes of sex or violence), reliance upon the conclusions from science are crucial. Concomitantly, strict adherence to and the knowledge-limits of scientific methodology assume an equally crucial importance. Why should we be any less troubled by inaccurate, unscientific, supposedly 'expert' testimony sending a former sex offender to his doom of probably natural-life preventive detention (with or without the 'garnish' of treatment) than we are by recklessly inaccurate DNA lab procedure?

Yet the court's concern over due process in civil commitments has focused exclusively on the substantive laws allowing commitment, ignoring the unfairness of `trial-by-witch-doctor' testimony by 'experts' who disregard, and sometimes oppose the knowledge-base and procedural rigors of the science governing their professional field. So, for instance, O'Connor v. Donaldson, 422 U.S. 563 (1975), held that "a state cannot constitutionally confine without more a non-dangerous individual ...". Interestingly, although overlooked in states like Minnesota, with a higher requirement for release than for commitment of sex offenders, O'Connor held that the state must also prove continued dangerousness at the time of any later request for release (Id., pp. 574–75). That holding remains good law to the present, but is mysteriously forgotten in sex offenders' judicial appeals for release.

However, by focusing on the law's substantive requirement for a finding of future 'dangerousness', the courts have ignored the emotional, excuse-making appeal in favor of commitment of sex offenders offered by unscientific or anti-scientific testimony by hired-gun 'experts'. As Scherr asks, "If expert predictions have so little reliability, how can their use satisfy due process?"[1]. The obvious answer is that it cannot.

Barefoot v. Estelle, 463 U.S. 880 (1983), illustrates how far the Supreme Court is willing to go to protect the sanctity of psychiatric

1 *Ibid., p 30.*

or psychological testimony against prohibition based on due process concerns. In that case, the court allowed a murder defendant to go to his death penalty based on troublingly flimsy psychiatric testimony. "The majority worried that an opposite conclusion would call into question the use of psychiatrists in other contexts, especially civil commitment proceedings. It saw no reason to assume that psychiatrists were any less reliable than laypersons in finding a likelihood of danger."[1]

The rejoinder to this fallacious argument is, of course, that opinions of dangerousness, or high likelihood of recidivism, by laypersons (non-experts) are not allowed by evidentiary rules in commitment cases, and for good reason: laypersons would simply be speculating on that question, unscientifically and highly emotionally. Hence, the court's comparison to lay opinion for ostensible rational support for its decision is inexcusable.

Even Justice Blackmun, writing a stinging dissent in Barefoot, distinguished civil commitment cases from others (such as death penalty cases) as involving only *short-term predictions* with *short-term consequences*, concluding therefrom that the constitutional stakes were lower in commitments. However, Justice Blackmun presided *before* the modern period began of renewed use or misuse of civil commitment of sex offenders, not as a substitute (as before) for criminal sentences, but now as a natural-life *extender* to them. There is nothing 'short-term' about such consequences. Hence, 'expert' testimony in such commitment cases should not be given a pass.

The Supreme Court, procedurally speaking, has rested its due process concerns on the requirement, enunciated in Addington v. Texas, 441 U.S. 418, 433 (1979), that a civil commitment must be supported overall by "clear and convincing evidence". However, in practice (as will be seen more closely in discussing the judicial commitment process in Minnesota), this requirement has not posed any real limit on commitment. Instead, it is paid only mere lip service in passing by judges, relying on unscientific or anti-scientific, impressionistic conclusions by prosecution experts, on a 'credibility contest' basis, as they slam the gavel on yet another commitment of a sex offender, when, in reality, the decisions (as reported on appeal) reek and drip with repulsion as to the sex offender's past crimes and with rank fears of reoffense, really based on nothing more than an anti-scientific contention that the past is an inevitable or presumptively near-certain prologue to a recidivistic future.

In Addington, at 429, the Supreme Court tellingly excused its choice not to require the criminal standard of 'proof beyond a reasonable

1 *Scherr, p. 32, citing Barefoot, at 898–903.*

doubt' to commitments by conceding that "given the *lack of certainty* and the *fallibility of psychiatric diagnosis*, there is a serious question as to whether a state could ever prove beyond a reasonable doubt that an individual is both mentally ill and likely to be dangerous" *(emphases supplied).* This is nothing more than fear-based grant of a pass from what otherwise is an absolute requirement of proof beyond the 'reasonable doubt' standard for depriving an individual of his liberty for any significant period of time.

Courts should never lower the standard of required proof merely to allow cases to be decided upon flimsy evidence, whether it be of guilt or of future recidivistic probability. Nonetheless, particularly as long as the reduced standard of 'clear and convincing evidence' reigns, in commitment cases, 'expert' testimony must be limited to the realm of facts derived from scientific method as applied to the case at hand. Anything otherwise is a sheer invitation to pure character assassination masquerading as expertise.

"Courts have also expressed the view that expert predictions are *pragmatically necessary* in commitment actions. In civil commitment cases, where the trier of fact is required by statute to determine whether a person is dangerous ... expert prediction may be the only evidence available ..." [Scherr, p. 39, quoting People v. Ward, 83 Cal. Rptr.2d 828, 832 (Cal. App. 1999)] *(emphasis supplied).*

Indeed, many states' commitment statutes, including those specific to sex offender commitment, require experts (typically called 'examiners') to testify to the defendant's dangerousness.[1] Such statutes, as Scherr notes, put pressure on courts to admit such predictive testimony regardless of its lack of grounding in science. However, legally, such statutes really only create a minimum quantum of proof required to support a commitment; they do not authorize, much less require, 'expert' testimony that defies or ignores the science of its own field.

In the functional reality of commitment cases, the fact that such 'expert' testimony is the only permissible evidence on the question of future probability of recidivism makes it absolutely essential that it not be impressionistic, but rather, completely well-founded on scientific method and scientific facts as derived from that method. We have already seen in considerable detail that even actuarial evidence can be extremely flawed in that regard due to the design of its RAIs.

Clinical assessment testimony is even far less reliable than that, due to its largely impressionistic nature. Such non-scientific and anti-

1 *Scherr, pp. 37–38.*

scientific grounds for 'expert' testimony have no advantage over lay testimony. Therefore, reliance on such 'expert' testimony makes the already largely diluted standard of supposedly 'clear and convincing evidence' an utter self-mockery.

Just as surely as a criminal conviction based only on expert testimony of DNA matches generated by faulty scientific lab procedures could never be allowed to stand against a due process challenge, so too no commitment based on unscientific or anti-scientific, supposedly `expert' testimony should ever be allowed to stand. Because it is clear that review of sufficiency of evidence has never served to prevent judicial reliance on such testimony, once admitted, the only apt and adequate remedy is to bar its admission.

While courts are in charge of their own rules of evidentiary admissibility, they have failed to use that power to create or enforce rules excluding 'expert' testimony at odds with, or outside of the realm of the scientific method. Courts have clung to what they see as a need for predictive expert testimony, and have time and again overruled challenges to even the most unscientific and anti-scientific evidence by citing that contention of need.

Au contraire!

Justice never has a need — or indeed any place — for testimony or evidence contrary to, or in disregard of the facts. If the reality is that predictions of future sex offense recidivism are not grounded, or are only inadequately based on principles of scientific method, such that such predictions are scientifically unreliable and if sex offender commitments are impossible without such predictions, then so be it.

Expert testimony is only expert when, and to the extent that, it is based on scientific method and on the facts reliably garnered by rigorous adherence to scientific method. Courts apparently cannot bring themselves to acknowledge this limit and to apply it to bar testimony or evidence that, although claimed to be expert, actually falls into the abyss of junk science (short of such adherence). This deprives commitment defendants, particularly and especially including sex offenders, of elemental procedural due process.

Since courts apparently will not acknowledge this and enforce the due process requirement against such baseless testimony, a clarifying constitutional amendment is in order, if such sex offender commitments are to continue at all. However, as will be discussed later, they should not continue, and the more fundamental, clarifying constitutional amendment would be to ban them, and all other forms of preventive detention altogether.

Sex Offender Recidivism as Weather: Attempting to Predict the Inherently Chaotic Course of Life

As Erica Beecher-Monas, in 'The Epistemology of Prediction', 60 Wash. & Lee L. Rev. 353, at footnote 293, points out that behavior of individuals is a "paradigmatic complex system". Individuals constantly interact with their environment and other individuals. As in weather, human behavior, with its many interacting components, is inherently unpredictable. Even weather predictions become very chaotic after six days. Hence, predicting human behavior, especially over long periods or a lifetime remainder, is impossible. Accurate measurement of initial conditions is a sine qua non even for short-term weather prediction, and many thousands of land-based stations and hundreds of ships collect data at no more than six-hour intervals to derive such short-term predictions. However, in contrast, no similar system monitors in detail the behavior of individuals. Worse, unlike weather monitoring, in the case of human behavior at the individual level, just which factors are relevant to prediction is "hotly debated".

Expertise at weather prediction requires feedback and opportunity for repeat performance, in turn requiring all that information gathering and regional reports, all at frequent intervals. Each of these conditions is lacking as to individual behavior.

Finally, even if one had all necessary data, predicting human individual behavior accurately is blocked by three facts about individuals. First, the human mind is a 'poster child' for nonlinearity; cause and effect cannot be reliably identified, much less predicted. The interacting systems of the mind are 'dynamic and fluid'. Second, because individual behavior is affected by the individual's environment, especially their relationships, it would be necessary to know, and to accurately predict, all such relationships and other environmental factors, now and in the future — an impossible feat generally. Third, and more specifically, wider systems, social, cultural, and political in nature, interacting among each other, envelop each individual and their most immediate social relationships. This, plus free will, plus both nature and nurture, all interact in ways that at best can be described as probabilistic, but subject to radical alteration by even the smallest of stimuli.

This excerpt from Beecher-Monas nails it. In a single sentence: Life is unpredictable. We have already seen the abysmal, less-than-pure-chance accuracy of so-called 'clinical risk assessment'. Therefore, testimony based on that non-scientific, mere impressionistic bases should never be admitted in any courtroom for any purpose.

Even so-called actuarial risk assessment (ARA), as applied to sex offense recidivism, is so rife with such profound problems that the very highest accuracy measured for any of its instruments, under ideal testing conditions and very large control group samples, has never eclipsed two-thirds. Indeed, as discussed supra, because control samples have been problematically small, and because average sex offense recidivism rates are so low, error rates, generated when trying to estimate higher, deviating probabilities of reoffense, are so high that the ARA approach collapses in that attempted application. It is, at best, highly doubtful that any modification of ARA technique can ever remedy such error rates, even apart from Beecher-Monas' categorical, unchanging observations about the limits of prediction. What is certain is that ARA does not currently have the threshold accuracy in predictions of percentages of probability of sexual reoffense to be deemed scientifically valid and reliable. Therefore, it too must be excluded as evidence that would both violate the general Daubert standard for expert testimony and evidence, and also deprive one under petition to commit of due process

But, were that not enough to end the debate, on top of it all, Beecher-Monas is correct: Quite apart from the errors, human experience, including both day-to-day experience and internal processes, is utterly dynamic, fluid, and unpredictably variable. Future behavior is a result of so many factors, many unknown, and some even unknowable, that predicting one's behavior even over the next several days is as challenging, if not more so, than predicting the weather accurately for that same period. Predictions of individual behavior over as little as the ensuing six months, let alone over the course of several years, or even decades (as some RAIs purport to do) is in complete defiance of the complexity theory, and therefore is doomed to inaccuracy. Human future behavior cannot reliably be predicted by probabilities. Therefore, all such predictive testimony is non-scientific and must accordingly be excluded. Since sex offender commitment depends on prediction, it must cease and be struck down on an as-applied basis.

Section Three

Minnesota

Chapter 8

The Sex Offender Commitment Process

A Classic Example Of Sex Offender Commitment As Pure, Politically-Driven Preventive Detention

Let's use Minnesota as a classic example of the hysteria and hatred behind commitment laws, and how those laws and practices unjustly, unfairly extend the incarceration of sex offenders to natural-life terms in a blatant dodge of the constitutional prohibition of double jeopardy.

Lest you think that this is just a blip on the radar or a footnote to history, this is a current issue involving a very-large-scale 'assembly line' comprising a 'commitment industry' of sorts.

Consider these facts:

- As of the start of 2011, Minnesota already had 656 committed sex offenders, who are incarcerated in high-security facilities — effectively prison clones (see discussion infra). Further, Minnesota promises to nearly double that number by 2020.
- Minnesota is the height of the 'sex offender commitment craze', having more committed sex offenders than every other state except the hugely populous pair, California and Florida. Nearly one out of every seven committed sex offenders nationwide is locked up in a Minnesota commitment facility.
- By far, Minnesota has the largest number per capita of sex offenders in commitment in the country.[1] Contrast these figures *per million residents* — Minnesota: 110 committed sex offenders, versus the average of all other 19 states with sex offender commitment laws: 27 committed sex offenders.
- Despite having only 1.7% of the nation's population, in 2010 Minnesota had almost 11% of the nation's committed sex offenders (State of Minnesota, Office of the Legislative Auditor, "Evaluation Report: Civil Commitment of Sex Offenders", 2011 [hereinafter "OLA Report"], pp. 1, 18).

According to Larry Oakes' Star Tribune article, MSOP costs are comparatively exorbitant – $134,000 per year to detain and treat each committed sex offender. In contrast, Minnesota's prisons spend only a third of that to do the same.

---

1 *Larry Oakes, "Locked in Limbo", Star Tribune, June 8, 2008, p. Al.*

Oakes in the Star Tribune further states that MSOP's budget tripled between 2004 and 2008, by then amounting to seven times the entire state expenditure to monitor all 3,500 sex offenders on probation. Thirty-one sex offenders can be kept on electronic home monitoring for less than the cost of keeping only one offender in MSOP. Even though all committed MSOP detainees amount to only about 3 percent of all predatory offenders in Minnesota, MSOP bums up half of the annual budget for controlling and tracking the other 97% of them.

So what can be causing these extreme numbers? Is Minnesota's batch of sex offenders really more dangerous than anywhere else? And are they really so much more dangerous, individually or collectively, than ever before? Or are there factors at work in the minds of Minnesota's electorate and its elected representatives and other officials? Factors, perhaps of excessive fear and hatred about sex crimes and those who have committed them.

Nor is this just a matter of numbers. It is also a troubling question of *whom* Minnesota is committing, and why, really. Among other states with commitment laws, Minnesota disproportionately commits the most *older* sex offenders — the group with, *by far the least* statistical likelihood of committing any further sex offenses after prison release. Over a third of all sex offenders committed in Minnesota are over 50 years old, and nearly half of those were in their 60s or older yet. One individual was recently committed at 84 years of age[1], and another, most recently, was committed to MSOP at age 88[2]. Something insane is happening here, all right, but it is on the part of those referring and petitioning such aged individuals for sex offender commitment, and on the part of local judges and appellate judges who approve such commitments. It doesn't take an advanced degree to see that something is seriously wrong here. No one of age 84 or 88 can be described as a credible sexual threat to anyone. Such commitment practices smack very loudly of *pure retribution* beyond the sentence already served.

So why is Minnesota so over-the-top about sex offender commitment, compared to anywhere else? Partly the answer lies in the fact that Minnesota's main sex offender commitment law (the 'Sexually Dangerous Persons Act') has by far the easiest set of elements for a prosecutor to prove to gain commitment of any given sex offender. Also, Minnesota's law about releasing a sex offender from commitment is by far the most difficult criterion for the sex offender to prove of any state having a sex offender commitment law. And third, the administrators of Minnesota's commitment program

1 *OLA Report, p. 6.*

2 *Ibid., p. 44.*

(known as the 'Minnesota Sex Offender Program' or MSOP) rigidly enforce an extremely conservative policy as to what comprises satisfactory completion by a sex offender of the years-long course of treatment in the MSOP commitment program. MSOP was created in 1994, but it 'inherited' about 30 sex offenders committed under an earlier law (discussed immediately infra). However, since then, to date (start of 2013) MSOP has released only two sex offenders — one in 1995, and the other early in 2012. The 1995 release was fairly quickly revoked, and the sex offender was re-incarcerated in the Moose Lake, Minnesota, MSOP facility. Shortly thereafter, he died there of an age-related cause.[1] But what are the underlying reasons that Minnesota has reacted so disproportionately on this matter? Well ... read on.

Really, commitment in Minnesota, as elsewhere, is just a political animal, not truly a measured reaction, for individual danger posed by any given sex offender, or for treatment calculated to reduce recidivistic tendencies. The historical narrative which follows demonstrates this beyond question.

Minnesota has had a sex offender commitment law on the books since 1939. That law provided for civil commitment of sex offenders with a 'psychopathic personality'. The Psychopathic Personality law was hastily enacted in response to a string of rape-and-murder crimes and other violent rapes, all perpetrated against children by strangers. Often, a single perpetrator was responsible for a series of these unspeakable crimes. The public hysteria and furore that ensued was extreme and sustained.

Just What Is 'Psychopathy', Anyway?

Before we get too far into the history of Minnesota's commitment laws regarding sex offenders, we need to understand the concept of 'psychopathy'.

In other words, in this broad definition, simply think: 'thug'.

Note in passing that the prevalence of antisocial personality disorder among prisoners suggests a causative relationship; the question is: which causes which. While it is often assumed that criminal motivations preceding incarceration are themselves a product of pre-existing APD, it is easy to intuit that the profoundly emotionally toxic experience of prison may actually cause APD in these not already suffering from it.

According to Fabian, supra, at pp. 313–314, psychopathy is not a formal diagnosis, but merely a 'clinical construct'. Most often,

1 *Ibid., p. 1, 19-21, 23, 25, 72, 85-87.*

psychopathy is clinically judged by use of the Hare Psychopathy Checklist Revised, 2nd ed. ('peL-R'). That checklist examines a so-called 'criminal personality', and also a 'propensity for criminal behavior'. It is said a psychopath will exhibit traits such as 'superficiality, egocentricity, manipulative demeanor, shallow emotions, and a lack of empathy, guilt, and remorse': impulsivity and irresponsibility are also often cited. Psychopaths engage in chronic antisocial conduct, diverse criminal behavior, and are not likely to obey rules and sanctions. Roughly 15–20% of imprisoned criminals are said to meet these criteria. In contrast, 50–80% of them can be said to meet antisocial personality disorder (APD) criteria.

However, returning from this brief digression, for our purposes, this 'thug' definition of psychopathy, embracing as many as one out of every five prisoners, while pointing up the urgent, profound need for far more `interventionistic' rehabilitation efforts in prison, doubtlessly incorporating psychotherapy, cannot meaningfully serve as any firm predictor of future acts of interpersonal criminality, much less of what type, and certainly does not, of itself, telegraph the future existence of any state of 'uncontrollable urge' toward such offenses of a violent or sexual sort.

Fabian adds[1] that the only portion of sex offending strongly associated with psychopathy is "amongst rapists who have high levels of sexual deviancy when measured by phallometric instrumentation" [citations omitted]. In layperson's terms, this subcategory refers to rapists strongly lustfully moved by fantasies of brutal sexual acts not likely to be consented to, and of force, and other means of imposition and domination, as opposed to consent. This is a cut above rapes not involving violent or brutal acts beyond threat and perhaps a wielded weapon to achieve such imposition or domination and in which the motivation does not include any eroticism of such coercion. Note in this connection as well that, in molestations, the incidence of such fantasies of sexual brutality or of hostile imposition or domination is far less than in adult rapes.

This is not to defend rape, of course, but aims only to distinguish sets of motivation from one type of offender to another. The point is that psychopathy, while worthy of detection and intervention, is only tangentially related to future sex crimes (original or recidivistic). Tests such as the PCL-R, which so broadly dredge for abstract signs of general psychopathy are therefore of very little utility in assisting in identifying an individual with unusually heinous sex crimes in mind, and of no utility whatsoever in pinpointing those with other or lesser sex crimes in mind.

---

1 *At p. 314.*

Moreover, today's motivation does not equal tomorrow's actions, particularly over a number of future years. Hence, even states of lustful motivation as disturbing as sexually psychopathic cannot reliably predict such conduct over any sustained future period. With this backgrounder in mind, as to the current state of forensic knowledge of psychopathy — as limited as it is — let's return to the history of sex offender commitment laws in Minnesota, starting with the law directed at those called (rightly or wrongly) 'psychopathic'.

There is an expression among lawyers and judges that 'hard cases make bad law'. Nowhere in the huge and ever-evolving body of American law has this ever been exemplified so radically and repeatedly as in the misuse of commitment laws intended to provide psychiatric treatment for the out-of-touch-with-reality psychotic (not the same thing as 'psychopathic') to ensure the permanent incarceration of sex offenders who have completed their prison sentences.

In reality, sex crimes almost never involve psychopathic attacks on strangers. From data supplied by Minnesota prosecutors in 2003, 32% of sex offenses were intra-familial, and another 50% involved acquaintances as victims. Another 8% involved some 'position of authority' over the victim. Only 7% involved strangers as victims.[1]

The MMPI Connection

By sheer coincidence, because of a long history of complaints against the psychiatric profession of loose, impressionistic diagnoses comprising malpractice, a team of psychological researchers at the University of Minnesota strove to construct a question-and-answer test capable of being given to anyone lucid to determine whether, and in what way(s), that individual varied from a pattern of response deemed 'normal'. These researchers devised scales dealing with such standard psychiatric concepts as depression, paranoia, and psychosis. The test they came up with became known as the 'MMPI', (Minnesota Multi-Phasic Personality Inventory). Even though a person's 'scores' on the MMPI turn on how they answer its myriad questions on a given day, the test is claimed to measure psychological 'traits'. This implies either a static permanence or a very long-term continuity of a given trait. Such 'trait-based' views of human psychology prompted strong and sustained debate in all of the sub-fields of psychology, save two: clinical psychology with either committed or seriously malfunctional clients; and forensic psychology involving either criminal defendants or commitment candidates. The result today is that the trait-based

---

1 *Minnesota Sentencing Guidelines Commission, "Sentencing Practices: Criminal Sexual Conduct (CSC) Offenses, Offenders Sentenced in 2003", p. 5.*

theory of psychology is largely scientifically rejected everywhere outside of these two realms.

Retention of that outdated approach in forensic and clinical psychology has nothing to do with science, but everything to do with politics, the helplessness of the test subjects in their particular circumstance, and a general 'full-employment' effect for members of those sub-specialties.

However, this general objection to use of the MMPI strays beyond the topic of this work. Suffice it to say that, as long as you are not seriously mentally ill and you don't wish to be falsely made that way, *never* agree to take the MMPI-2 or any other MMPI-based test.

Now to explain where the MMPI fits into the history of sex offender commitment. For many years prior to the MMPI, psychiatry and psychology had struggled to find a way to fit individuals who perpetrated horrific acts of violence, sexual violence, and terroristic domination upon strangers into psychological theory. However, such individuals did not fit into any of the existing categories of mental illness. Largely for this reason, a consensus of feeling (not through scientific procedure) arose by the 1930s that 'psychopathy' was a matter of 'defective personality'.

Based on the aforesaid string of heinous, violent crimes, and on public imaginings spurred by such media portrayals as Peter Lorre's riveting performance as a compulsively child-killing maniac in "M", a desperate need was felt to identify those who perhaps already had perpetrated, or might one day perpetrate such crimes. The MMPI team was approached for this task.

Partly because true psychopaths are hard to find until they are caught, the team simply contacted the warden of Minnesota's prison at Stillwater, asking him to select certain inmates with violent crimes as a sampling thought likely to reflect 'psychopathy'. However, those initially nominated by that warden did not comprise a large sample, so another culling of inmates was added with lesser crimes, but whose criminal records suggested a history of violence.

Certain test questions were added to the MMPI to comprise an additional scoring scale for psychopathy. Some of those questions were constructed through consultation with psychiatrists treating those already committed because of violent acts. However, other questions were drafted merely on the basis that some forms of sexual attractions or interests, such as pedophilic or pedosexual orientation, supposedly bespeak a psychopathic tendency. Still other questions were drafted from consultations with that warden and his prison staff.

As with other MMPI scales, the yes/no answers to these questions were compared to the 'normal' control population to whom the test was also administered (largely, incoming freshmen, male and female, at the University of Minnesota in 1937–38). Questions to which a higher proportion of those prison inmates responded in a given way, or in an opposite way, compared to those college freshmen were deemed indicative of psychopathy.

Of course, partly because of the questions themselves, and partly because of difference in outlook between such radically divergent populations, it is actually the case that the so-called psychopathy scale really just identified prison inmates by specifics of the unique outlooks of longtime prison inmates (i.e., because of their status as such), and it also identified those willing to admit pedosexual attractions or other unusual sexual interests. Note: Especially in 1930s America, young college students straight from home and high school certainly were not willing to make such admissions. But contrast this with the fact that those highly educated and intelligent are over-represented among convicted sex offenders today.[1]

The bottom line: The MMPI 'psychopathy' scale does not reliably identify psychopaths or give any useful indication of who might be more likely than usual to have psychopathic tendencies. Yet for 70+ years, that scale has been used as at least part of the rationale for commitments and for hasher criminal sentences. Another old saying holds that if the only tool one possesses is a hammer, everything starts to look like a nail. The result for almost three-quarters of a century is a long line of unfortunates incorrectly labeled as psychopaths and committed on that basis.

'Psychopath': Scary Word, No Real Meaning

Interestingly, in 1939, the Minnesota Legislature enacted a law concerning itself with only *sexual* misconduct, incorrectly labeling such as 'psychopathic'. Even to the present, the Minnesota statute in question speaks to sexual concerns, defining one who has a 'sexual psychopathic personality' as one who:

(1) is "irresponsible for personal conduct with respect to sexual matters" due to "conditions" (unspecified), or "emotional instability, impulsive behavior, lack of customary standards of good judgment, or failure to appreciate the consequences of personal acts";

(2) has engaged in "an habitual course of misconduct in sexual matters"; and

(3) exhibits "an utter lack of power to control the person's sexual impulses."

---

1 *OLA Report, p. 82.*

Someone meeting these three qualifications is deemed by that statute to be "dangerous to other persons".

Of course, the terms of the first two elements of that statute are chock full of vagueness of boundless breadth. "Irresponsible for personal conduct with respect to sexual matters" could be brought to bear on swingers-club members or rave-party attendees, just as easily as (indeed, far more accurately than) cunning criminals bent on sexual atrocities. And indeed, if "emotional instability", "impulsive behavior", "lack of customary standards of good judgment", and even "failure to appreciate the consequences of personal acts", are reasons for commitment, then massive numbers of Americans are in serious trouble. Even the second element, "an habitual course of misconduct in sexual matters", read in laypersons' understanding, would render vulnerable to commitment numbers beyond counting of adulterers two-timing boyfriends (or girlfriends), bigamists, and probably tens of millions additionally, if "misconduct" includes sexual sin in the Catholic or Mormon sense. Note that, in '*In re Alverson*, 2007 WL 447159, at *6, 9' (Minn. App. 2007, unpublished[1]), contacting minors by internet, using alcohol, and accessing and possessing (legal) pornography were deemed part of the "habitual course" of "misconduct", even though not illegal.

Even as to crimes, as few as two such crimes — even in the context of a single incident with a single victim or co-participant — can suffice as the necessary "habit" in that second element.[2] Nor need these crimes be recent, and prior offense(s) can have been separated from the crime of current incarceration or from each other by many years or even multiple decades.[3]

Moreover, *conviction* of, or even merely arrest for any sex crime is not required, and out-of-court accusations, *even if never made to police at the time*, are often used to fulfill this element — a highly troubling aspect in its own right.[4] Even charges of which the defendant was acquitted can be used to establish the 'habit', an equally troubling aspect.[5]

---

1 *Note that almost all sex offender commitment appeals are "unpublished" decisions, depriving them of any "precedential" value. This allows Minnesota's Court of Appeals to decide such cases on whim and prejudice, and to be as inconsistent as they want to be, with impunity.*

2 *In re Gleason, 1998 WL 218223, at *2 (Minn. App. 1998, unpub.*

3 *In re Rask, 2009 WL 511943, at *2 (Minn. App. 2009, unpub.); In re Fisher, 2005 WL 2209079, at *8 (Minn. App. 2005, unpub.).*

4 *See, e.g.: In re Monson, 478 N,.W.2d 785, 789 (Minn. App. 1991); same as to SDP Act (infra); In re Moore, 2009 WL 2747980, at *2-3 (Minn. App. 2009,unpub.).*

5 *In re Jasmer, 447 N.W.2d 192, 195 (Minn. 1989).*

True, the third (final) element of this 'sexually psychopathic' commitment formula, "an utter lack of power to control the person's sexual impulses", sounds definite enough. However, in practice reflected by case law, this is hardly the case. The problem starts with the term "sexual impulses". The 1939 legislature clearly intended to address only sexual attacks driven by irresistible, strong and transitory impulse (in the psychologically narrow meaning of 'impulse').[1] However, case law in recent decades has broadened out application of the term 'impulse' beyond all recognition.[2] Now, according to Minnesota appellate cases, if one commits a sex crime of any kind (or some different kind of crime, under circumstances reflecting a sexual motivation), then because crimes by definition are deemed to inherently involve harm and a victim, and a consequential penalty upon the perpetrator, such misconduct *must* have been the result of a momentary 'impulse'. That is obviously a nonsequitur, but one upon which commitments have been held to stand.

Alternatively, other decisions, more candidly grappling with the fact that a sex crime stems from an attraction to children, for instance, style that lifelong or very long-term attraction as a 'sexual impulse'[3], in a desperate, intellectually dishonest effort to make such crimes 'fit' the commitment definition under the Sexually Psychopathic Personality (SPP) law (as renamed in 1994).

This is ludicrously at odds with all human experience. Beyond Dr. Franklin's observation (supra), this is simply judges twisting a required term beyond recognition to fit more sex offenders within it, thereby maximizing the judicially desired end of sex offender commitment. Such tacitly conspiratorial agreement to collectively engage in such intellectual dishonesty to reach a desired result, especially where the lifetime liberty of individuals lies in the balance, is an unconscionable practice that casts the entire judicial system of decision-making into disrepute.

A far more grievous distortion, however, utilizes this fiction that any sex crime necessarily arises from an 'impulse' (since, one supposes, it does not reflect 'good judgment') to justify an inference that an 'habitual course' (perhaps of only two crimes) inherently reflects 'an utter lack of power to control' sexual impulses. This particular nonsequitur ignores, of course, that each such crime could have been decided upon

---

1 *See: State ex rel. Pearson v. Probate Court, 287 N.W.2d 297, 302 (Minn. 1939), affirmed: 309 U.S. 270 (1940).*

2 *Cf : In re Blodgett, 510 N.W.2d 910 (Minn. 1995); In re Luhmann, 2007 WL 2417341, at *4-5 (Minn. App. 2007, unpub.); In re Bieganowski, 520 N.W.2d 525 (Minn App. 1994); In re Pirkl, 531 N.W.2d 902, 905 (Minn. App. 1995).*

3 *Bieganowski; In re Adolphson, 1995 WL 434386 [Minn. App. 1995].*

in advance, carefully planned, and carried out in organized, step-wise fashion[1].

In the particular case of crimes with minor victims, simply holding an intellectual belief that acts of oral sex upon volunteering victims is morally acceptable has been held to prove an 'utter lack of control' of 'sexual impulses', despite long advance deliberation of the sexual crime, and equally long advance 'grooming' of the victim[2].

In truth, even though sexual passion is typically experienced by a perpetrator while committing a sex crime, only rarely does a sex crime occur on purely momentary impulse, whim, or sudden urge. Assertions to the contrary by accosted sex offenders are almost invariably merely efforts to avoid being held criminally accountable for the current crime.

Most sex crimes involve such detailed planning and mental rehearsing that, were they instead homicides, they would unquestionably be found to have been 'premeditated'.[3] This is *anything but* an instance of "an utter lack of power to control a sexual impulse".[4]

Thus, the Sexually Psychopathic Personality law in Minnesota is bent back upon itself by judges daily, to prevent that law from being nearly useless on its very terms.

This is 'bad law'.

Prelude to Mass Insanity

"A person need not be 'psychopathic' as measured on a commonly used instrument for assessing psychopathy, the PCL-R, in order to be committed as an SPP."[5] Conversely, the fact that the person is a 'psychopath' as measured by the PCL-R does not mean the person satisfies the SPP commitment definition; "even though the names 'sexual psychopathic personality' and 'clinical psychopath' are similar, they are not the same."[6]

---

1 *Cf: Pirkl; Bieganowski, supra.*

2 *Adolphson, supra.*

3 *Cf : Pirkl.*

4 *See also: In re Preston, 629 N.W.2d 104 (Minn. App. 2001), in which, despite massive advance planning, extensive grooming that preceded the sex crime, and waiting on the part of the perpetrator for the most opportune occasion to commit the sex crime, he was held to have been uncontrollably impulsive.*

5 *Citing In re Luhmann, supra; In re Kirckof, 2006 WL 3007995, at *7 (Minn. App. 2006).*

6 *Citing In re Whitley, 2010 WL 1192307, at *6:7 (Minn. App. 2010)]" (John L. Kerwin, "Civil Commitment of Sexual Psychopathic Personalities and Sexually Dangerous Persons in Minnesota: Legal Overview," Hennepin County Attorney's Office, Minneapolis, MN, 2010, p. 9).*

Effectively, Whitley thereby concedes that Minnesota's so-called Sexually Psychopathic Personality law has nothing to do with mental or emotional pathology; instead, it is simply a deliberately broad or vague dragnet of a legislatively invented standard. In other words, it simply identifies a disfavored class of individuals for permanent or indefinite preventive detention — a hallmark of a 'bill of attainder'.

By 1980, judicial use of Minnesota's Psychopathic Personality law (as then known) had diminished almost to a trickle of cases per decade, primarily because excessive use in earlier years had eventually posed an embarrassment to prosecutors and judges in rural counties, where many residents knew the committed individual personally beforehand and, on an intuitive basis, were disimpressed by the contention that the individual secretly held uncontrollable sexual impulses.

This was part of a nationwide trend. In all, 26 states had enacted some form of sexual psychopathy laws by 1960. However, after 1960, 15 of those states repealed them outright. Several factors contributed to this repeal movement, one being the fact that the psychiatric establishment objected that 'sexual psychopath' was purely a legal construct, not a valid diagnosis. Another objection was the lack of evidence that many such committed sex offenders could be cured or rehabilitated. Also during this repeal period, the trend in criminal justice turned away from rehabilitative efforts toward sheer retribution as the primary goal in response to crimes, particularly those deemed to personally victimize persons in a physical way.[1]

In Minnesota, before 1990, the Psychopathic Personality law was not used at the end of a prison sentence, but instead only as a substitute for one. Hence, in 1990, there were only 30 sex offenders under civil commitment in Minnesota. Yet we must hasten to note that, under that earliest sex offender commitment law in Minnesota, "not a single person convicted of a sex offense and then civilly committed was ever released".[2] By the late 1980s, nonetheless, a movement began to start using 'psychopathic personality' commitments as a *supplement* to a prison sentence, not a substitute for it.

Eric S. Janus, writing in 'Closing Pandora's Box: Sexual Predators and The Politics of Sexual Violence', 34 Seton Hall Law Rev. 1233, at pp. 1234–35 (2003–04), observes that such commitment laws were chosen due to their "bypass of constitutional protections". In Minnesota, a task force recommended such a law as a means to avoid the criminal procedure bar on hearsay, Indirectly, this would

1 *See: Psychiatry and Sex Psychopath Legislation: The 1930s to the '80s (Group for the Advancement of Psychiatry, 1977).*

2 *Jenny Roberts.*

also allow commitments to be based on extrajudicial accusations that were never even charged against the commitment defendant. That task force also favorably noted the avoidance of the criminal burden of proof beyond a reasonable doubt through such a commitment law, effectively resulting in confinement as an incarceration substitute, upon a lesser standard of evidence. And last, that task force also observed that such commitment was not barred by double jeopardy or ex post facto prohibitions For this reason, recommended the task force, such commitment, as an incarceration supplement, could 'make up' for sentences thought to be too short.

Over the ten years after 1990, the number of committed sex offenders would grow fivefold — to 149 in the year 2000, and another 286% of that in the next ten years — to 575 in 2010. The causes for this follow.

In 1991, the Minnesota Department of Corrections (often hereinafter, DOC) "began screening sex offenders in its custody [just before their respective releases from prison] for possible referral to county attorneys for civil commitment ... This change brought more cases to the attention of county attorneys ... In part the decision to refer sex offenders to county attorneys was a response to a growing public concern about crimes committed by sex offenders. After several rapes and murders in 1987 and 1988, the Attorney General convened a task force to review current policies and practices and to prevent sexual violence against women. Among other recommendations, the task force recommended greater use of the civil commitment statute for sex offenders released from prison ...".[1]

If Indefinitely Detaining a 'Dangerous Person' Isn't Preventive Detention — What Is?

Thus, things were bad enough when the Psychopathic Personality law was the only sex offender commitment law in Minnesota. However, in 1994, the Minnesota Legislature became dismayed that one notorious, murderous sex offender was ruled not to have the requisite "utter lack of power to control" his presumed sexual 'impulses'.[2] Hence, the legislature created a task force "to study issues relating to the *confinement* of sexual predators ...".[3]

Tipping the legislature's hand to show that its intent was preventive detention of sex offenders, not their treatment, Section 20 identifies

---

1 *OLA Report, p. 4.*

2 *In re Linehan, 5128 N.W.2d 609, 613 [Minn. 1994] — "Linehan I"; Even courts tire of lying now and then.*

3 *1994 Minn. Laws, Chapter 636, Art. 8, §20; emphasis supplied.*

that task force goal as "confinement of sexual predators" by looking at "options, both *civil* and criminal, for *dealing with* sexual predators". *(emphases supplied)*. Generally, such Sexually Violent Predator (SVP) laws were recognized immediately as being "designed to extend [a sex offender's] confinement [at the end of his sentence] for society's protection".[1]

Looking to steal a little of the spotlight, then Minnesota Governor Carlson called the state legislature into special session for the sole purpose of enacting a broader sex offender commitment law. The legislature convened in special session (one day only) on August 31, 1994, hastily passing that task force's recommended bill.

'Broader' is a gross understatement. The resulting Sexually Dangerous Persons Act (SDP) offers an alternative (not a replacement) means to commit a sex offender. By this act, "the Legislature allowed for the commitment of persons who did not exhibit an 'utter' lack of power to control their sexual impulses. The new sexually dangerous person category also removed the requirement that the offender's history of sexual misconduct be 'habitual'."[2]

This SDP law, too, has three elements. However, their coverage is nearly universal. The first two elements, combined, are subject to a 'swearing contest' in court between forensic psychologists, armed with dueling 'actuarial instruments' mentioned earlier. For reasons of personal and institutional bias, as well as politics of judicial re-election, decisions almost always go against the hapless sex offender, who was looking forward to prison release at long last.

Those three elements are, specifically, one who:

1 "has engaged in a course of harmful sexual conduct";
2 "has manifested a sexual, personality, or other mental disorder or dysfunction"; and
3 "as a result, is likely to engage in acts of harmful sexual conduct."

Note that this new SDP Law expressly states that "it is not necessary to prove that the person has an inability to control the person's sexual impulses".[3]

The first of these SDP law elements includes any of a wide array of designated sex crimes, each of which is presumed 'harmful' — either

---

1 *"Proof of Qualification for Commitment as a Mentally Disordered Sex Offender", 51 Am.Jur. Proof or Facts 3d 299 [1999], Section 7; emphases supplied.*

2 *OLA Report, p. 24.*

3 *Minn. Stat., § 253B.02, subd. 18c(b).*

physically or emotionally.[1] Under this new SDP law, prosecutors need not show an utter lack of power to control sexual impulses. Note that no conviction is required by these elements, again allowing commitment consideration of allegations, including of alleged decades-old sexual misconduct that may be advanced by surprise for the first time only in the course of the commitment proceeding itself.[2] In fact, under Moore, one need not ever have had any sex offense convictions![3]

As with the other commitment law, as few as two crimes, even if very close in time to each other, can comprise the required "course" of "harmful sexual conduct".[4] In other words, application of this first element is potentially nearly universal in the case of sex offenders exiting prison.

The second element ("disorder or dysfunction") can also be applied nearly universally. It should be noted that this element was written in contemplation of the Diagnostic and Statistical Manual of Mental Disorders (DSM)[5], and that the term 'dysfunction' was included to cover situations where all of a 'disorder's' criteria in the DSM are not presented. But the latest edition (DSM-V) allows an evaluator to "use clinical judgment" to apply a diagnosis of a "disorder" in the absence of one or more criteria of its definition.[6]

Especially worthy of note, in Linehan III, Linehan argued that an antisocial personality disorder (APD) diagnosis was an invalid basis for commitment, since it is defined by past criminal behavior, and is therefore just another way of stating that one has a criminal record. The Minnesota Court of Appeals rejected that argument, citing Linehan's supposed current mental processes (but drawing that conclusion from psychologist testimony inferring such processes from such criminal conduct).[7]

The claimed 'disorder' need not be sexual in nature, or have anything to do with sexual conduct or inclinations.[8] Yet, inconsistently, the *sheer fact* that one suffers from a disorder (even if diagnosed as a

---

1 *Minn. Stat., § 253B.02, subd. 7a.*

2 *In re Stone, 711 N.W.2d 831, 837-38 (Minn. App. 2006); In re Jackson, 658 N.W.2d 219, 226 (Minn. App. 2003); In re Moore, 2009 WL 2747980 (Minn. App. 2009, unpub.).*

3 *Accord: Martin v. Mooney, 2007 WL 1306409 at *13-14 (U.S. Dist. Ct., Minn. 2007).*

4 *In re Taylor, 2002 WL 31890941, at *6 (Minn. App. 2002).*

5 *Then 'Jr', now 'r'. In re Linehan, 557 N.W.2d 171, 185 (Minn. 1996, "Linehan III").*

6 *DSM-IV-TR, xxxii (2000).*

7 *Ibid., p. 184-85.*

8 *In re Krych, 2008 WL 1800140, at *3 [Minn. App. 2008, unpub.].*

definitional 'stretch', as supra) is held as sufficient evidence that one is unable to adequately control sexual 'impulses' (another stretch).[1]

Sex crimes can be divided conceptually into two categories: (a) those involving children (below or at pubescence); and (b) those not. As to the first of these categories, appellate commitment decisions universally find that such a sex crime involving a child inherently bespeaks 'pedophilia', as used in those decisions to denote the specific definition in the DSM-IV-R, or -V, of a declared 'sexual disorder' (not a 'mental illness'). Effectively, between the unscientific definition-by-fiat of this 'disorder' and the operation of this second element, any sex offender with a crime involving children qualifies for commitment under this second element.[2]

Those whose sex crimes did not involve a child can also be deemed to fulfill this second element. Its reference to "... personality ... disorder is a 'buzz phrase' invoking the aforesaid alternative 'diagnosis' of an 'antisocial personality disorder'. Obviously, rape of anyone, including an adult victim [category (b) above] is about as antisocial an act as can be perpetrated. The hazy definitional terms of that DSM 'disorder' are sufficiently vague as to be called into service to support such a diagnosis based on such acts alone. Other sexual assault crimes, and crimes of deliberate sexual effrontery, such as 'flashing' one's genitals, can be said to be similarly antisocial by their nature as well.

Moreover, in Minnesota, as in almost all other states, sex offender treatment participation in prison is mandatory. In such treatment, intense, often confrontational discussion of one's specific aspects of motivation will be had. Typically, such a 'category (b) sex offender' will admit to some role of anger at, or an urge to degrade or emotionally hurt, the victim. This will satisfy the definition of 'antisocial personality disorder'. Even if no such admission is forthcoming, the assigned therapist in that prison treatment program will often be called as a pro-commitment witness, if only to opine that such acts and other undenied facts inherently do comprise that disorder.

In sum, therefore, it is a very unusual case indeed in which the sex offender does not satisfy the almost inherently applicable second element.

The third element is where 'actuarial instruments' show up. Actually, by later U.S. Supreme Court decision, it is not enough that a sex offender be merely 'likely' (as in 'more likely than not') to engage in further acts of harmful sexual conduct. That court dictated that, to support commitment, such further predicted acts must be *highly* likely.[3]

---

1 *In re Fulgeseth, 2004 WL 422695 at *9 [Minn. App. 2004].*

2 *See: In re Fugelseth.*

3 *Kansas v. Hendricks.*

Applying that decision to SDP commitment, the Minnesota Supreme Court held in In re Linehan[1] that the second element must require that the disorder or dysfunction be current; and that the reason for such likely future harmful sexual conduct is that "the disorder or dysfunction does not allow the person to *adequately* control his or her behavior" *(emphases supplied).*

However, one must note that case law exists holding that 'untreated' 'pedophilia' is deemed to *inherently* hamper one's control of their sexual behavior — another point of law at odds with known psychological facts. Most individuals who have a sexual interest in children never actually engage a child in sexual activity. Often, incidentally, these are first and loudest to condemn one accused or convicted of sex crimes with children, as 'cover' for their own celibate pedosexual attraction. Notwithstanding the fact that celibacy is the rule, not the exception, among pedosexuals, under this judicial view any pedosexual nearing prison release for any sex crime is subject to commitment merely by virtue of that label. To illustrate how extreme this gets, the requisite lack of adequate control has been held to be presented even where one's last sex offense happened a very long time ago.[2]

Let's step back a minute to witness a 'constitutional dodge' in action. In the 1997 decision in Kansas v. Hendricks, the U.S. Supreme Court defined the control requirement of the constitution as "difficult, if not impossible to control," and confirmed that such a *serious* lack of control is required to commit by adding later in that opinion that it must be a "*special and serious*" lack of control. In Minnesota (always rebellious and provincial), however, the later decision in In re Linehan[3] engages in semantic contortionism to equate that constitutionally required standard to the clearly *lesser* standard of a disorder or dysfunction not allowing one "to *adequately* control his sexual *behavior*".[4]

Nota bene that this Minnesota standard does not just differ in *quantum*, but *differs as to which party the effective burden of proof falls upon.* It is obviously incumbent upon the *prosecutor* to present sufficient proof on the *Hendricks* issue of a sexual impulse "difficult if not impossible to control". But under the *Minnesota* standard, it would appear that the found existence of a 'sexual impulse' carries with it an implicit irrebuttable *presumption* of the existence of *at least some level of problem controlling such impulse*, so that the sex offender commitment defendant or respondent must carry a *burden of proving*

---

1 *"Linehan IV", 594 N.W.2d 867, 876 (Minn. 1999).*

2 *In re Brown, 2006 WL 44354 [Minn. App. 2006]), and even when a 10-year gap existed between such last sex offense and a sole prior sex offense (In re Robb, 622 N.W.2d 564, 573 [Minn. App. 2001]).*

3 *"Linehan IV", 594 N.W.2d 867 (Minn. 1999).*

4 *Linehan IV, at p. 876 & n. 4; emphasis supplied.*

that his control is 'adequate'. Moreover, note that unlike the Hendricks standard referring to controlling the *impulse*, the Minnesota standard under Linehan IV refers to control of one's "sexual *behavior*".

This distinction turns out to be critical in practice, since Minnesota appellate decisions often turn on a finding that the sex offender failed to prove that his sexual *behavior* was under control, even though he may have offered proof that he was able to control any *impulse* to reoffend. Basically, this subverts the Hendricks standard from one of concern over *irresistibility of impulse compelling* future recidivism to a conceptually different, and far lesser standard of, concern over the *mere likelihood* of future recidivism, regardless whether driven by impulse, or simply a product of a deliberate, perhaps long-contemplated *choice* to reoffend. *Locking people up due to the latter concern is not a matter of mental or emotional disorder, but instead is purely an exercise in preventive detention.*

However, five years after Hendricks, the U.S. Supreme Court again spoke on this standard for commitment of sex offenders, in Kansas v. Crane[1], *somewhat* retrenching from the "difficult if not impossible" standard of Hendricks to a revised requirement of "proof of *serious difficulty* in controlling behavior" *(emphasis supplied)*. Still, anyone can see that the Linehan IV standard of "inadequate control" is far more subjective and permissive of commitment than the Crane standard of "serious difficulty in controlling behavior."

By the time of Crane, Linehan's case had gone to the federal habeas corpus stager. The following year, the Eighth Circuit federal Court of Appeals decided that case[2], In Linehan v. Milczark, the 8th Circuit, *invented a standard of its own* from a phrase in Crane ("sufficient to distinguish"), explaining the impact of Crane's 'serious difficulty in controlling behavior' standard, by not just looking at the question of 'serious difficulty', but by *conflating* with that standard 'findings of past sexual violence and resultant likelihood of future sexually dangerous behavior', into a *combination* of required findings [that] will *adequately distinguish* an offender subject to civil commitment, who has *difficulty* controlling his behavior *because* of a disorder of dysfunction, from the more typical offender with behavioral problems, *who is best dealt with in the criminal system.*[3] In essence, in Milczark, the 8th Circuit, departing from Crane, allows Minnesota to use its finding of past crimes and of the sheer existence of a disorder or dysfunction, to determine that 'difficulty' (not Crane's 'serious difficulty') in controlling one's behavior is presented. Indeed, the sentence quoted even allows 'likelihood' of recidivism

1 *534 U.S. 407, 413 (2002).*

2 *Linehan v. Milczark, 315 F.3d 920 [8th Cir. 2003].*

3 *Ibid., p 927; emphases supplied.*

testimony (actuarial, based purely on statistics of others' experience) to take a place in this determination of difficulty to control — an ultimate kind of bootstrapping, since that 'high likelihood' requirement is the ultimate issue in both SDP and SPP commitments in Minnesota.

Adding it all up, if any forensic psychologist reviews the record of one's past and current criminal offenses, concludes therefrom (without ever meeting the defendant) that one is suffering from any 'disorder' (even if that 'diagnosis is 'fudged' by a lack of one or more definitional elements), a committing court can conclude that the sheer fact of that 'disorder' inherently prevents 'adequate control' of sexual behavior (in spite of all offender-specific evidence to the contrary), all as allowed by the foregoing Minnesota case law *(See later section, addressing some preposterous, outrageous examples of Minnesota appellate decision-making about sex offender commitments).* In the sex offender commitment case, In re Ramey, 648 N,.W.2d 260, 268 (Minn App. 2002), for instance, that appellate court declared:

> "... The meaning of the phrase, 'adequate control' is clear: an offender's history of harmful sexual conduct and the high likelihood of future dangerousness, coupled with a mental illness or dysfunction, demonstrates that an offender will find it difficult to control behavior." *Ibid.*

Indeed, in the later case, In re Garza, 2008 WL 2889700, at *8 (Minn. App. 2008), the same court reduced the self-control issue to *just one factor*: "In other words, if there is clear and convincing evidence that appellant is highly likely to reoffend, *then there is* clear and convincing evidence that he is unable to control his sexual impulses".

Even though this chain of reasoning effectively requires *nothing more* that a record of at least two sexual acts (no conviction required; one-victim-only is sufficient; mere accusation OK), under Linehan v. Milczark, this is proclaimed to satisfy Crane's 'serious difficulty standard' — as if the committed sex offender is a highly compulsive sex maniac literally unable to stop himself from reoffending at the earliest opportunity in an assaultive manner upon any convenient stranger.

When nothing more than word games, with matters of bedrock definitional importance, in the grave context of a potentially natural-life commitment, allow such a twisted reconceptualization of an individual so at odds with actual ground truth about that individual, something has gone very desperately wrong with the judicial decision-making process.

Consider, for example, In re Martin, 661 N.W.2d 632, 638-40 (Minn. App. 2003), holding that the 'adequate control' issue is a 'legal' issue, not a factual one. In the eyes of courts, 'legal issues' are defined by precedent, often comprising *just such word games*, and they may be decided with little or no regard for the actual facts. Further, it allows the appellate court to overrule a trial court's finding of one's ability to adequately control oneself (see: In re Martin, supra). This effectively allows the issue to be politically decided contrary to the facts. When judges can act in these ways, a constitutional amendment is in order.

Contrast this holding of inadequate control as sufficient to support commitment with the alternative law's (SPP's) requirement of an "utter lack of control". This is another reason that SDP commitments far outstrip commitments based solely on sexual psychopathy. Nonetheless, prosecutors regularly alternatively plead petitions for sex offender commitment based on either law, and 38% of such commitment cases have ended in dual commitment under each law. Put another way, the SDP law was either the sole basis or part of such dual bases with SPP in a total of 89% of such commitment cases.[1]

This use of the SDP standard of 'high likelihood', satisfied by carefully 'cherry-picked' ARA predictions of high percentages of probability, translates to a 'Minority Report'-style preventive detention — except that *no one ever truly knows any individual's future.*

Never before has American law allowed preventive detention other than in criminal bail decisions. A slippery slope has been trod upon. Never before has anyone been incarcerated in America merely for being in an unfavorable statistical grouping.

In sum, by way of comparison to other states with sex offender commitment laws, "Minnesota laws specifically allow for commitment for offenses that involve emotional harm, as well as those involving physical harm or violence. In contrast, statutes of most states require a violent offense for [sex offender] civil commitment ... unlike most states, Minnesota does not require that the offenses resulted in convictions.[2] Indeed, 70 of those committed to MSOP to date have *no known convictions.*"[3] In commitment trials in Minnesota, judges side with prosecutors in 4 out of 5 cases, confirming the low standard and vague elements needed to commit.[4]

Larry Oakes, in 'They're All Close Calls Now'[5], wrote that judges in Minnesota have commented that the state's sex offender commitment statutes are so vague and widely applicable that virtually every sex offender can be committed under it, on nothing more than guesswork by a small cadre of psychologists paid to use flawed, inaccurate 'risk

---

1 *OLA Report, p. 25.*

2 *Ibid., p. 20.*

3 *Ibid., p. 7.*

4 *Ibid., p. 36.*

5 *Star Tribune, June 8, 2008, p. Al.*

assessment'. These psychologists are usually limited to lists kept by the state attorney general and county courts.

Only about 25 psychologists have provided the supposed basis for nearly all sex offender commitments in Minnesota, earning $10,000 in taxpayer-paid fees for each case. For this, they offer up a prediction as to whether a given sex offender is likely to commit another sex crime.

Critics object to psychologists testifying as supposed experts on whether an offender fulfills legal constructs such as 'sexual psychopathic personality' or 'sexually dangerous person', unknown to psychological science. Dr. Jeffrey Hardwig, president of the Minnesota Psychiatric Society, objects to civil commitment as a means to extend a criminal sentence.

Even armed with that boundless new SDP law, "... over the 12 years prior to December 2003, DOC had referred 333 sex offenders to county attorneys, or about 26 per year".[1] Considering that the sum total of sex offenders in commitment in 1990 was only 30, this was an enormous increase in the rate of commitments. Yet 2003 brought yet another story of political reaction to an isolated incident.

In 2003, Alfonso Rodriguez, jr., a rapist, was passed over for referral for potential sex offender commitment and was released from prison. Late that year, he kidnapped and killed a young woman. In immediate and sustained reaction, the Minnesota Department of Corrections radically increased its rate of referral of sex offenders to county attorneys for possible commitment, starting with 235 offenders at one time in December, 2003. Over the next five years, it continued referring offenders at an average of 157 per year, a rate many times higher than in earlier years.

This last figure reflects a six-fold increase in referrals per year from the pre-December 2003 average. All because of Alfonso Rodriguez. No doubt the Minnesota DOC felt stung by the Rodriguez incident. But the guilt lies squarely on that department. Rodriguez had vowed in the presence of prison staff that, upon release, he would sexually reoffend, specifically by raping some young woman. And yet the DOC did nothing to stop Rodriguez. More specifically, DOC officials declined to seek his commitment.[2]

Apparently, this threat was ignored, and Rodriguez was not referred for commitment consideration. Alternatively, Rodriguez could have been placed on ISR (intensive supervision) that could easily have included house arrest enforced by an electronic anklet serving as an out-of-proximity detector. The house arrest could have been

---

1 *OLA Report, p. 5.*

2 *"2003: A Pivotal Year Causes Commitments to Surge", editor inset, Star Tribune, June 8, 2008.*

accomplished as a halfway house, from which unauthorized departure is prevented by locked doors.

Indeed, one form of electronic anklet widely available at reasonable price in 2003 included a GPS locator, always broadcasting the releasee's whereabouts. Rodriguez was not given any anklet and hence he was allowed free range without intensive supervision at all.

So free was he that he drove to North Dakota and there kidnapped his next victim as she left work at a mall. Undetected in all of this, he drove her back to Minnesota, where he committed that rape and ensuing murder.

Problem One was the exceptionally horrific criminal bent of Alfonso Rodriguez. Problem Two was that no one in the DOC paid any attention to his admitted intent to commit further horrific deeds. But, from 2004 to date, approximately 425 additionally committed sex offenders have paid the price for the DOC's negligence as to Alfonso Rodriguez — even though almost none of those 425 are possessed by anything like Rodriguez' sheer evil.

Rather than supporting the need for a commitment program, the Rodriguez case stands for the propositions that:

1 Commitment selection simply does not work. Rodriguez was passed over, incorrectly deemed an insufficient threat. Inherently, no one can accurately predict the future, particularly as to any individual's actions in the future. Science has not made seers of psychologists, nor does it hold out any promise of being able to do so anytime in the foreseeable future. By our very nature as human beings, and by reason of the vagaries and happenstances of life, we all bounce like billiard balls off each other and off the banks of our experiences in our environments. Because those banks are ever-changing, and the positions of others and the 'bounce characteristics' of each interaction constantly change and are unpredictable, it is impossible to predict our paths in life or where we will wind up.

2 By nothing more forensic than simply listening to Rodriguez, corrections staff could (and should) have realized his exceptional dangerousness and, although obligated by law to release him, could have placed him under such restrictive and closely monitored and surveilled conditions that any opportunity for sexual offense would have been nil — all for a tiny fraction of the cost had he been committed.

Instead, looking to pass the buck, the Minnesota DOC chose to ramp up commitment referrals of sex offenders to the point that, in the ensuing seven years (to the end of 2010), twice as many new commitments took place as had ever taken place before. Moreover, the Minnesota DHS (administrative overlord of MSOP) now calculates that, by 2020, the number of committed sex offenders will *double over that 2010 total*, given a projected lack of any significant number of releases from commitment. This is tantamount to illustration-in-action of the bureaucratic principle: 'If it doesn't work, do more of it!'.

Nor was this increase in commitments the only outfall from the Rodriguez Horror. Also in 2003 ... "Gov. Tim Pawlenty [of Minnesota] issued an executive order prohibiting releases from the [Minnesota sex offender commitment facilities] unless required by law or ordered by a court. Although Pawlenty is no longer governor, Pawlenty's order remains in effect."[1] Interestingly, the rape/murder by Rodriguez followed by one year a similar incident in Massachusetts, in which an unsuspecting 30-year-old woman (Alexandra Zapp) was killed by a convicted sex offender in a Burger King restroom. In an identical reaction, Massachusetts doubled the rate of its own sex offender commitments over the next five years.[2] Obviously, Rodriguez was responsible for his own bad intent and the crimes he committed in that terrible incident. However, it would appear from this closely parallel, 'round up the usual suspects' reaction of two states that politicians in office were not above 'playing to the electorate' by this 'mass preventive detention' response.

Despite the horror of rare crimes such as Rodriguez', they remain rare. To the contrary of those doing their utmost to spread public hysteria and to whip up unwarranted, lynch-mob furor, sex crimes are not a growing social menace, nor even a constant blight; in fact, in the last 30 years the incidence of sex crimes of every type has been falling — indeed, in the last 10 years, plummeting precipitously. 'Sex Offender Recidivism in Minnesota' (a report by the Minnesota Department of Corrections, St. Paul, MN, April, 2007) cited a drop from 19% sex offense reconviction rate in 1990 to just 3% in 2002 — *before* the huge 'commitment round-up' prompted by the Rodriguez incident.

The Minnesota DOC, having ramped up such post-release restrictions and surveillance, takes substantial credit in Minnesota, although this phenomenon is nationwide, in states without commitment laws (30), as well as in those with such laws (20).

At this point it is apt to consider this, because in Minnesota the number of committed sex offenders has spiked and re-spiked repeatedly, cumulatively, from 30 in 1990 to over 650 currently, and

---

1 *Larry Oakes, "OK'd for Transfer, but Going Nowhere". Star Tribune [Minneapolis], June 11, 2008, p. Al.*

2 *Jonathan Saltzman, "Push Is On to Keep Sex Criminals Locked Up". Boston Globe, Oct. 25, 2005, p. Al.*

to more than 1100 as a projection by 2020 — a 40-fold increase. New commitments have risen to more than 50 each year currently.[1] Moreover, past growth rates, properly projected, indicate that the DHS's projection of 1100 detainees is likely to be a grievous underestimate.

In a required report to the Minnesota Legislature in January 2011, 'Options for Managing the Growth and Cost of MS01-1: Facility Study' (hereinafter, the MSOP Report), MSOP does not mention non-growth of MSOP detainee population as an option. On the contrary, that MSOP Report assumes that *MSOP will not release any detainees through at least 2022*. That is *permanent* preventive detention.

The sex-crimes outlook is in fact *better now* than it was in 1990 — not 40 times worse. Sex crime recidivism was low then, but it is *much lower now*, notwithstanding that 81% of registered sex offenders in Minnesota currently *live in its communities* on some form of probation or parole (that is, *neither incarcerated nor committed*).[2]

Surely nothing about the present situation requires or warrants preventively detaining this enormous number of individuals, just on the shotgun-fear that one, or even as many as a *few* among all those detained *hundreds*, may secretly hold a Rodriguez-like bad intent. Beyond the inherently tyrannical nature of such preventive detention as a pure bill of attainder, this 'round up the usual suspects' approach is a classic exercise in swatting flies with a sledgehammer: it is overreaction, inflicting catastrophic, potentially lifetime loss of liberty upon hundreds with no evil intent, and it cannot guarantee that the truly vicious sexual-assault recidivist will be detained.

Is Commitment to High-Security, Prison-Like Facilities Even Necessary? A Comparison to the Texas Sex Offender Civil Commitment System

The OLA Report, on page 16, describes the very different sex offender commitment system in operation in Texas:

> "... The program in Texas is exclusively an outpatient program. The civilly committed [sex offender] population primarily lives under GPS surveillance in halfway houses in four locations throughout Texas. Activities of the offenders outside of the halfway house are greatly restricted. Violations of the conditions of commitment — including failure to participate in treatment — are a felony in Texas and may result in a lengthy prison

1 *Ibid., pp. 3–5.*

2 *OLA Report, p. 9.*

> sentence. However, according to those managing the Texas program, *no civilly committed sex offender has been charged or convicted of a new sex offense.*"[1]

These halfway houses are designed and operated specifically for the committed sex offenders. Texas provides outpatient treatment for them.[2] It also provides close supervision and monitoring.[3] This halfway house commitment system suffices to prevent sexual reoffense by those committed. It should be noted that New York also houses at least some of its committed sex offenders in community settings.[4]

Despite the larger population of Texas and a far larger group of imprisoned sex offenders, and despite having enacted its sex offender commitment system in 1999, as of 2007 Texas had committed only 66 sex offenders to its halfway-house-based commitment system. This clearly reflects either a statute with a higher standard to commit, or administrative policies disfavoring use invocation of that commitment statute, except in truly extremely egregious cases.

The fact that no halfway-house-resident committed sex offenders have committed any recidivistic sex crimes from that environment assumes far greater meaning when one considers that only the very 'worst of the worst' have been thus committed by Texas. The lesson to be drawn must be stated in the alternative: either (a) even those regarded as having the most extreme likelihood of sexual reoffense are not the 'recidivating machines' they are feared to be; or (b) whatever their level of probability of such reoffense, even these worst offenders can be satisfactorily managed in a halfway house context, successfully preventing reoffense.

This in turn has greater significance to the public purse when one contemplates the comparatively trivial cost of housing in a halfway house, as compared to Minnesota's high-security commitment facilities, with one-to-one staffing ratios to detainees. The annual cost per committed sex offender in Texas is only $27,000 — a figure roughly comparable to the average annual cost per inmate in Minnesota prisons, and in sharp contrast to the $120,000 annual cost per detainee in Minnesota's prison-like MSOP-Moose Lake commitment facility (MSOP Report, p. X-Xi). While Minnesota's annual MSOP budget has recently topped $70 million, the entire sex offender commitment program budget in Texas is a mere $900 thousand — less than 1170th that of Minnesota's cost.[5]

---

1 *Emphasis supplied.*

2 *Ibid., p. 16.*

3 *Ibid., p. xi.*

4 *Ibid., p. 44.*

5 *Monica Davey & Abby Goodnough, "Locked Away" [series title]: "Doubts Rise*

The valid question then becomes: is Minnesota's high-cost, high-security choice, reflected by MSOP, even necessary at all? The Texas experience would answer 'No'.

Even Anita Schlank, former clinical director of MNSOP (and an adamant proponent of commitment, with treatment duration of many years) conceded at a symposium held in November, 2002 (i.e., *before* the 'commitment explosion' that began just over a year later in the wake of the Alfonso Rodriguez kidnapping, rape, and murder of Dru Sjodin) that, in her estimate, 25% of MSOP's detainees could be safely managed with proper supervision in the community.[1] Given the far more inclusive, effective standard for commitment used in Minnesota since that later 'commitment explosion', one can assume that even such an MSOP partisan as Anita Schlank would now revise that percentage greatly upward.

If one assumes that commitment is necessary for some (i.e., at most, only a small fraction of those currently under commitment in Minnesota, along the lines of the 66 committed sex offenders in Texas), then Minnesota would do well to abandon its current program in favor of the Texas approach.

As to all other Minnesota sex offenders who have been, or might be, referred for commitment, the Minnesota DOC requires all sex offenders to go through 'intensive supervised release' (ISR), as part of statutorily mandated 'conditional release', specific to sex offenders. The requirements of ISR include a lengthy initial residence in a halfway house, during and following which 'ankle bracelet'-style proximity and locating devices are installed on a leg of each releasee. These make it possible to know when any releasee has left his authorized area and to know exactly where he is. Moreover, ISR agents, unlike regular parole agents, are assigned only about 15 releasees to supervise. As a result, they are able to constantly monitor their releasees in a rapid, random rotation that convinces each releasee that he can be under direct visual surveillance at any moment, and that he can be found and accosted, if necessary, within minutes, with the coordinated help of local law enforcement agencies. In this intensive supervision context, to actually carry out any sexual crime would be a practical impossibility. To date, no releasee under ISR has committed a sex crime.

Minnesota's report by the Office of the Legislative Auditor, supra, after comprehensive investigation, concluded: "... Community placements can be effective from a public safety standpoint provided

---

as States Hold Sex Offenders after Prison", New York Times, March 4, 2007, p. Al.

1 *E.Janus, "Closing Pandora's Box" [etc.], supra, at 34 Seton Hall L. Rev. 1239.*

that appropriate safeguards are taken and intensive supervision of offenders is provided on a continuing basis[1] ... The most effective known technique for reducing risk of relapse is intensive supervision" in the community; community "aftercare can be made sufficiently 'tight' to reduce risk to a minimum for many offenders.[2]

Hence, again, one is compelled to ask what further, indispensable purpose commitment to a high-security, high cost facility even serves that cannot be obviated through use of ISR and, where absolutely necessary, Texas-style halfway-house-based commitment?

In short, Minnesota has bought an unconscionable boondoggle that unnecessarily relegates those who have finished their prison sentences to additional life-without-parole incarceration in such high-security commitment facility, in which officials have no serious intent to release anyone.

The Comparative Experience of California Highlights the Baseless Extremism of the Minnesota Sex Offender Commitment System

Civil commitment of sex offenders merely because they are feared to be likely to recidivate is wrong-headed, and is draconian and tyrannical. It is also the very 'poster child' of the particular violation of any individual's reserved constitutional rights known as a 'bill of attainder', whether or not politically-swayed-and-biased courts choose to acknowledge that fact. The fact that they have not done so to date only further points up the basic dishonesty of the entire commitment regime, including those very courts themselves, who play mere word games to ignore and avoid the heinous threat to the personal liberty of everyone posed by the very existence of such ad hominem laws.

Having said this important manifesto, however, further light can be shed on the utterly over-the-top extremism embodied in the Minnesota sex offender commitment system by comparing it to the analogous California commitment system, and the headaches that playing politics and buck-passing has foisted upon that more limited, moderate commitment system. Read on.

Before getting into the commitment comparison, a comparison of sex offender recidivism rates is in order. Just as in Minnesota itself,

---

1 *OLA Report, pp. 44-45) Accord: Robert A. Prentky & Ann W. Burgess, Forensic Management of Sexual Offenders, pp. 236, 243 (2000).*

2 *Kim English, "The Containment Approach: An Aggressive Strategy for the Community Management of Adult Sex Offenders", 4 Psychology, Public Policy & Law, 218, 219 (reporting on supervision methods that "can exert significant control over offenders' opportunities to commit new crimes").*

fairly recent statistics from California (from a much larger pool of sex offenders released from prison) show a clear and consistent very low rate of sexual recidivism. According to 'Sex Offenders Unlikely to Commit Second Crime'[1], a California study of more than 4,000 sex offenders released on parole in 2002 showed that just 3.2% of them were re-imprisoned for another sex offense in the ensuing five years. These figures are consistent with a 2007 Minnesota study that derived that same percentage for released sex offenders. Indeed, in the Minnesota study, a huge drop was noted: of sex offenders released in 1990, the 3-year post-release sexual reoffense rate was 5%, but for those released in 2002, the figure was only 1% (as measured by the same standard: re-imprisonment). The article noted that "the main factor in reducing sexual reoffending is supervision after release — which has become more intensive in many states".[2]

In 1996, California enacted its own 'Sex Offender Commitment Program'. That program, unlike Minnesota's, provided a commitment term (two years). It also limited commitment to those who had committed sexually *violent* offenses. However, in 2006, California passed 'Jessica's Law', which, among many other restrictions on sex offenders, added more crimes to the list of 'sexually violent offenses' that qualify an offender for commitment. Even so, that law retained a requirement that the offender must have committed a 'predatory act' (not just any means of committing a sex crime). Jessica's Law also changed the commitment term from two years to 'indeterminate'. However, unlike Minnesota, an annual evaluation is required, allowing for periodic assessment of a committed offender's eligibility for release.[3]

As of May, 2011, 530 sex offenders had been committed under this California program, of whom eight had been granted conditional release and were then being treated and supervised by California's Department of Mental Health (DMH) in communities. It is important to note that California's population is approximately ten times that of Minnesota. Since Minnesota then had over 600 sex offenders under commitment, California's per capita rate of such committed sex offenders is less than one-tenth that of Minnesota. It is also important to note that, in California, such commitments are made to the general state hospital system. There is no special administrative unit for, or any commitment facility exclusive to sex offenders. This implies that, unlike in Minnesota, accommodations for committed

1 *New Scientist, 7.5.2008 (Vol. 19, Issue 26), p. 6.*

2 *Ibid.*

3 *Prison Legal News, April, 2012, p. 28: "Thousands Referred, but Very Few Qualify for Commitment as Sexually Violent Predators in California".*

sex offenders are hospital-like, rather than the stark, high-security-prison-like special facility in Minnesota for such committed sex offenders.

Like Minnesota, California allows its California Department of Corrections and Rehabilitation (CDCR) to refer sex offenders for commitment consideration. However, in contradistinction to Minnesota, such a referral is not made to a prosecuting attorney, but instead to DMH itself. DMH screens such referrals and, if deemed appropriate, recommends individual cases for commitment proceedings (which the appropriate district attorney may then (but is not required to) bring to court.

Much as happened in Minnesota in reaction to the Alfonso Rodriguez incident, in California, in reaction to the passage of Jessica's Law, correctional authorities vastly ramped up the number of sex offenders pending prison release who were referred for commitment consideration.

Before Jessica's Law, the number of referrals made by CDCR to DMH had gradually risen to 1,850 per year. However, in 2007, the first full year in which Jessica's Law took effect, CDCR referrals rocketed up to 8,871. By 2009, such referrals declined modestly to 6,675. Since then, however, referrals have continued at this high pace.

Here, however, is where the comparison starts to favor California over Minnesota in terms of the sanity of its decision makers. Rather than approaching commitment as a political act, California views commitment as a psychiatric decision, and one of very last resort. Thus, DMH recommends only a very small number of cases for commitment proceedings every year.

In fact, unmoved by the politically motivated expanded definitions of commitment eligibility in Jessica's Law, the rate of DMH commitment recommendations remained the same in 2009 as it had been in 2005: 50 per year. Thus, those commitment recommendations came to less than 1% of all those CDCR referrals. This indicates the impression of unwarranted hysteria that almost all of those referrals reflect. An audit performed in 2011 by the California State Auditor at the request of the state legislature found that the CDCR process generating all those referrals is inefficient and overloads the DMH with unnecessary work.

Just as significant is the fact, also observed by that report, that, even among that slender rate of DMH recommendations each year, only 20% (average: 10 per year) result in 'Sexually Violent Predator' (SVP) commitments. If this rate were transposed to Minnesota, with its comparative 10% state population, judicial commitments to MSOP would average only 1 per year.

Recall, comparatively, that Minnesota in fact commits more than 50 sex offenders to MSOP every year. In a state as populous as California, this would transpose to some 500 commitments each year. Whether in Minnesota of California, the enormity of such large numbers cannot be abided.

Also of note by way of contrast to the careful, conservative screening of California's DMH, in Minnesota, of DOC referrals direct to county attorneys, judicial commitments range from 34 to 67 percent. This range reflects a substantial ongoing tendency of 'rubber-stamping' by county attorneys as to commitment petitions and of 'rubber gaveling' by judges in issuing commitment judgments. Even worse, appellate challenges to such 'railroaded' commitments are only very rarely successful. In Minnesota, sex offender commitment is a political act and a disgrace to notions of law, rather than true psychiatric screening, à la California.

So here's the question that must be asked to determine whether California's low sex offender commitment rates have had any adverse effect on public safety: what of all those sex offenders referred by CDCR who were not recommended by DMH for commitment? That 2011 audit examined this as well. It found that, among all 13,512 offenders referred to DMH for SVP evaluation from 2005 through 2010, but who were found by DMH not to meet SVP criteria, a slight majority did violate some parole condition not involving a felony. However, only 133 of that group of many thousands were convicted of *any* new felony, and of those, *only one* was convicted of a sexually violent offense (as broadly defined by Jessica's Law). By comparative recidivism standards applicable to other types of felons, that audit found even that number of non-sexually violent felonies was extremely low.

These figures, lower on commitments (as compared to approximately 350 in that period in Minnesota), and even more infinitesimally low on recidivism than in Minnesota (indeed, even among those deemed high-enough-risk by California corrections officials to refer for commitments), clearly show up Minnesota's extremism in its own commitment policy to be completely unwarranted by the facts.

Hence, in all, California's vastly more conservative sex offender commitment program serves the goal of public safety as effectively as Minnesota's massive and all-inclusive MSOP. Per capita, the cost of California's commitment program is minimal, while MSOP's cost per capita is astronomical. Most important, California's program, interposing the state's general psychiatrists of its DMH as evaluators, rather than advancing directly from corrections referral to county attorney commitment petition decision as in Minnesota, reduces the deprivation of the liberty interest of sex offenders (who have paid their debt to society and are otherwise entitled to mandatory prison release) to those very few who, by psychiatric standards, are truly highly likely to imminently commit heinous, sexually violent crimes.

As to all other sex offenders, the California recidivism experience confirms that of Minnesota's Department of Corrections: sex offenders can be completely adequately managed, and recidivism prevented, by means of adequate post-release supervision, requirements and restrictions, monitoring and surveillance, augmented by in-place community notification and registration laws.

Vastly overbroad sex offender commitment laws and commitment boondoggles, such as that currently in place in Minnesota, are unneeded, bureaucratically bloated and obscenely expensive. They are a precedential threat to the rights of every individual. They should be abandoned in favor of the correctional post-release supervision programs that, since fully implemented after Minnesota's 'Rodriguez incident', have proven that they work and that they preserve public safety effectively.[1]

Minnesota DOC Treatment as Betrayal

MSOP-DOC Site Is a 'Commitment Trap'

Currently, the Minnesota DOC operates *two* treatment programs for sex offenders. The longstanding program, 'Sex Offender Treatment Program' (SOTP), operates in the usual manner as other prison-based treatment programs for sex offenders around the country, and with the same aim: to equip its clients for life after release without sex-offense recidivism. The operating assumption of such programs is that it is within the sex offender's power to refrain from committing additional sex offenses. Its technique is to educate sex offenders about the harms of sex crimes, to convince them that committing sex crimes will result in their apprehension and long imprisonment (potentially, a life-without-parole sentence), and to introduce and encourage practice of individual techniques to avoid and to manage temptations toward illegal sexual conduct.

The other program is known as 'MSOP-DOC Site' and is located within the prison at Moose Lake, MN. That program is run by the very same personnel who operate the 'Minnesota Sex Offender Program' (hereinafter, MSOP) commitment facility immediately adjacent to that prison.

---

1 *Sources: California State Auditor, Bureau of State Audits, "Sex Offender Commitment Program", Report 2010–116 (July, 2011); "Thousands Referred but Very Few Qualify for Commitment as Sexually Violent Predators in California", Prison Legal News, April, 2012, p. 28.*

MSOP's Claim about MSOP-DOC Site's Purposes, if Sincere, Is a Failure

MSOP claims that the dual purposes of MSOP-DOC Site treatment are to "reduce the number of offenders who need to be civilly committed and [to] reduce the length of their stay at MSOP facilities if they are committed".[1] This telegraphs MSOP's very pessimistic view of its assigned sex-offender prison inmates. The OLA Report, at p. 50, notes that, "... of those who have participated in the [MSOP-DOC Site] program in the past ten years, about 66 percent [two-thirds] have been civilly committed". MSOP-DOC Site has only seven clinical staff.[2] Deducting the considerable staff time devoted to initial assessments and dossier-compiling (see infra), precious little actual treatment is provided by MSOP-DOC Site, contrary to its self-billing as the DOC's 'intensive' treatment program. By administrative rule, the SOTP program is obligated to provide twelve hours of therapy every week.[3] In contrast, MSOP-DOC Site, operated by MSOP, is not covered by that rule. MSOP states that MSOP-DOC Site participants get treatment under the Dept. of Human Services rule applicable to MSOP's commitment facility (only 6 hours per week).[4] Given that high percentage of commitment and MSOP's practice of non-release from commitment, even assuming the bona fides of the MSOP-DOC Site statement of purpose, that program has been an abject failure. However, the actual purpose and operation of MSOP-DOC Site are considerably different from this public statement.

The Real Purpose: Commitment Trap

Many of those committed were previously enrolled in treatment at MSOP-DOC Site. Indeed, as to these, their commitments are largely based on testimony of staff from that treatment program and on its records. Obviously, since virtually no one has been released from commitment in MSOP, the stated goal of reducing length of stay in commitment has not been achieved, and by DHS projection of continued non-release as an MSOP policy, this purported 'goal' will not be achieved in the foreseeable future. Thus, it is fair to question the bona fides of this claimed goal. Moreover, because two-thirds of MSOP-DOC Site participants ultimately get committed at the prompting of, and volunteered adverse testimony by, MSOP-DOC Site staff[5], the bona fides of the other claim (i.e., of reducing the number of those committed) is also open to serious question.

---

1 *OLA Report, supra, pp. 49-50; accord: "Options for Managing the Growth and Cost of [MSOP]: Facility Study" [report to Minn. Legislature, January, 2011 — hereinafter, "MSOP Report"], p. 11.*

2 *MSOP Report, p. 13.*

3 *OLA Report, p. 62.*

4 *Ibid.*

5 *Ibid., p. 50.*

More specifically, one can alternatively view MSOP-DOC Site as an elaborate 'commitment grooming device', for the secret purpose of compiling 'dossiers' of adverse evidence and notes for adverse testimony at later commitment trials by MSOP-DOC Site staff themselves, including both assessment personnel and therapists. In this view, by selecting specific imprisoned sex offenders thought to be most vulnerable to a commitment attempt, MSOP's elaborate assessment protocol and comparatively limited treatment regimen (supra) amount primarily to a 'victim selection' means for commitment. Before getting too specific, a little more background is needed.

Upon entering into a prison-based treatment program, a sex offender is 'evaluated'. Ostensibly, this initial phase of psychological and related testing and interviewing is simply to give treatment staff a clear picture of matters that, in that sex offender's circumstance, need to be addressed through treatment.

Before proceeding further, note that other sections of this work explain that, by their respective natures, both clinical risk assessment (CRA) and actuarial risk assessment (ARA) are highly subjective and are open to vastly varying views. In commitment trials for instance, psychologists testifying from either CRA or ARA perspective typically strongly disagree about numerous aspects of each of those approaches to recidivism in risk assessment, and even about the ultimate issue of that offender's likelihood of sexual recidivism.

Bearing that in mind, a little-known fact of this assessment phase in prison-based treatment programs is that such treatment program staff will *always* write up their initial findings with the most dire spin possible on every finding, and with the most pessimistic prognosis. In traditional sex offender treatment programs, provided a given sex offender is not terminated prematurely from the program, progress reports are written up in a gradually more positive and optimistic manner as treatment progresses. In programs ending with 'graduation' (successful completion by the sex offender), the final report will reflect the most positive and optimistic statements of all about the sex offender. This is not an accurate reflection of transition by the offender from very poor to very good prognosis so much as it is a means by treatment program officials to maximize the appearance of effective results by the program, when later audited by outsiders.

In contrast, however, there is no graduation or successful completion from the MSOP-DOC Site prison-based treatment program. It is open-ended expressly because it is a prelude to commitment-based treatment thereafter. Yet the same approach to initial assessment is used, casting each entering sex offender as having extreme and uncontrollable impulses to reoffend sexually. Because that same overly conservative, 'never let them go' view in MSOP's commitment facilities also pervades the prison-based program with the same staff and supervisors, *nothing a sex offender can do in that prison treatment program will ever significantly change that initial, overly pessimistic assessment.*

Most damningly, the OLA Report (p. 28) provides a figure of 42% of offenders referred by the DOC as having wound up committed during the sample period 2004-2008. Obviously, matching this 42% to the 66% of MSOP-DOC Site participants who actually got committed, and even considering that a somewhat higher percentage than 42% might specifically apply to MSOP-DOC Site itself, it remains clear that *virtually every MSOP-DOC Site participant is probably referred for commitment,* a collective result obviously reached because of commitment advocacy by MSOP-DOC Site staff.

The General 'Commitment Trap' Model

Without identifying MSOP-DOC Site particularly, the Minnesota DOC does concede that having been in a sex offender treatment program *increases* the odds of being referred by the DOC for commitment consideration. The DOC connects this to 'more dangerous offenders' (for which read, those selected by MSOP-DOC) by further conceding that these are more likely to be in treatment.[1] Further confirming this indirectly, the MSOP Report itself[2] notes that "... almost 90% of the clients reviewed had had at least one sex offender treatment admission prior to their commitment". Whether through MSOP-DOC Site or elsewhere, at the very least, it can be reliably concluded from this that *the surest way for an imprisoned sex offender to get committed is to participate in sex offender treatment.*

Blaming The Trapped

Returning to MSOP-DOC Site specifically, that program excuses the large percentage of its participants who get committed as purportedly being a result of 'failure' by those participants or of those participants purportedly 'needing more' treatment when their prison release date occurs. Essentially, this is a 'blame the victim' ploy, in which the unfortunate treatment participant gets to play the role of victim. MSOP is effectively misusing MSOP-DOC Site to turn out participants as 'commitment fodder', even though on average these individuals were in MSOP-DOC Site for five years or more at the time of their release dates.

Note that the MSOP Report argues that even 'successful completers' of sex offender treatment can be apt candidates for commitment, on the apparent implication that post-treatment-completion events can demonstrate the need for further treatment in commitment. Obviously,

---

1 *Ibid., p. 41.*

2 *Ibid., p. 20.*

this would have to be something serious, one would think, such as some post-release sex crime, or an attempt at one, or at least undeniable specific preparations for one. Au contraire! Note that most such 'successful completers' attained that status during the imprisonment that then perversely culminated in their commitment regardless. That is to say, *they never were released* from prison on that sentence (but instead, they were taken immediately to county jail to await commitment proceedings). Hence, they had no opportunity to engage in recidivism, such that claims that they *would or might* have done so once released are pure speculation. Nor can it be said, contrary to MSOP's adverse prediction, whether they *would or might* have failed at 'community-based' treatment or *would or might* have violated any terms of their ISR or CR restrictions.

"Successful? Who Cares?"

According to the MSOP Report, p. 21 "... successful participation in treatment was not associated with a significant reduction in commitment rates ...".

MSOP's 'Insufficient Data' Dodge

So, by MSOP's own assertion, participation in prison-based treatment does not help a sex offender to avoid MSOP commitment — even with 'successful completion'. Interestingly, notwithstanding compiling statistics on this, MSOP fails to provide any *further* information based on the same data, claiming 'insufficient data'. This is most suspect. More specifically, that Report claims that no data is 'available' as to referral numbers or percentages on such treatment participants or successful completers, even though referral is an act taking place before one's release date, and even though the MSOP study looked at release dates from 2004 to 2010 — all in the past. As to commitment data on these, the MSOP demurred, claiming that data would be 'incomplete' because 'resolution of civil commitment may take several years'. A review of recent appellate decisions in such cases shows no cases that had been pending more than two years. In sum, it appears that MSOP is throwing up a smoke screen to hide highly material data, especially about its subsidiary, MSOP-DOC Site.

Justifying Commitment from the Trap: The 'Zero-Percent Public Safety Guarantee' and 'More Treatment Needed' as Commitment-Standard Substitutes

Recall again that MSOP's position as a rationale for commitment is that "in some cases, the reductions achieved through treatment, when weighed against the case as a whole, remain insufficient to guarantee public safety ...".[1] In light of observations, supra, as to the

1 *Ibid.; emphasis supplied.*

unattainability of the 'zero-percent public safety guarantee', which is MSOP's operating principle, and the *only partial* reduction in sex offense recidivism, which is the optimal outcome of sex offender treatment, and MSOP's belief and practice that *even decades of MSOP's own* highly intensive treatment are not enough to safely release their detainees, MSOP personnel naturally deem *every* MSOP-DOC Site participant as at least being 'in need of more treatment' of the MSOP-commitment kind. Hence, almost all MSOP-DOC Site participants only 'graduate' to face a commitment petition.

Contrary to the 'highly likely' constitutional requirement for sex offender commitment, MSOP-DOC Site staff urge courts to commit *every* such MSOP-DOC Site participant who is petitioned, since *none* of them (or anyone else) can 'prove the negative' of such a 'zero-percent guarantee' as to himself. Despite that this turns the commitment standard on its head and incorrectly places the burden of proof on the commitment defendant (respondent), judges unquestioningly consume everything such MSOP staff say, deeming them to be the quintessential experts on commitment to their program, and accepting their 'need for more treatment' rationale as sufficient excuse to commit.

"Just the Bad facts, Ma'am"

Worthy of note here in connection to points made elsewhere, MSOP excuses such high rates of commitment of treatment participants by saying: "... Risk assessments are partially based on actuarial scores. These tools are designed to address static factors. Static factors are not impacted by treatment completion or dynamic changes ... The legal criteria for civil commitment emphasize the static factors and do not recognize or give credit for positive impact on dynamic factors that are often the case in successful treatment"[1], or the positive impact of any other [i.e., non-treatment] dynamic factors, such as age.

One may fairly observe that the 'legal criteria' for commitment do indeed leave room for consideration of all such ameliorative, 'dynamic' factors in any given case. However, what apparently is happening is that in the case of MSOP-DOC Site and other DOC treatment programs, no such ameliorative changing factors are noted in a participant's file, and hence are not passed along either to prosecutors or to courts in commitment proceedings. Evidently, staff of those treatment programs are firm believers in the quote misattributed to Oscar Wilde: "If you have nothing bad to say, say nothing at all".

In sum, such a sex offender has nothing to gain from entering the MSOP-DOC Site program and, indeed, will find only that, by participating in that initial assessment, he has given such assessment

---

1 *Ibid., p21.*

staff substantial 'ammunition' to use against him by way of adverse testimony at any later commitment hearing. In essence then, MSOP-DOC Site serves as a candidate-selection process for later commitment, and as an adverse 'dossier-building' process to provide prosecuting attorneys the maximum amount of testimony and evidence in favor of commitment. In short, MSOP-DOC Site is a 'commitment trap'.

Thus, it should be no surprise that intelligent sex offenders who become aware of this 'commitment trap' nature of that program, when ordered into it by DOC officials, simply refuse and take the harsh disciplinary consequences (release delayed by one year). No one in their right mind, knowing this about MSOP-DOC Site, would ever enter it.

The 'Disclosure Trap'

The MSOP Report, on p. 21, also discusses the topic of disclosure (in pre-commitment treatment) of additional sex offenses by a given sex offender, vis-à-vis the impact of such disclosures on commitment evaluation.

> "Additional offender disclosures made during treatment are encouraged and expected. It may be that in commitment proceedings, however, the increased perception of risk associated with these disclosures offsets, to some extent, the perceived reduction in risk achieved through the treatment process." *Ibid.*

It should be recalled at this point that an exception to the therapist-client privilege exists as to disclosures of past sex offenses. This is no empty gesture: Sex offenders making such disclosures usually find that, such information having been passed along by therapists, acting as 'mandated reporters' under such laws, a law enforcement investigation ensues. Quite often, this results in belated criminal charge(s), when an applicable statute of limitation allows it, and where corroborating victim statement can be obtained.

So why would any sex offender make such disclosures in treatment? Is it purely out of the goodness of one's heart? Not really. Overbearing interrogation is the reason. Typically through fraudulent misuse of a polygraph exam as an interrogation tool, treatment staff assert to a beginning treatment participant that (whether in fact true or false) such polygraph exam results 'prove' the existence of undisclosed offenses. They follow this assertion with a threat to terminate that offender's treatment participation if he does not think about it and then come up with more unprosecuted 'offenses'.

Treatment participants fear the consequences of such termination, including a perceived greater chance of commitment referral.

This causes them to make such further disclosures, notably often including entirely fictional offenses. However, paradoxically, and despite successful treatment completion, they later get committed, in part on the rationale that such additional, 'admitted' prior sex offenses inherently, statistically, raise their risk of reoffending, either in disregard of, or overwhelmingly countervailing, the risk-reducing effect of treatment.

This is known as the 'disclosure trap'. For those who are determined to participate in treatment despite my general warning, supra, I warn them of this disclosure trap and strenuously suggest that they not admit or even mention any prior unprosecuted sex offenses and that they not make any up as a 'therapist mollifying' tactic. Over the years of hearing accounts by those who participated in prison-based sex offender treatment, nearly all of those 'disclosures' I have learned of ended badly for the treatment participant.

I am well aware of the justification advanced in favor of 'no privilege' laws as to sex offenses divulged to therapists, counselors, and clergy, among others. All of those rationales strike me as either wrong-headed or over-the-top, or both. Regardless of that old debate, however, unless or until legislatures repeal such laws, or at least carve out an exception for sex offender treatment-generated disclosures and make that restored privilege applicable to commitment proceedings as well as to criminal cases, such disclosures must be avoided as the hornets' nests they are.

Confirming that my advice was correct, the Minnesota Court of Appeals, in Stevens v. Ludeman,[1] held that the Fifth Amendment right against self-incrimination did not apply to statements disclosing previously uncharged sex crimes. In a phenomenal case of double-talk, that court ruled that neither the 'incrimination' nor the 'compulsion' element of self-incrimination was established by the detainee.

The ostensible basis for the supposed lack of incrimination was testimony by an MSOP representative that MSOP detainees could participate in treatment without disclosing identifying information about the victims.

Let's get real, folks. Put this instead in the context of police interrogation. If a police officer arrested you, demanded confession of the time, place, and manner of a crime from you, and refused to let you go unless you complied with that demand, and then used that information, in conjunction with other information derived from further investigation stemming from the divulged information, to deduce the identity of the victim(s), and then charged you with that

---

1 *2008 WL 2574475 (Minn. App. 2008].*

crime, that demand surely would be ruled by any judge to have been a violation of the Fifth Amendment right against self-incrimination. However, according to Stevens, the same demand by MSOP treatment staff does not comprise that same violation.

In the same comparison, *any* interrogation while being detained by police is always held to satisfy the 'compulsion' element of that self-incrimination violation. Yet, according to Stevens, the potentially *permanent* detention by MSOP is somehow not the 'same' as such potentially temporary police detention. The only way out of MSOP detention is to complete treatment and satisfy authorities that one has materially changed.

So when an MSOP demand for disclosure is coupled with a threat of non-advancement in treatment, it is merely a thinly disguised threat not to release one — ever — unless one disclosed everything but the names of victims of such past, uncharged crimes. Stevens turned a deliberately blind eye to this basic fact in order not to rule the obvious: the MSOP disclosure demand is a blatant self-incrimination violation. Until supervening case law or legislation overrules this, however, my advice to MSOP detainees and to sex offenders in treatment elsewhere must stand.

DOC Commitment Referrals

Sex Offenders as Piñatas, and Everyone Gets a Swing!

Starting in 2004, DOC referral of sex offenders to county attorneys for commitment consideration is now formalized, compared to earlier years. While one might think formalization includes procedural protections for the sex offender under scrutiny, the reality is that one staff group and two individuals each have the power under current rules to make such a referral.

First, screening of each sex offender nearing release is done by a three-person group consisting of a DOC psychologist, a correctional facility staff person, and a DOC probation services staff person. This group can make a referral without any further approval by anyone. If that group does not make the referral, an 'independent legal counsel' contracted by the DOC, having reviewed the psychologist's report, can make that referral by himself. Finally, if neither that group nor that contracted legal counsel makes that referral, the Commissioner of Corrections can independently refer any inmate for commitment who has been deemed by the End of Confinement Review Committee (ECRC) to be a Level 3 (highest recidivism risk) sex offender.[1]

---

1 *Ibid., p. 28.*

The general philosophy behind this three-alternative means to referral was to increase referrals from just those sex offenders who met the commitment standard to also include others who any of those alternative decision makers believed *might* qualify. The result has been a large increase of referrals. In turn, a large increase in commitments has resulted from that massive increase in referrals.[1] As that report notes, "... the revised referral policy increases the chance of referring an offender who will not reoffend or whose tendencies to reoffend could probably be *managed through supervision and treatment in the community* ..."[2].

Intriguingly, referral rates are substantially higher in both Hennepin and Ramsey Counties (containing, respectively, Minneapolis and St. Paul), exhibiting an apparent bias against sex offenders whose crimes occurred in those counties.

The DOC Referral Process: Pure Politics at Work

Initial screening includes looking for any one or more of a number of listed factors.[3] One of these (speaking of political considerations) is whether the offender has ever been charged with possession, sale, or distribution of child pornography, crimes whose connection, if any, to recidivism of 'hands-on' sex crimes is uncertain and controversial at best.

Another factor in this list is whether a sex offender has two or more sex offense convictions, even if they were sustained in the same prosecution or did not arise from a recidivistic act after release from prison. The existence of two or more acts, separately charged, as to the same victim or victims, closely connected, who were victimized as part of one set of relationships, also has a dubious causal or actuarial effect as to recidivistic tendency.

Two actuarial instruments (MnSOST-3.1 and Static-99) are filled out by corrections staff working only from DOC records and court files, supplemented with pure guesses as to anything not of record required by either of these actuarial instruments. This ARA process transpires in secret, unknown to the offender in question. Cases deemed sufficiently probable are forwarded to the Screening Committee and Independent Legal Counsel for Review. A high percentage of individuals considered by these are referred for commitment each year.[4]

Although the referral process is spelled out in the governing DOC 'policy', a given individual under scrutiny for such a referral

---

1 *Ibid., p. 29.*

2 *Ibid., emphasis supplied.*

3 *MSOP Report, p. 33.*

4 *Ibid.*

is not afforded any hearing or other mode of submission of relevant information. Moreover, the policy's criteria are, on the whole, vague and overbroad, resulting in a substantial number of referred individuals whose tendency toward recidivism is clearly less than that of others not referred.[1]

One example of a sweeping, all-encompassing criterion is the determination of any mental disorder or dysfunction. "Application of diagnostic criterion for sexual offenders remains controversial as it relates to predicting risk."[2] This, for instance, concedes that merely calling someone a 'pedophile' (one of those diagnostic categories) does not increase his risk.

Whether such criteria offer 'waffle room' or are based on impression, particularly on a point capable of arousing strong emotional reaction, such as strong fear or loathing, the application of such criteria becomes an exercise in politics. Unfortunately for the offender in question, however, the politics of sex offender management are all one-sided: a contest to see who can pile on the most and worst collateral consequences of conviction — in this case, finding justification to refer for commitment. Because this referral process is anything but scientific, and relies on numerous subjective judgments, with little or no consistent guidance by way of rules and other guidance, and in the absence of any opportunity for input on behalf of the sex offender in question, the process becomes very much like a witch hunt of yore. Elemental fairness is utterly lost in this secret process.

> "Amid intense controversy over Rodriguez, the Minnesota Department of Corrections [in December, 2003] stop[ped] following a 1991 state law requiring it to screen sex offenders due for release for possible civil commitment and make recommendations to prosecutors. Instead, it beg[an] referring all Level III [sex] offenders due for release to counties for commitment consideration. It immediately g[ave] county attorneys 235 names — including names of 135 inmates *already* released — *in addition to* the 14 already recommended for commitment that year. The total for 2002 had been 13.
>
> "Corrections referred the names of 170 offenders in 2004 and 145 in 2005 before reversing course and starting to screen offenders again and make commitment recommendations."
>
> *Larry Oakes, "2003: A Pivotal Year Causes Commitments to Surge", Star Tribune, June 8, 2008*

1 *Ibid., p. 34.*

2 *Ibid.*

The only thing that article leaves out is that, as the OLA Report painstakingly tallied, unlike any year before the 2003–05 period, in all years *after* 2005, even though based on *supposedly* individualized scrutiny, the annual number of commitment referrals has *remained substantially in excess of 100*. These new annual numbers are at least seven times higher than years up to 2003 (and including it, up to the December mass-referral). Thus, it is a perfect fit to the observed numerical pattern to conclude that the Minnesota Department of Corrections is still engaging in mass referrals every year, and that it simply covers that fact with the superficial appearance of an individualized screening. Otherwise, it becomes impossible to explain why 12 to 14 referrals per year were adequate until 2003, and ever since only numbers 7 to 8 times higher are now deemed adequate.

This pattern confirms that the DOC referral process in Minnesota is utterly political, rather than truly forensic.

Confirming this, simultaneously with, and partly causing, such mass referrals, in December 2003, then-Governor Pawlenty and the Commissioner of Corrections agreed to a strategy of referring all 'Level 3' sex offenders to county prosecutors for commitment petition consideration, taking corrections officials completely out of the referral decision loop.[1] This lasted for the next two years, after which referral decision-making reverted to corrections officials — a political hot potato tossed around.

Lack of Criminal Procedural Rights

At the outset of this section, note that a prosecuting attorney is not restricted by the aforementioned DOC 'referral' process. Even without a referral, a prosecuting attorney in Minnesota (called 'county attorney', identical to 'district attorney' or 'state's attorney' in other states) may file a commitment petition under one or both of Minnesota's two sex offender commitment laws at any time, not just before a sex offender is released from prison. This includes while a sex offender remains on any of Minnesota's forms of parole, or after one's sentence has entirely ended, or even if one never went to prison at all (i.e., received a probationary sentence). It is also important to note that it is not necessary for a non-imprisoned or post-release sex offender to have committed any new sexual offense (or, in the case of offenders on probation or parole, to have violated any condition of that status) in order to qualify for commitment.[2]

---

1 *Paul Gustafson, "Level 3 Offender Reviewal Changed," Star Tribune, Dec. 5, 2003, at p. 1B.*

2 *"Sex Offender Civil Commitment Fact Sheet", Office of Ombudsman for Mental Health and Mental Retardation, January, 2004, available at: www.ombudmhdd.state.mn.us/cctrc/sexoffendersccfactsheet.htm*

Significant differences in procedural rights exist in sex offender commitment proceedings, as contrasted to such rights in criminal prosecutions. All of these differences are adverse to the sex offender in commitment cases. In essence, despite that a judgment of commitment of a sex offender in Minnesota effectively spells a natural-life re-sentence for his most recent crime, Minnesota denies those petitioned for such commitment most of the rights afforded to criminal defendants.

Unlike criminal trials, for instance, in a sex offender commitment trial[1]:

1 there is no constitutional right to decision by jury;

2 the exacting criminal standard of proof beyond a reasonable doubt does not apply (unless the law of a given commitment state so provides);

3 the sex offender cannot refuse to testify (i.e., has no Fifth Amendment right to remain silent); and

4 the 'sentence' (i.e., confinement) is indefinite, and probably lifetime.

The OLA Report[2] adds: "In addition, hearsay evidence is allowed in a commitment trial, while it is not permitted in a criminal trial. The court may also hear testimony about offenses that did not result in convictions and may consider evidence about offenses even if it is hearsay evidence."

Also, while a sex offender, like a criminal defendant, has a right to counsel, including appointed counsel, the sex offender in a commitment proceeding, unlike a criminal defendant, has no constitutional right to reject such representation and to represent himself instead. This is an artifact from general provisions applicable in most commitments. Most traditional commitments, of course, did not involve sex offenders but rather, those so delusional or otherwise out of contact with reality that self-representation would be simply impossible. To date, apparently no sex offender has yet raised a constitutional claim of a right to self-representation.

As a general matter, one U.S. Supreme Court case, Specht v. Patterson[3], declared that sound logic and fundamental justice would seem to dictate the applicability of the constitutional procedural safeguards normally applicable in a criminal case to a sexual psychopathy commitment proceeding, despite the superficially 'civil'

---

1 *"Civil Commitment vs. Criminal Trials", (editor's inset), Star Tribune, June 8, 2008, p. Al.*

2 *p. 26.*

3 *386 U.S. 605, 18 L.Ed.2d 326, 87 S.Ct. 1209 (1967).*

nature of the latter proceeding. However, a later U.S. Supreme Court decision expressly rejected a sex offender's constitutional claim of a right to a jury in a commitment proceeding, apparently ignoring that earlier declaration in Specht. Nonetheless, 15 of the 20 states with sex offender commitment laws permit jury trials in such proceedings simply as a matter of state law. However, Minnesota does not so allow. In Minnesota, the commitment case is decided by a district court judge.[1]

Specht v. Patterson held that a failure to grant such procedural safeguards in sex offender commitment proceedings as the right to confrontation violated the due process requirement of the 14th Amendment to the U.S. Constitution. Yet currently, this holding has been forgotten by bench and bar alike, even in the modern, post-Crawford v. Washington era.

Insofar as confrontation concerns the right to cross-examine, or to call as a witness and adversely examine a clinical or forensic expert for the prosecution submitting an adverse report in evidence, the right to confrontation has been held by various states to apply to such proceedings, including a right to discovery of such reports in advance of trial.[2] Yet courts have not recognized in sex offender commitment trials the same right as in a criminal trial to confront declarants of out-of-court accusatory statements of a testimonial nature (Anno.: "Applicability in Proceedings under Statutes Relating to Sexual Psychopaths of Constitutional Provisions for the Protection of a Person Accused of a Crime".[3]) Some states, such as Virginia, rather than treating this as a confrontation problem, simply hold that a prosecution expert's opinion, to the extent it relies on an out-of-court, unadjudicated accusation, lacks an adequate factual foundation, and must therefore be struck.[4]

Of some comfort, the laws of 14 of the 20 states with sex offender commitment laws provide for a probable cause hearing prior to proceeding with the commitment process (Karsjens, et al. v. Jesson, et al. (hereinafter, "Karsjens").[5]

Although the Supreme Court, in Kansas v. Crane, supra, held that the standard of 'clear and convincing evidence' (a lesser standard than 'proof beyond a reasonable doubt') is constitutionally sufficient as to

---

1 *Minn. Stat. Chapter 253B; Joelson v. O'Keefe, 544 N.W.2d 905, 911 (Minn. App. 1999).*

2 *See, e.g.: In re Parker, 71 Cal. Rptr.2d 167 (4th Dist. 1998); People v. Austin, 321 N.E.2d 106 (Ill. App. 2000; Comm. v. Dooley, 232 A.2d 45 (Pa. Super. 1967].*

3 *34 A.L.R.3d 652, 675.*

4 *See, e.g.: Lawrence v. Comm., 689 S.E.2d 748 (Va. 2010).*

5 *U.S. Dist Court (Minn.), Case No. 11-cv-3659-DWF-JJK: First Amended Complaint, Para. 54).*

the statutory elements to commit a sex offender, lesser courts in some parts of the country insist on the reasonable doubt standard as to untried accusations of sex crimes, which in part are alleged to form the basis for such commitment.[1]

Again of some comfort, as a matter of state law, half of the states with sex offender commitment laws require satisfaction of the reasonable doubt standard to commit. This does not apply to Minnesota, however, where even uncharged accusations and such testimony by prosecution 'hired gun' expert witnesses is judged by that lesser 'clear and convincing' standard (In re Martinelli[2]). In Minnesota, such testimony about uncharged offenses need not even be given by a claimed victim themselves, but can be offered by hearsay testimony by someone else to whom that allegation was made.[3] This would never be allowed in a criminal trial. It is permitted in commitment trials only because they are arbitrarily classified as 'civil', rather than 'criminal'.

Likewise, some states (but not Minnesota) have applied the right to remain silent in civil commitment proceedings.[4] Some judicial districts, including the one in Minnesota in which most sex offender commitments occur, assign one specific judge to hear all such commitment cases. Although this is hailed as allowing development of judicial expertise with such cases, by the same token, it can breed a subtle form of institutional bias, in that such a judge may come to believe in application of what they think they personally 'know', rather than deciding the case solely on the record before them. Requiring decision by jury, with its strict instructions not to do that very thing, would at least cure this potential source of bias.

The lack of criminal procedural rights, coupled with the use of a lesser burden of proof on the prosecutor in a sex offender commitment proceeding reduces the profound importance of such a proceeding to the level of a mere lawsuit, even though personal freedom from incarceration is at stake. This simply should never be so. Courts, unfortunately, have ruled that the U.S. Constitution does not require such rights in a sex offender commitment proceeding. Therefore, legislation, or better yet, a constitutional amendment appears to be needed.

---

1 *See, e.g.: U.S. v. Shields, 522 F.Supp.2d 317 (D. Mass. 2007); U.S. v. Comstock, 507 F.Supp.2d 522 (E.D.N.C. 2007).*

2 *649 N.W.2d 886 (Minn. App. 2002).*

3 *Sex Offender Civil Commitment Fact Sheet.*

4 *See: State v. Zanelli, 569 N.W.2d 301 (Wis. App. 1997) (comment to jury forbidden on defendant's refusal to be interviewed); In re Commitment of Zanelli, 589 N.W.2d 687 (Wis. App. 1998) (lack of Miranda warning barred admission of defendant's earlier incriminating statement to police on untried accusation); Haskett v. State, 263 N.E.2d 529 (Ind. 1970) (refusal to answer questions by examining psychiatrists protected from contempt of court penalty).*

Is the Question Really 'Civil' vs. 'Criminal'?

Or Should the Focus Be on Loss of Liberty?

The reality of the aforesaid 'civil versus criminal' dichotomy, placing sex offender commitments in the civil category, is open to serious question. Both criminal trials and such sex offender commitment trials are based on *crimes* — convictions and accusations of crimes, whether charged or uncharged. Both involve the potential for an adverse ruling resulting in incarceration of the sex offender — the only difference being in what facility such incarceration takes place. Thus, e.g., in Comm. v. Page[1], commitment to what amounted to a prison was struck down, due to lack of a full array of criminal trial rights. In re Kramer[2], the court ruled that the practical effect of a civil sex offender commitment — life without parole — required criminal proceedings.[3]

Currently, sex offender commitment facilities are becoming more and more prison-like, both in Minnesota and elsewhere. Some such facilities in other states are simply in a different building within the secured compound of an existing prison. Effectively, as such commitment facilities are becoming further administratively divorced from state government units responsible for other kinds of commitment facilities, sex offender commitment facilities, in restrictive, high-security operation, are becoming more like maximum-security prisons every year. The only claimed distinction — the availability of treatment — is illusory, since modern prisons offer (and often require) treatment participation by sex-offender prisoners.

Functionally then, an end-of-imprisonment commitment simply extends a sex offender's incarceration, potentially to a natural-life additional term. In Minnesota, where only one sex offender has ever been successfully released (after approximately 25 years), this natural-life incarceration prospect is nearly certain.

Figures from Development of the MnSOST-3 Screening Tool Show That Only a Handful of Hundreds Committed in Minnesota Presented Recidivism Probability Percentages of 50% or More

As noted in other sections, a comparison of two studies in Minnesota of sex offender recidivism revealed that, against a former average sex-crime recidivism ratio of approximately 17% for offenders released in the 1990s, sex offenders released in the later range 2003–2006 committed a new sex crime over a 4-year period post-release only 3.4% of the time.

---

1 *159 N.E.2d 82 (Mass. 1959).*

2 *64 Cal. Rptr. 686 (Cal. App. 1967).*

3 *Accord: People v. Allen, 106 Cal. Rptr. 2d 43 (Cal. App. 1989); People v. Capoldi, 139 N.E.2d 776 (Ill. 1957).*

As a replacement for the notoriously inaccurate MnSOST-R, the MNSOST-3 was in development in this same period, and was able to use the results of this newer study showing reduced current rates of recidivism to derive its tables of predicted percentages of probability of sex-crime recidivism. The overall sample used in that newer recidivism study included in its total (nearly 2,700 sex offenders who passed their correctional release dates) some 134 of the then more than 500 Minnesota sex offenders who had been committed by then under sex offender legislation. Nothing would suggest that there was anything exceptional about these 134; they appear to be an average, random 'slice' of that 500+ total.

In constructing their tables, MnSOST-3 developers excluded these from their tabular calculations. Nonetheless, those developers later used the MnSOST-3 tool retrospectively on the 134 excluded commitment detainees. The developers' findings as to these detainees are shocking:

> "The average MnSOST-3 value for the 134 civilly committed [sex] offenders (who, but for commitment, would have been in the 2003–2006 sample) was 10.5% ... *Only four* of the [134] offenders [3%], however, had a MnSOST-3 value greater than 50%, and only 9 [7%] had an *upper* 95% confidence interval [CI] that exceeded 507... " *(emphases supplied).*
>
> *Grant Duwe & Pamela Friske, "Using Logistic Regression Modeling to Predict Sexual Recidivism: The Minnesota Sex Offender Screening Tool-3 (MnSOST-3)", Sexual Abuse: A Journal of Research and Treatment, Vol. No., pp. 1–28 (2012), available online at www.sax.sage.com (at p. 17).*

Note that the four offenders cited were *subsumed within* that nine offenders, making 7% the most *generous estimate* in comparison to a '50% standard' for commitment. In actual fact, however, the true legal standard for sex offender commitment ('highly likely' to recidivate) should be interpreted as requiring a percentage *vastly in excess* of 50%, such as 70% or higher. In essence, this shows that most sex offenders committed in Minnesota actually have a recidivism rate (10.5%) only modestly above the overall average for all sex offenders released from prison. In turn, this means that nearly *nine* who would not have recidivated (at least, within that four-year period of that study) were committed for each one who *would* have recidivated, but for commitment.

It gets worse. Duwe & Freske, supra, at p. 21, describing the potential of the MnSOST-3 to overstate recidivism predictions, noted the fact that Minnesota disproportionately relies far more on non-prison sentencing for sex offenses, compared to other states' sex offender sentencing practices. This means that sex offenders in prison in Minnesota can fairly be categorized as 'the worst' sex offenders, relatively speaking.

With this in mind, the good news is that only 1% (N=25) of the 2,535 sex offenders in the sample were at or above a predicted recidivism percentage of 40% (used by MnSOST-3 as a cut-point). Yet in that same four-year period (2003–2006), over 300 sex offenders were committed. Comparing this total of 25 offenders to that 300 total committed offenders, this means that more than 11 out of every 12 committed in that period would have been rated on the MnSOST-3 (had it then been ready) as being *less* than 40% likely to reoffend — a figure not even rising to a 'more likely than not' (51%) standard, much less to the actual 'highly likely' standard for commitment.

Thus, clearly, MnSOST-3 shows that Minnesota's 'commitment binge' has been completely unwarranted, locking up *many times* the number of sex offenders as to whom a credible case could be made for a claim of being 'highly likely' to reoffend. It appears that all those committed in Minnesota should petition for state 'habeas corpus' relief on the ground that their MnSOST-3 scores and consequent predicted recidivism probability fall *unfathomly below* the standard for commitment, proving whatever earlier ARA evidence and testimony used against them to have been flatly incorrect in Minnesota in modern times.

The Stupidity and the Horror of Minnesota Case Law on Sex Offender Commitment

The 'Linehan Legacy' can be seen as non-science and bad law, and the non-scientific 'Monahan Factors' of impressionistic violence prediction seen as baseless, judicially adopted factors for impressionistic sex-crime recidivism prediction.

In Linehan I (supra), the Minnesota Supreme Court stated:

> "The trial court, in predicting serious danger to the public, should consider the following factors if such evidence is presented:
>
> (a) the person's relevant demographic characteristics (e.g., age, education, etc.);
>
> (b) the person's history of violent behavior (paying particular attention to recency, severity, and frequency of violent acts);
>
> (c) the base rate statistics for violent behavior among individuals of this person's background (e.g., data

showing the rate at which rapists recidivate, the correlation between age and criminal sexual activity, etc.);

(d) the sources of stress in the environment (cognitive and affective factors which indicate that the person may be predisposed to cope with stress in a violent or nonviolent manner);

(e) the similarity of the present or future context to those contexts in which the person has used violence in the past; and

(f) the person's record with respect to sex therapy programs."[1]

While Linehan I preceded the SDP law and concerned only the SPP law, that same court later held in Linehan III (557 N.W.2d at 189) that the same factors may be considered in determining likelihood of reoffense under the SDP law. It is important to note that the six factors declared in Linehan I were taken directly from a book by John Monahan, Predicting Violent Behavior: An Assessment of Clinical Techniques (1981).

Three points should be observed in this regard.

First, Monahan was specifically addressing prediction of *violence*, not of sexual offense. Neither of the parties in Linehan I requested the court to adopt such factors; it did so on its own as a matter of judicial notice. The problem with application of Monahan's violence-prediction factors to even just SPP commitment trials is that sexual psychopathy is not the same as violence based on common anger or even on antisocial tendencies. The Supreme Court of Minnesota merely *assumed* that factors that may prompt pure violence are the same that may prompt, or elevate the likelihood of sexual assaults. In this, that court is guilty of having played a grievous game of armchair psychologists in a matter of utmost gravity: commitment detention of at least many years' duration and, based on sex offender commitment history, probably natural-life duration.

Second, as we have already seen, most sex offender commitments in Minnesota are based on the other (SDP) law; only 15% rest solely on the SPP (sexual psychopathy) law. In ruling in Linehan III that Monahan's 'violence factors' apply equally to SDP commitments, where *no violence* is required by the definitional elements of that law, and to which prosecutors typically resort specifically because no violence was involved, the Minnesota Supreme Court compounded its unscientific mistake. In short, *violence* prediction factors have *no place*

1 *Ibid., 518 N.W.2d at 614).*

in an inquiry into the likelihood of a non-violent sexual offense (e.g., a typical child molestation, in which no coitus occurs, no force is used, and the victim is willing). Those committed on judicial application of such inapplicable scientific considerations have a clear due process violation claim. This amounts to most of those committed to date. Oops!

Third, a preceding subsection (supra) squarely addresses the inaccuracy (and hence uselessness, and due process violation by use) of so-called 'clinical risk assessment' (CRA). Even on consideration of factors deemed predictive of sexual (not violent) offenses, CRA has been shown to produce predictions of future recidivism that are incorrect 70–90% of the time (id.); hence the uselessness and impropriety of their use in a sex offender commitment trial. Nonetheless, not only have prosecutors continued to use CRA so-called 'expert' witnesses, but also, knowing that courts *still* remain under 'marching orders' to consider the Monahan violence factors, prosecutors take pains to elicit testimony about the presence of such factors (or as many as can be asserted to be present) in the case at bar. By tying the CRA prediction in such a given case to that set of factors, most of which have no known correlation to *sexual* re-offense, particularly of the nonviolent kind, prosecutors are causing such so-called CRA experts to further corrupt and pollute their already-incorrect and unreliable predictions by those inapposite considerations — yet another due process violation.

Linehan Paved the Way to Precedential Adoption of Numerous Other Unscientific 'Factors' Which Do Not Reliably Indicate Probable Sex Crime Recidivism

Apart from the 'Linehan/Monahan factors', a veritable pot pourri of other 'factors' is often cited, including, e.g., the following:

(a) an 'escalation' over time in the person's history of sexual misconduct (but often based on inaccuracies or trivial differences, such as one charged offense one time, versus two the next, when in fact the first instance also included a second, uncharged offense);

(b) the offender's asserted 'lack of remorse' or 'lack of empathy' (this most often thrown at commitment targets who have always staunchly maintained their innocence);

(c) reoffense while under a suspended sentence — which could be for *any* (nonsexual) offense;

(d) reoffense on probation despite known consequences (but, compared to the penalty for a significant sex offense currently even if not on probation, the probation setting is a wash);

(e) 'inadequate insight' (that is, the "degree to which the offender appreciates the gravity of his condition"). This is a classic: in every case of any type, in which psychologists or psychiatrists are called in to 'medicalize' it, typically to justify a commitment, they *always* haul out this old chestnut. The fallacy: one who truly is not mentally ill will naturally deny it, but the psychologist or psychiatrist will then seize upon that denial as 'evidence' that one is mentally ill. This one is no 'factor'; it's just a rhetorical trick.[1]

Beyond such earnest questions as to the *applicability* of each such 'factor', the overarching objection to reliance upon such other factors is that, although each of them has an initial intuitive appeal, the fact remains that not one of them has ever been scientifically shown to have any *actual* correlation to later recidivism. They simply *sound* like bad omens. This is not science; it just amounts to condemning a man to probable lifetime commitment on the most troubling-sounding aspects of his past.

At best, this comes down to just another avenue by which to launch the fallacious argument that one's past behavior is the best predictor of one's future behavior. *Au contraire!* As pointed out in rejoinder, it is an established fact that most who commit a sex offense do not recidivate. Statistics *also* show consistently that most who commit a second sex offense do not commit a third, and so on. Even for recidivists, the odds are that they will not do so again. So the past is not a reliable predictor of the future, even purely from a statistical point of view. More fundamentally, even *were* one in some statistical cohort deemed more than 50% likely to reoffend, the mere fact of being so *categorized* does not inform the court — or anyone — whether this particular sex offender will be among those within that category who do reoffend or those who *don't*. At its very core, what is wrong with sex offender commitment-as-preventive-detention, is that no one can predict the answer to this question; judges are simply playing dice with the lives of those who have completed their prison sentences. 'Factors' which have not been actuarially established just attempt to cover this up; they do not improve the guesswork, they worsen it.

Linehan Invites Misapplication of ARA by Permitting Lifetime Extrapolation of Predicted, Short-Term Recidivism Probability

Another troubling fact is that Linehan III hastened to point out that the SDP Law "does not limit the prediction by time period".[2]

---

1 *Collectively on these, see, e.g.: In re Castonguay, 1999 WL 1216127, at *6 (Minn. App. 1999); In re Foley, 2005 WL 1154334, at *5 (Minn. App. 2005); In re Peria, 2007 WL 235632, at *3 (Minn. App. 2007).*

2 *Ibid., 557 N.W.2d at 190.*

The real aim of this observation was to encourage prosecutors to elicit ARA (actuarial risk assessment) testimony as to *possibilities* of recidivism over the entire remainder of a given sex offender's life, thereby *increasing* the reported percentage of likelihood. Although considering whether a sex offender will ever reoffend sounds fair and to the point on the face of it, the reality is that, because sex offenders must be dead (most very old first) before they can be included in such lifespan recidivism samples, those samples are so few and so small as to be statistically insignificant in their subdivided cohorts of particular *types* of sex crimes, age at commission, whether, how many, and when of recidivistic instances, relationship to the victim, etc. Thus, statistics emerging from these samples are *not 'generalizable' or reliable*, are open to self-serving interpretation either way, and widely and inconsistently vary between one study and the next. Therefore, the testimony which Linehan III invites is the most unreliable, least scientific kind of conclusion.

Damned by Double-Standard: Of Recent and Remote Prior Offense, Of Good Conduct and Bad

Moving on, under Minnesota case law, the fact that one's past sex offense(s) was remote in time, and that even one's current offense is old, given the typically long prison terms imposed in recent decades, is disregarded — as if those past offenses were committed only yesterday. Yet a truly recent current offense, or a prior not long before it, is treated as a severe sign of probable future recidivism: a genuine double-standard. Likewise, one's 'model prisoner' conduct is often disregarded ("Good behavior in the artificial environment of a prison is not determinative"[1]). Even good conduct on parole has been cast aside as another 'artificial environment'[2]. Of course, given current ten-year minimum paroles in Minnesota for sex offenses, this judicial policy effectively bars most sex offenders from establishing their good behavior on parole. Even a sex offender whose parole expired within the last few years would be credited only with those last few years' good behavior, ignoring such initial ten years of non-recidivism and good behavior.

Yet the fact that one reoffends, or even merely engages in 'inappropriate sexual conduct' while in prison is deemed to support a finding of high likelihood of reoffense — another double standard.[3]

---

1 *In re Linehan, 503 N.W.2d 142, 147 (Minn. App. 1993); see also: In re Hollie, 2009 WL 2596071, at *4 (Minn. App. 2009); In re Eberhardt, 2007 WL 738719, at *2 (Minn. App. 2007).*

2 *In re Hammill, 2009 WL 3818393 at *3 (Minn. App. 2009).*

3 *In re Preston 629 N.W.2d 104, 114 (Minn. App. 2001); In re Swedeen, 2007 WL 2770440, at *7 (Minn. App. 2007).*

In sum, it is very clear: the accused in a sex offender commitment trial cannot establish proof of anything that will be accepted as valid proof of a non-likelihood (or lesser likelihood) of reoffense, but virtually any argument by a prosecutor of the supposed significance of any converse of the very same kind of fact will be accepted as full *prima facie* proof of a very high probability of reoffense. The playing field is very badly tilted.

Aging Revisited: Judicial Rejection of Sound Science as to the Drastically Reduced Sex Offense Recidivism with Increasing Age

In another blatant 'stacking of the deck', in case after case, the Minnesota Court of Appeals has refused to recognize the plain and statistically well documented truth: that advanced age or disability act as a profound damper on sex offense recidivism.[1]

In one case, that court relied upon a so-called expert's testimony that "an extrafamilial pedophile ... is not subject to typical patterns of desistance with age".[2] That case stands for the proposition that you can get an 'expert' to say anything you want them to, regardless of falsity; and the fact that an 'expert' has said something under oath does not make it scientifically correct. As observed in a preceding subsection, all pedophiles, including extrafamilial-offense ones, have vastly reduced recidivism rates past age 50, and nearly nil recidivism at age 70 and beyond.

In the same vein, consider also In re Poole[3], in which that appellate panel wrote: "The court found that because *molesters abuse after age 70*, Poole's age of 61 is not relevant". In point of scientific fact, the Wollert meta-analysis proves that sexual abuse is actually perpetrated only rarely by anyone over age 70, including previously recidivistic pedophiles. Unreasoning, dominating fear, and a willingness to uncritically accept anything asserted by a so-called expert, that appears to confirm such base fears, won the day in Poole.

Perhaps more extreme, and certainly more revealing of the myths, baseless assertions, and factual distortions is the case of In re Dunlavey[4]: at the time of his commitment, Dunlavey was 74 years old; his physician testified to his physical infirmities, including congestive heart failure, needle-dependent diabetes, underactive thyroid, shortness of breath, and difficulty walking. Having met Mr. Dunlavey, the author can assure the reader that he was then a fat,

---

1 *See, e.g.: In re Lindsay, 2007 WL 1323597, at *4 (Minn. App. 2007); In re Braylock, 2006 WL 3409875, at *3 (Minn. App. 2006); In re Dunlavey, 1998 WL 2423 (Minn. App. 1998).*

2 *In re Gorden, 2006 WL 1806464, at *5 (Minn. App. 2006).*

3 *2000 Minn. App. LEXIS 624 (Minn. App. 2000). Emphasis supplied.*

4 *1998 Minn. App. LEXIS 68 (Minn. App. 1998).*

bloated old man, barely able to walk with a walker. To call Dunlavey "a large, powerful man" (as does that judicial opinion) takes exceptional brass, even for such a consistent prosecution-shill as psychologist Gilbertson, whom that opinion was quoting. Yet the Court of Appeals also adopted speculation that Dunlavey "could pose a threat to the safety of vulnerable nursing home residents and visiting children" if not committed. One is compelled to wonder: how? — by limping or waddling over to them with his walker and panting out (due to shortness of breath) some obscene suggestion?

The Court of Appeals also seized upon Dunlavey's longstanding protestation of innocence ("denies his offenses"), adding that he "lacks remorse". This dirty rhetorical trick needs to cease. Perhaps Dunlavey was telling the truth in protesting his innocence. If so, there obviously is nothing to be remorseful for. 'Lack of remorse' should be a valid factor only for offenses that are *admitted*, indeed, ones for which anyone would be remorseful, unless one were truly heartless, such as crimes of exceptional brutality. Politically incorrect though it may be, many sex offenses do not measure up to that standard.

Finally, Anita Schlank (then clinical director of MSOP) relied in part on the fact that Dunlavey had not successfully completed treatment. The implication is, of course, that no sex offender should ever be released without treatment, on the implicit premise that, without treatment, any sex offender is too 'dangerous' to release. This, however, is poppycock. Statistics by the Minnesota Department of Corrections (report to the legislature, 1997, on adult offender recidivism) point out that recidivism rates for sex offenders were virtually identical, *with or without treatment.*

In another case worthy of focus, Braylock v. Jesson[1], an illustration is presented of the highly artificial excuse-making for not releasing even those who clearly no longer present a threat to anyone. Ben Braylock, 79 years old when the Court of Appeals decided his case, was committed in 2006 to MSOP. In 2008, he petitioned for a provisional discharge from that commitment. This Court of Appeals opinion rejected that petition.

> "Braylock testified that if discharged, he planned to reside with his son and daughter-in-law. They in turn testified that they would ensure that Braylock followed the requisite supervised release conditions of parole, including that he have no contact with minor children. They also testified, as did another son and two stepdaughters of Braylock, that they supported his discharge, would report any violations of his supervised-release conditions to his

1 *2011 Minn. App. Unpub. LEXIS 249 (Minn. App. 2011).*

> parole officer, and did not believe that Braylock would pose a danger to anyone if discharged to reside in his family's home. His pastor also supported Braylock's discharge and testified that he would report to law enforcement authorities any failure of Braylock to comply with the conditions of the discharge ..."[1].

Yet despite all this, the Court of Appeals discredited these assurances by Braylock's family, because they "believed that he did not commit the sexual-assault offenses". Contrary to the opinion of the Court of Appeals, it appears that Braylock's family's efforts would be altogether adequate "to monitor his access to adolescents". In any event, let's get factually grounded. Here is a 79-year-old man. It stretches sanity to believe that he physically could, or even would try to, sexually assault anyone. The alternative surmise that he might now try to proposition teenage girls (victims of his crimes 21+ years beforehand) at his current age is so comical as to provoke laughter. This is a case of pure vengeance in action, under only the thinnest gossamer of superficial disguise. 79 years old. Commitment as a weapon. Utterly barbaric.

It is time to put away the hysteria and continuing retribution, courts; it embarrasses you and it has no place in decisions of such gravity. Your opinions will read in posterity as mean-spirited and venomously spiteful. This will ultimately be seen by calmer, wiser heads as anathema to concepts of justice. It is not merely some old men that are being judged, it is also you, the American judiciary.

To cast these senior citizens as being 'highly likely' to reoffend (the required constitutional standard) is either the depth of forensic incompetence or the height of judicial prejudice and unrestrained emotionality masquerading as logical reasoning.

Treatment as a 'Can't Win' Factor

Also in the 'can't win' department, that appellate court also held that where a person had previously participated in sex offender treatment, but later reoffended (his current conviction), the fact that he recently successfully completed a new prison-based sex offender treatment program did not have any effect on his conjectured high likelihood of reoffending yet again.[2] But capping this category is In re Peria, supra, in which the sex offender was deemed 'highly likely' to reoffend, even though he was on a long-term 'chemical castration' drug therapy that essentially extinguishes one's libido entirely. In a

---

1 *Ibid.*

2 *In re Braaten, 2006 WL 2474274, at *6-7 (Minn. App. 2006).*

stupendous example of judicial double-talk, the court opined that sexual urge was only one part of his supposed 'dangerousness'. Really? What else do the statutes allow an SPP or SDP commitment for, other than *sexual* recidivism danger? (rhetorical question). Separately, a different offender's argument against commitment showing that MSOP 'treatment' is a sham was ruled irrelevant.[1] — Can't win!

Forced Defendant Testimony as a Rhetorical Trap

Here's another 'can't win' instance. A sex offender has no right against self-incrimination in a commitment proceeding, unlike in a criminal prosecution. Of itself, that's inherently just wrong. But it gets worse. Having forced the defendant to testify adversely, here's one common rhetorical trick used against such a hapless defendant: "If a person acknowledges that there is a risk that he will reoffend, this is taken as an admission of his dangerous propensities. But if he states that he will not reoffend, this is taken as a lack of insight and is counted as a risk factor".[2]

'Really Dumb' Says It All!

And here's the Really Dumb Department: even a pending federal deportation proceeding has been held not to render SPP/SDP commitment pointless.[3] Even where the offender in a commitment proceeding is currently serving a prison sentence long enough for him to complete a prison-based treatment program, a 'prison placement' is unacceptable as a less-restrictive alternative to commitment to MSOP, according to that same court.[4]

Let's see:

1 Prison is too insecure to be a 'less-restrictive environment'? Hmmm ...

2 He will have enough time in prison to complete treatment, but should be committed anyway, just because? Hmmm ...

On a related point, one particularly notorious sex offender, who was exceptionally singled out for SPP commitment early in his decades-long prison sentence, challenged his placement in a prison not providing sex offender treatment, as opposed to one that did (Minnesota has three, one of which is in a high-security prison), or as

---

1 *In re Hince, 1997 WL 311662 (Minn. App. 1997).*

2 *Eric S. Janus, Failure To Protect: America's Sexual Predator Laws And The Rise Of The Preventive State, Cornell Univ. Press, 2006, pp. 33–34.*

3 *In re Richards, 738 N.W.2d 397, 400 (Minn. App. 2007).*

4 *In re Johnson, 2005 WL 89862, at *6 (Minn. App. 2005); In re Hopson, 2006 WL 3199160, at *5 (Minn. App. 2006).*

opposed to a commitment treatment facility.[1] Rather than to sensibly adjust this misplacement in an inappropriate prison, the Minnesota Court of Appeals spitefully doomed Thomas to serve out nearly all of that sentence before being able to raise that challenge, calling that 'right to treatment' challenge unripe until his prison release was imminent. This effectively ensured that all of Thomas' commitment time would be consecutive to his prison sentence. There was no reason to do this other than sheer spite. Decisions like this point up that sex offender commitment in Minnesota *isn't about treatment*; it's all about maximizing the duration of incarceration of sex offenders — years, perhaps decades, after their prison release dates have come and gone, to no actual effect.

Check-Box Testimony Jumping the Conclusion of the Legal Standard as Judicially Accepted Excuse-Making for Sex Offender Commitment

Minnesota appellate precedent allows experts to testify on the 'ultimate question' of whether the sex offender under scrutiny fulfills either the SPP or SDP legal standards for commitment[2], even though those sets of 'elements' are merely legislative formulations having no correspondence to psychological or psychiatric science, concepts, or definitions. Indeed, the Minnesota Rules for Civil Commitment, Rule 23, *requires* such experts to address those statutory standards. Yet, in so doing, such 'experts' step outside of the area of their expertise. In this, they are simply giving any other *layman's* opinion as to a matter of law. In all other areas of expert testimony, this is not allowed because it deprives the adverse party of basic fairness and due process. This *de facto* exception without rational basis for distinction makes a mockery of the trial process. Only judges are empowered to opine as to satisfaction of statutory standards in any court case.

Dirty Laundry: "Just Give Us Something We Can Use"

Also as to matters of proof, even a prior charge of a sex crime that ended in a dismissal, or even in an acquittal, can be used identically to a prior conviction in a Minnesota sex offender commitment proceeding.[3] This applies even to uncharged allegations of offenses, even from decades ago, and even if not asserted until now. This is the heart of unfairness to a commitment defendant. Any defense of this 'smear tactic' evidence (usually via hearsay) involves a tacit presumption that the defendant did in fact commit such alleged, but unconvicted crimes. Because commitment courts will almost always credit such accusations as supposedly possessing the status of 'clear

1 *In re Thomas, 1995 WL 465611 (Minn. App. 1995).*

2 *In re Jackson, 658 N.W.2d 219, 226-27 (Minn. App. 2003).*

3 *In re Jasmer, 447 N.W.2d 192, 195 (Minn. 1989).*

and convincing evidence' just because the accusation is made and nothing more (apparently an instance of the emotionally appealing, but logically baseless claim of presumed truth in 'coming forward' with such an accusation), this unfairly shifts the burden to the defendant to flatly prove that the accusation is false — an utter impossibility in cases of allegations of acts claimed to have occurred many years ago.

Repetitive Attempts to Commit: Outrageously Unfair, but Judicially OK'd

Even worse, where the prosecuting attorney ('county attorney' in Minnesota) in one county dismisses a sex offender commitment case, or the judge rejects commitment, the legal doctrine of double jeopardy does not apply, and the separate legal doctrine of 'collateral estoppel' (a wider form of res judicata) has been held by the Minnesota Court of Appeals not to bar a county attorney in one of the alternative counties of such commitment jurisdiction over the defendant from filing a new commitment petition (even if not alleging any new or different facts) and thereby starting the proceeding all over again.[1] In cases of dismissal before the commitment trial, even the *same* county attorney can refile a petition and start over again. If at first you don't succeed, try again. Just ignore the aspect of misuse of the commitment process as endless harassment.

Gagging the Defendant: The Insidious Extermination of the Right to Self-Representation

As noted elsewhere, appointed counsel is inescapable for those unable to afford to retain an attorney. The subject sex offender in a commitment proceeding is forbidden to represent himself, even though virtually all sex offenders are mentally competent.[2] This procedural rule is a holdover from commitment of psychotics, who are *unable* to defend themselves due to delusions. In *no other kind of case* is self-representation forbidden. In most instances in other states, representing oneself often proves to be a disastrous mistake. However, in Minnesota, particularly in the context of sex offender proceedings, in which appointed counsel typically act as assistant prosecutors, clients often beg the court to be allowed to fire that unchosen lawyer, and to proceed pro se. If that's not an indictment of the abysmal state of sex offender commitment defense in Minnesota, I have no idea what would be.

Presumption of Admissibility as a Shift of the Burden of Proof: Non-Confrontation — Lies and Damned Lies

Because the Confrontation Clause applies only to criminal trials (a constitutional fact that needs to be fixed), a subject sex offender

---

1 *In re Anderson, 2007 WL 738719 at *1 (Minn. App. 2007).*

2 *In re Irwin, 529 N.W.2d at 371 Minn. 1995).*

(i.e., through his lawyer) has no right to cross-examine prosecution witnesses, and in the case of at least some witnesses in commitment trials, is often banished (with his lawyer too) to another room, where all they can do is listen to that witness' direct examination.[1] Surely, this must at least violate notions of procedural fairness and due process.

But, as if all this is not bad enough, the Rules of Evidence themselves do not apply in a sex offender commitment trial.[2] All of the considerations of evidentiary fairness go out the window. In comes all manner of slander and calumny. This is enforced by a presumption in favor of admissibility, invented expressly for commitment cases.

Hence, the burden *falls upon the subject* sex offender to show that any hearsay accounts of uncharged accusations of sex crimes are false or unreliable. If the distance of the long past and current unavailability of refuting witnesses and of proof of alibi prevent him from satisfying that burden, any such surprise hearsay testimony can be *admitted.*

The frequency with which prosecutors suddenly pull these 'rabbits out of their hats' strongly suggests the existence of a furtive industry in last-minute invention of just such practically irrefutable lies set in decades past. The judicial countenancing, of this vicious trash as evidence when a man's liberty is in peril — potentially permanently — is an unconscionable disgrace that can be explained only in terms of fear and loathing of the subject sex offender substituting for impartial, reasoned judgment.

"Where Do I Sign?"

But this cavalcade of judicial horrors continues. The statutory requirements for *specificity* of findings that govern other kinds of commitments do not apply to sex offender commitment, according to Minnesota appellate cases.[3] This exemption includes findings relating to less restrictive alternatives.[4]

Moreover, such cases have OK'd the 'rubber stamp' practice of a commitment trial court adopting the prosecutor's proposed findings of fact verbatim, without any individualized court comment about any of such findings.[5] See also to same effect: In re Jones[6], wherein it was held that the district court had sufficiently fulfilled its duty to 'scrupulously assure' that such findings it adopts verbatim will allow 'meaningful review' on appeal by merely adding the 'boilerplate' statement that the

---

1 *Irwin, 529 N.W.2d at 372–73.*

2 *In re Williams, 735 N.W.2d 727 (Minn. App. 2007).*

3 *Linehan III, 557 N.W.2d at 190.*

4 *In re Ayers, 570 N.W.2d at 25.*

5 *In re Fernandes, 2006 WL 2947642 at *2 (Minn. App. 2006).*

6 *2001 Minn. App. LEXIS 1250 (Minn App. 2001).*

court "carefully reviewed the proposed findings of fact submitted by (the prosecution) and concluded that these findings accurately, completely and properly describe the evidence presented at the trial". That opinion fails to explain, however, that this same statement or similar verbiage is *always* included in trial court findings documents using such verbatim adoption of proposed findings. What a crock!

Between these two rulings, it becomes clear that the Minnesota appellate courts have tacitly authorized commitment trial judges to ask no other questions of prosecutors except: "Where do I sign?".

Judicial 'Credibility' Assessments of Conflicting Expert Testimony as a Means to Dismiss an Inconvenient Scientific Truth

No matter how unscientific, indeed *anti*-scientific, the testimony of prosecution expert witnesses, and regardless how unequivocally such 'junk science' testimony has been demolished by the testimony of defense experts, supported fully by academic literature, judges in sex offender commitment trials typically sweep all that firm refutation aside by citing (without any documentation from the record) the supposed greater 'credibility' of the prosecution expert(s). This is a standard for witness evaluation that is wholly inappropriate to expert witnesses (as opposed to lay witnesses testifying, for instance, about something they claim to have seen, heard, or experienced).

In the case of expert witnesses, the question does not revolve around such courtroom observations as whether an expert witness fidgets nervously in testimony or stammers under cross-examination. Instead, the expert witness is merely the conduit to report scientific facts that can be verified through examination of the sources cited and comparing them to other scientific publications that perhaps appear to differ or to engage in scientifically supported distinction. Additionally, expert witnesses commonly apply scientific knowledge to the facts of the case at bar. In this role, the question, once again, does not devolve to examination of a witness's personal behaviors scrutinized for signs of deception or uncertainty. Instead, the issue is simply: how well founded and scientifically correct is that application? Again, this can be verified through scrutiny of sources and other publications.

Sadly, R. Prentky, E. Janus, et al., "Sexually Violent Predators in the Courtroom: Science on Trial"[1], were forced to note "... the increasing tendency ... for experts to stretch or distort the science — to introduce bad science — in response to the strong advocacy pressures inherent in SVP proceedings".

When experts differ in a trial, either about the underlying scientific principles or about their application or lack of applicability to the

---

1 *Psychology, Public Policy, and Law, Vol. 12, p. 357 at 360 (2006).*

case at bar, correct judicial analysis of the competing merits of those opposing experts' respective scientific testimonial contentions is not to be judged by their comparative rhetorical style or appearance of confidence, for instance, but rather purely by close evaluation of the science cited as the basis for such testimony. Despite glibness and airs of confidence, an expert witness can be dead wrong.

Therefore, a lack of such analysis in a sex offender commitment judge's decision, and instead wholesale dismissal of the expert testimony and supporting scientific evidence offered by the defense on supposed (but unspecified) 'credibility' findings (whether of lack of 'credibility' or some unspecified comparison of credibility) is nothing more than a cover-up for a wilful bias to accept whatever a prosecution expert says, in a preconceived judicial plan to justify commitment of the sex offender at bar.

This course is chosen by such a biased judge because he knows that appellate courts will almost never examine a trial court's finding as to 'credibility'.[1]

It should be particularly noted that *virtually all* of the 'credibility' decisions cited in Minnesota appellate reports favor the prosecution. Mere odds-defying coincidence? You decide.

Just Who Is Being Committed, and Why on Earth Are They?

Just as outrageous as the 'stacked deck' of the sex offender commitment process is who is being committed, and under what circumstances. MSOP has justified its existence, and sponsoring legislators and certain overzealous prosecutors have justified the 'need' for Minnesota's sex offender commitment laws on the contention that those committed are uncontrollable sex maniacs, operating under irresistible impulses to rape women or small children. Really? Consider these examples:

- Ben Alverson, then in his early 20s, engaged in sexual relationships with two girls, ages 13 and 14. After serving a three-year sentence, he was placed on parole. His subsequent commitment was based on a technical violation of rules of that parole.
- Dwayne Peterson, 28, has no sex-crime convictions, charges, or uncharged accusations. He only had sexual fantasies about children and wrote to them. His 'sex offender' commitment was based solely on the fear that one day he might commit a sex crime.[2]

1 *In re Ramey, 648 N.W.2d 260,269 (Minn. App. 2002); Linehan III, 557 N.W.2d at 190; In re Black, 2007 WL 1470592 at *5 (Minn. App. 2007).*

2 *Larry Oakes, "Locked in Limbo", Star Tribune, June 8, 2008, p. Al).*

Clearly, such examples don't fit the foregoing violent, impulsive predator stereotype. Alverson apparently had no prior record, was therefore not recidivist at all, and had been thought so innocuous by the criminal court judge that he gave Alverson a minimum sentence. Peterson, more preposterously, had no sex crime at all — only some prosecutor's fear that he might someday commit one.

Let's add these further examples.

Harley Morris was 61 years old in 2011, when he was committed as a 'sexually dangerous person'. Really? Mr. Morris did have one sex-crime conviction, in 1995: attempted second degree criminal sexual conduct, for which he served all of his prison sentence. In case you were wondering, that charge means that he was convicted of a mere failed attempt at a grope. In 1968 (some 43 years before commitment), he had been accused of rape. However, that accusation was then officially determined to be unsubstantiated. Clearly no 'clear and convincing evidence' there. In the late 1970s to early 1980s, Mr. Morris engaged in pimping prostitutes for about seven years — perhaps not the most savory of businesses, but obviously not the same as sexual assault. In a phenomenally 'politically correct' move, the Minnesota Court of Appeals rested his commitment in part on that pimping, by claiming that pimping "had a sexually harmful component", thereby allowing that court to hold that the indispensable element of a 'course of harmful sexual conduct' was presented. Not a stretch, you say? No more than spandex.[1]

And this one, which is really troubling.

Gessell v. Jesson[2], at which time (2011) Mr. Gessell was 25 years old, and had already been committed as an SDP since age 19. Mr. Gessell's 'string' of sex crimes consisted of the following:

- At age 12, he was adjudged delinquent after pleading guilty to a fifth degree (a misdemeanor) for 'sexually assaulting' his 8-year-old sister. I'm guessing that, at fifth degree, it couldn't have been much of an 'assault' and that whatever actual sexual conduct that took place in this incident must have been relatively minor (no pun intended).

That's it — no more sex crimes (only that one), or indeed, any more crimes at all.

For this 'heinous' offense, young Master Gessell was placed in various lock-up juvenile placements, including treatment programs for juvenile 'sex criminals'. According to the august Judge Kalitowski

---

1 *In re Morris, 2011 Minn. App. Unpub. LEXIS 1114 (Minn. App. 2011).*

2 *2011 Minn. App. Unpub. LEXIS 1034 (Minn. App. 2011).*

of the Minnesota Court of Appeals, young Mr. Gessell (ages 12–19) was cited by treatment staff for "inappropriate sexual behavior" — "masturbation, voyeurism, making sexual gestures toward others, engaging in sexual contact with peers, and stalking others in treatment settings" (whatever that really means). On the whole, it doesn't sound too unusual for most teenage boys. Yet for nothing more than this, rather than being released, Mr. Gessell was committed as an SDP. To date, Mr. Gessell has been locked up for 13 years for a misdemeanor crime (maximum jail term: one year). Worse, according to the Minnesota Court of Appeals, Mr. Gessell must remain 'indefinitely' committed, and could remain so for the rest of his days on earth — which could be as few as the next 70 years or so. Does it strike you yet that something seriously insane is going on in the legislative and judicial chambers of Minnesota?

Think that all commitments are from prison? Think again! Consider the case of Robin Razmyslowski, who, six months after his release from prison, and while *successfully* participating in community-based sex offender treatment, was suddenly snatched away for commitment to MSOP, even though he did all that was asked of him and was a model releasee, and had completed a post-release period of house arrest, and remained on electronic home monitoring.[1]

A case similarly illustrating the extremism of sex offender commitment in Minnesota is In re Eberhardt[2]. Mr. Eberhardt had not committed a sex offense since 1984 — some 22 years before his commitment. This is not to say he led an altogether exemplary life thereafter. According to that appellate opinion, he spent the 'majority' of the intervening years incarcerated. The 'Overview' of that opinion by LEXIS editors reports that: "The district court found that the lack of recent sexual offense was countered by appellant's recent conviction of a felony, his drinking and attitude toward drinking, and his use of cocaine on the eve of entering jail" on his most recent felony conviction. However, none of this was sexual in nature. Hence, one must ask: how do these nonsexual matters 'counter' the lack of any sexual offense? Indeed, that opinion concedes that Eberhardt had just spent the last four and a half years 'in the community' without any sexual offense or any indication that one was in the offing.

The appellate opinion affirming Eberhardt's commitment cites testimony by 'experts' that "Eberhardt's relapse prevention plan was 'completely lacking". Come off it, please! A relapse prevention plan is necessary only when one does have a current inclination to commit sex offenses. The fact that, in his multiple periods of release since that

---

1 *In re Razmyslowski, 2005 Minn. App. Unpub. LEXIS 412 (Minn. App. 2005).*

2 *2007 Minn. App. Unpub. LEXIS 243 (Minn. App. 2007).*

1984 sex offense, Eberhardt had not committed another one stands as strong evidence that he did not have any such inclination later. Judicial reliance on such supposedly expert mumbo-jumbo as a presumed need for a 'relapse prevention plan' effectively indulges a further tacit presumption that, absent such a plan, recidivistic sex offense is highly likely to ensue. Judicially jumping that conclusion improperly shifted the burden to Eberhardt to prove that no such sex offenses were likely. When the burden falls upon a commitment defendant to prove that commitment is not warranted, a form of 'presumption of guilt' has been judicially indulged. Consider this: how, exactly, does anyone prove a negative? Answer: at best, it is very difficult, perhaps impossible, especially against such a presumption.

Notwithstanding the court's sniping about Eberhardt's drinking and cocaine use during his periods of freedom, the fact that he did not commit any sex offenses even while thus intoxicated actually bespeaks a lack of such likelihood of future sex offenses. That individual judges, or individual panels of appellate judges could come to the opposite conclusion out of sheer displeasure over alcohol and drug consumption, and base a potentially lifetime incarceration commitment on such consumption, demonstrates beyond question that sex offender commitment in Minnesota is grounded on nothing more than arbitrary whim, judicial prejudice, and personal dislike of, or displeasure with, the defendant. This is worse than a bill of attainder (see infra), it is an 'anti-popularity contest', with those most disfavored in general being relegated to permanent detention.

The Ipsedixitism of 'Hired Gun' Testimony by Prosecution Forensic Witnesses

Does a man who has already successfully completed sex offender treatment have some assurance that he will not be targeted for commitment? Not in Minnesota. Consider the case, In re Pirkl.[1] While Mr. Pirkl was incarcerated, he obtained both sex offender treatment and chemical dependency treatment. He successfully completed both of those treatment programs. At his commitment hearing, a prosecution expert opined (with no apparent factual basis) that Pirkl had "shown signs of faking his recovery", and thus his successful completion of treatment could not be trusted. Notwithstanding such successful completion, his commitment was based on this bare assertion by a single, bought-and-paid-for, so-called 'expert'.

See also: In re Sveen,[2] to same effect. Despite 47 months of sex offender treatment in prison, ending in Sveen's successful completion,

---

1 *531 N.W.2d 902 (Minn. App. 1995).*

2 *2011 Minn. App. Unpub. LEXIS 638 (Minn. App. 2011).*

experts at Sveen's commitment trial opined that he had gained little from treatment and did not learn enough to significantly reduce his likelihood of reoffending. Really? After 47 months? Notwithstanding prison treatment staff thoroughly testing Sveen and certifying that his treatment completion was successful?

Just who are these 'expert' witnesses, anyway, to have such a crystal ball to defy such a treatment history and such certification by treatment therapists?

Sexual Minority Membership as Ipso Facto 'Irresistible Impulse'

In re Smallwood[1] points up one unfair presumption. Again based on 'expert' testimony, the trial court found that Mr. Smallwood had a 'sexual disorder' known as 'paraphilia', which can loosely be described as sexual attraction to unusual activity. Let's call it 'kinkiness', which about sums it up. Merely because of that fact, the expert testified that Smallwood could not "adequately control his sexual impulses".

Really? Well, first, shouldn't the court determine *whether* Smallwood had what could fairly be termed 'impulses', rather than mere sexual attractions or interests? The leap of logic here seems to be that, in the case of any *unusual* sexual interest or attraction, any such sexual response must be inherently elevated to the level of uncontrollability, hence 'impulse'. There is no science, however, behind this mere assumption. Prentky, Janus, et al., "Sexually Violent Predators (etc.)"[2] point out that "... Jackson, et al. (2004) pointed out that the 'mere presence (of a paraphilia) is not sufficient to meet the legal criteria (for commitment). The paraphilia must also impair the offender's ability to control his behavior'.".

Worse, even if one could fairly describe such unusual attractions as 'sexual impulses', where is it written, exactly, that the sheer unusual nature of some sexual attractions make such impulses inherently beyond adequate self-control? This again is not science, it is simply retained, partisan witnesses making it up as they go, to justify their exorbitant pay. The trial court relied on this baseless presumption and committed Smallwood.

Even If the Monahan/Linehan Factors Were Magically Incised in Tablets of Stone, the Very Devil Is in Their Application

We have already discussed the so-called six-factor 'Linehan test', originally based on a 1970 article about violent psychopaths (not 'sexual psychopaths'), which set forth those six factors to predict near-term violent episodes. Even though the Minnesota statute *named*

1 *2012 Minn. App. Unpub. LEXIS 230 (Minn. App. 2012).*

2 *supra, at p. 364.*

Sexual Psychopathic Personality (SPP) has virtually nothing to do, by definition, with violent psychopathy, the Minnesota Supreme Court, on its own motion (and apparently the private readings of one of its justices) incorporated those six 'Monahan factors', first into its judicial factors for finding 'sexual psychopathy', and second (and in fact totally unconnected to clinical psychopathy), into its factors for finding one to be a 'sexually dangerous person'. This was bad enough.

But it is in the way those factors are applied where the outrages truly start. Take, for instance, In re Pyron[1], in which the appellate court noted that, if released, Mr. Pyron would be required to register with the state as a sex offender, and such registration, in turn, would cause him difficulty in obtaining housing and employment. The court went through all this, not in sympathy, but to the contrary, to declare that Pyron would thus suffer stress (the fourth Monahan factor). Thus, supposedly, Pyron would be more likely to sexually recidivate, opined that court. So, in other words, this is how we commit: create problems for a guy (by the registration requirement) who will already face reintegration difficulties due to the sheer prejudice, fear, and loathing applied by whole communities against sex offenders, and then claim those very problems as a ground to commit. Wow! How convenient!

It gets worse. The first 'Monahan factor' is 'the offender's demographic characteristics'. Monahan never explained this, so it has become a free-for-all to simply say some things that *sound* bad or adverse about the offender's background. In Pyron's case, the 'hired-gun experts' found these facts in this category:

1 Pyron had never been in a monogamous, stable relationship;

2 a "poor relationship history";

3 a history of family instability; and (wait for it)

4 he had been "abused as a child".

Let's skip over the boundless vagueness of these terms, although that would be good ground for criticism of itself. Getting right down to it, the fact remains that none of these cited facts in Pyron's case are scientifically verified predictors of a subsequent sex offense, where one has not committed a sex offense to date. Each of these facts pre-dated Pyron's original sex offense. Ergo, citing any of these 'demographic' facts is sheer postdiction, a blatant form of junk science.

The fifth Monahan factor relied upon by Minnesota courts is a 'similarity of past and present contexts'. On this, the court in Pyron merely noted that Pyron would be "returning to an environment where he would continue to have access to his victim pool" and which would be "similar settings in which he offended in the past". Let's deconstruct

---

1 2008 Minn. App. Unpub. LEXIS 1045 (Minn. App. 2008).

this just a bit. The concept of a 'victim pool' is just a makeweight argument. Whether a given sex offender is a rapist of adult women or a molester of children, the fact is that women and children are found ubiquitously in all non-incarcerated and noncommitted settings, with only rare exception (e.g., cloistered monasteries). Therefore, any hired-gun 'expert' can always fall back on this truism that any sex offender, if released, will once again have "access to his victim pool". Likewise, nearly all sex offenses are committed in ordinary communities, only immaterially indistinguishable from each other when it comes to their potential as sites for such crimes. Hence, again, any testifying 'expert' can create this makeweight argument against any sex offender whose release plan calls for either return to his former home community or to any other typical community — a setting similar to that in which he previously committed a sex crime.

Finally, the sixth Monahan factor is the offender's record of participation in treatment. We have already seen from Pirkl that even superb treatment completion will not suffice to prevent commitment. So this is purely a one-way factor, by which to heap further criticism on an offender.

Apparently being a good sport about all this character assassination of his client, Pyron's lawyer did not challenge the scientific baselessness of all this 'auguring of the entrails', instead confining his defensive rejoinders to the matter of actuarial base rates, a poor strategy. Shrugging that off, the appellate court affirmed Pyron's commitment on all the junk science of the foregoing 'Monahan factors'.

"Unconstitutional as Applied? We Can't Hear You!"

In re Travis[1], the court held that a sex offender under a prosecution petition for commitment cannot challenge the constitutionality of Minnesota's sex offender commitment system on an 'as-applied' basis as a denial of substantive due process. Essentially, Travis' argument was that, since no one had ever been successfully released from MSOP, and since MSOP treatment had merely been a series of experiments ultimately abandoned, each such abandonment forcing MSOP detainees to restart treatment ab initio, repeatedly, with no true progress possible, MSOP treatment was a mere sham serving as a cover rubric for real sheer preventive detention. The Court of Appeals overruled the trial court's order requiring the prosecution to respond to that argument against commitment, relying on the doctrine of 'unripeness'. Basically, the appellate court was saying that such a claim of unconstitutionality could not be raised by a sex offender unless already under commitment and 'deprived' of treatment. In this way, Travis closed the courthouse

1 767 N.W.2d 52 (Minn App. 2009).

doors to all such claims of 'as-applied' unconstitutionality as a defense to a commitment proceeding itself. But of course, no controversy could be more 'ripe' than that. One who is being petitioned into commitment clearly has a present stake in that outcome, and should be able to raise any applicable constitutional defense.

The true gist of the Travis ruling is the Court of Appeals' argument that, in an 'as-applied' challenge, one should not be able to cite the experience of those already committed to show that MSOP treatment is a mere sham and cover-up for surreptitious preventive detention. However, there is no legal basis for limiting 'controversy' and 'ripeness' in this way. Any evidence is valid and permissible to show that actual application of commitment statutes, in daily or yearly administration of commitment, including the question of the reality of treatment, as cast in grave doubt by lack of releases and by constant complete re-creation of the treatment regimen every few years to date, is a mere façade, behind which hides permanent preventive detention, with no intent of releases beyond a few intended only to defuse that very claim of unconstitutionality.

Therefore, the Travis holding itself is just a dodge, by which to prevent probing of the truth and of making that case in *the context most meaningful*, i.e., *whether one's current proposed commitment is unconstitutional.* Minnesota jurisprudence has slipped to a new low of politics trumping justice.

Everything the Judges 'Know' Is Wrong!

Many matters have been cited in Minnesota appellate opinions upholding commitments as indicating a high likelihood of future sex offense recidivism. Yet many such supposed 'factors' have been scientifically debunked. For instance, A.J.R. Harris & R.K. Hanson, "Clinical, Actuarial and Dynamic Risk-Assessment of Sexual Offenders: Why Do Things Keep Changing?",[1] reveals that "Many evaluators had assumed that having been *sexually abused as a child, not displaying victim empathy*, and having low self-esteem would be related to sexual recidivism; this turned out not to be the case". Further[2], they add that, based on results of one large Canadian study ("Dynamic Supervision Project"), three attitude items (namely, "the offender's acceptance of *attitudes supportive of sexual entitlement, rape, and sexual activity with children*") were dropped from a revision of one 'dynamic' RAI (Stable-2007), "due to *lack of association with sexual recidivism*". Last, from that same study, those authors found that "... *emotional collapse, collapse of social support*, and *substance abuse* were not related

1 *16 Jour. of Sexual Aggression, No. 3, pp. 296–310 (Nov., 2010), at p. 298.*

2 *At pp. 302–03.*

consistently to sexual or violent recidivism." *(emphases supplied).*

As to the last finding as to substance abuse, firstly recall that the MnSOST-3 and 3.1 instruments link substance abuse to sexual recidivism incorrectly by only affording a reduction to the score derived from that instrument where an offender has successfully completed both sex offender and substance abuse treatment programs (conversely elevating one's predicted likelihood of sexual recidivism otherwise, making commitment more likely).

As to lack of victim empathy, the commitment of Dennis Linehan[1] in part relied on Linehan's "... lack of remorse, based on Linehan's unconvincing display of regret at the [commitment] hearing". That opinion, at p. 190, also relies on Linehan's alcoholism. In re Roth[2] also rested commitment in part on a compromised ability for empathy on Roth's part.

As to the foregoing 'attitudes', In re Blodgett, supra, at 510 N.W.2d 915, requires commitment courts to consider, inter alia, "the offender's attitude".

As to having been "sexually abused as a child", In re Pyron, 2008 Minn. App. Unpub. LEXIS 1045 (Minn. App. 2008), in part relies upon that fact in upholding Pyron's SDP commitment.

As to "collapse of social support", In re Burnham[3] based Burnham's sex offender commitment partly upon his lack of social support. Likewise, In re Freeman[4] cited partial support of commitment that Freeman had no family ties and was abandoned at a young age. Also, In re Ponicki[5] rested commitment in part on Ponicki's currently significantly reduced social support.

In sum, Minnesota's trial judges have been swayed to approve commitment of countless sex offenders in part because of testimonial assertions by psychologists that have been proven to have nothing to do with the question of tendency to commit future sex crimes.

How appalling does it have to get?

---

1 *In re Linehan, 557 N.W.2d 171, 177 (Minn. 1996).*

2 *2011 Minn. App. Unpub. LEXIS 747 (Minn. App. 2011).*

3 *2005 Minn. App. Unpub. LEXIS 434 (Minn. App. 2005).*

4 *2005 Minn. App. Unpub. LEXIS 377 (Minn. App. 2005).*

5 *2009 Minn. App. Unpub. LEXIS 1216 (Minn. App. 2009).*

Section Four

Quackery and Obfuscation at their Worst

Chapter 9

Commitment as Treatment, or as Lifetime Preventive Detention?

MSOP 101: Conceded Problems with Treatment

Upon arrival at MSOP Moose Lake campus immediately following commitment, each committed person is required to sign a form declaring whether or not they intend to participate in treatment in MSOP. Those choosing to participate in treatment are then supposed to be evaluated (anew) and be given an individual treatment plan.[1]

MSOP treatment consists of three 'phases': Phase 1, in which 'patients' learn how to comply with MSOP facility rules and learn basic treatment concepts; Phase 2, in which patients must discuss and work through their sexual offenses and patterns of sexual abuse; and Phase 3, in which the focus is on community reintegration. Phase 3 takes place at the other MSOP site, on the grounds of the Minnesota Security Hospital in St. Peter, MN. As a last portion of Phase 3, patients are electronically monitored and live on those grounds in a house not within the secured perimeter[2].

The MSOP treatment program was designed to be completed within four years[3]. Yet currently, 75% of MSOP detainees (80% of who participate in treatment) have been under civil commitment for three years or more — many for more than a decade, some as long as, or longer than, 20 years. Indeed, notwithstanding that MSOP has been in operation more or less in its current configuration for 20 years (since 1992), 64 percent of its treatment-participating detainees *currently remain in Phase 1*, while *only 12 percent are in Phase 3*. It was not until February, 2012, that the first patient in MSOP history was deemed to have completed that treatment program — *after 18 years in commitment.* It takes no advanced degree in rocket science (or clinical psychology) to know that something is very wrong with MSOP.

In the investigation resulting in the aforementioned OLA Report, MSOP officials offered excuses that can be classed overall as "problems in the treatment program over the last ten years (that) have likely affected the progress of some sex offenders".[4]

---

1 *Karsjens, supra, First Amended Complaint, Paragraph 63.*

2 *Karsjens, ibid, para. 66.*

3 *Ibid, Para. 66.*

4 *Ibid, p. xxi.*

Really? What is the excuse as to the first ten years?

That OLA Report[1], for instance, passes along the excuse that treatment-participating detainees get stuck in Phase 1, which focuses on following rules and learning how to participate in treatment groups, rather than addressing the detainee's sexual offenses or how to prevent reoffending. That report[2] conjectures that this may be because MSOP does not promote "positive treatment participation".

Again, really?

How long *should* it take to learn the rules and the etiquette of group therapy participation: one month, maybe two months?

The OLA Report, at p. 58, also cites "years of inconsistent and unstable clinical leadership" as another excuse for lack of releases and aggregate movement toward release. More specifically, that report cites "frequent leadership changes" as contributing to a "lack of continuity" in MSOP's treatment program, noting that MSOP "has had three executive directors and four executive clinical directors in the last seven years" (i.e., 2004–10). That report explains the impediment caused by this constant turnover thus:

> "Due to these many leadership changes, the content of the treatment program at MSOP facilities has changed multiple times since 2003. With each change in leadership and the treatment program, clinicians and clients have needed to learn the new program. Also, clients have had to be reassessed according to new program requirements. At times, clinicians have lacked supervision to help them make good clinical decisions."

Upon reflection, *it should be clear that it is highly unlikely that so many MSOP* leaders and especially clinical leaders would have left for personal reasons or due to frictions with staff. Far more likely is that their respective departures had everything to do with sequential failures and realizations of inherent flaws in the various treatment approaches over the years. Thus, those departures have actually been indictments of MSOP treatment approaches themselves.

This view would seem to be supported by the additional fact that MSOP has had persistent problems with filling clinical supervisor positions (only four of eight such slots filled as of January, 2011).[3]

> "With a dearth of clinical supervisors, MSOP has been unable to assure that all clinicians are implementing a therapeutic style consistent with best practices or

1 *p. 64.*

2 *Ibid.*

3 *Ibid., p. 60.*

applying the treatment model in the way clinical directors envision ...".

In fact, there is also a shortage of therapists in MSOP. The OLA Report[1] cited one-quarter of therapist positions in MSOP as being vacant as of November, 2010. That report explains: "Clinicians may not want to work for MSOP because of its reputation for program instability and not releasing any clients".[2] MSOP's goal is to have a client-to-therapist ratio of 8:1. However, at times, that ratio has been as high as 25:1.[3] That report explains one crucial impact of this therapist shortage thus: "When clinicians are overworked, those clients who have the most trouble or who speak the loudest may get the most attention. Clients who are well behaved and may be progressing nicely in treatment may not be noticed".

Despite its claim of intensive treatment, in fact, MSOP delivers less treatment hours per week than the Minnesota Dept. of Corrections prison-based sex offender treatment program.[4] This obviously impedes detainee progress in treatment. Another conceded adverse impact on treatment is a recent (2008 to date) emphasis on institution security, resembling prison architecture and operations.[5]

Most importantly, the lack of releases from MSOP has bred a pronounced hopelessness among detainees. This in turn has profoundly dampened their motivation to participate meaningfully in treatment.[6] Between such hopelessness and a sense of chronic daily stress in MSOP, many have asked to have their parole revoked, opting for prison life instead.[7] It should be obvious that any environment more stressful than daily life in prison cannot hope to deliver therapy successfully.

Most MSOP 'Therapists' Are Un-Degreed Quacks

"Civil Commitment ..." (OLA Report), at p. 61, admits that MSOP's current administration inherited "clinical staff who had been promoted into clinical positions even though they lacked a background in therapy. For example, some clinicians were formerly *security staff, with backgrounds in criminal justice. Some have only a high school diploma ...".*

---

1 *Ibid.*
2 *Ibid, p. 61.*
3 *Ibid, p. 60.*
4 *Ibid., p. 62.*
5 *Ibid, p. 68.*
6 *Ibid.*
7 *Ibid.*

This is an outrage! In any other mental health treatment context, hiring poseurs with no advanced college degrees (M.A. or Ph.D.) specific to clinical psychology as therapists would result in class-action lawsuits, license revocation of both such quack therapists and the entity that had knowingly hired them, and license revocation of their clinical supervisors for fostering this act of inherent mass malpractice of mental health therapy. Any under-educated, let alone completely uneducated, person posing as a clinical psychology professional, regardless of whatever on-the-job 'crash coursing' offered by supervisors, inherently lacks the knowledge and skills to be able to carry out this most delicate of all therapeutic regimens.

The fact that such clinical supervisors and *their* bosses (MSOP administrators) conspired to allow and foster that use of unqualified, hopelessly uneducated persons to fill civil service positions for which it was blatantly obvious that they held no credentials, and to pretend to be delivering mental health therapy as to which they had no clue, testifies voluminously about their *real, unspoken* knowledge that the 'treatment', which they publicly argue is the rationale for MSOP's existence, is worthless and inherently incapable of changing such basics as sexual orientation — notably, pedosexuality, pedophilia, or paraphilias (formerly 'fetishes'). Effectively, the true thinking must have been to the effect that, since the underlying concepts upon which such 'treatments' are based are junk science, and such 'treatment' itself is therefore inherently ineffectual. It really makes no difference that those who occupy 'therapist' positions are incompetent charlatans with no professional education whatsoever. No indictment of the entire model of sex offender treatment could be more damning than this.

Of course, the casualties of inherently flawed 'treatment' and its underlying concepts are MSOP's detainees, who are thus in reality being actually just subjected to natural-life preventive detention with no real hope of release.

Apparently to downplay this egregious malpractice, MSOP officials told investigators from the Office of the Legislative Auditor of repeated leadership changes before 2008 that were cited as responsible for many poor practices then, including this matter of therapeutic mis-staffing[1], citing a high "clinician turnover and difficulty in re-filling those positions" as excuses. Essentially, the theme of this apology is, 'things were chaotic before, but now we've reformed our operation'.

More specifically, "... since 2008, MSOP administrators have required new clinicians [therapists] to have master's degrees and be licensed-eligible ..." to assure that they "have a clinical background that equips

1 OLA Report, pp. 58–61.

them to do intensive treatment required in the program".[1] However, "as these [new] staff are often inexperienced ... [they] learn to do their job *through on-the-job training and mentoring by other clinical staff*".[2] The first underscored phrase connotes that such advance-degreed professionals are still required to conform their therapeutic practice to the flawed treatment model and its underlying, equally flawed concepts. Given this limitation, any hope for real improvement is ill-founded.

The second underscored phrase in the quote above connotes that the hold-over, incompetent therapists with no professional education are purporting to guide these new, degreed therapists. Note specifically that, as of January, 2011, only 11 new, degreed therapists had been hired, out of 48 such positions (leaving five vacant).[3] Given these numbers, the continuing influence of holdover therapists without applicable education remains strong. Indeed, also as of January, 2011, only four of eight clinical supervisor positions were occupied, and two of those four positions had been recently filled. About this, that same report notes MSOP's inability to ensure that therapy actually comports with the current treatment model.[4] This undisciplined chaos confirms the view that treatment is not really going on in MSOP, but rather only the personal approaches of 43 therapists, mostly uneducated.

In this way, all of the 'witch-doctoring' ways of those charlatans are being 'passed down' as 'treatment gospel', notwithstanding its utterly non-scientific and often anti-scientific nature. This can be expected to confuse the new, degreed therapists and to 'hamstring' their performance. In this way, the legacy of incompetence is perpetuated, regardless of the academic preparation of the latest therapists.

Worse, hiring these new degreed therapists has the effect of adding an *appearance* of professionalism to what remains a deeply flawed set of underlying concepts and the treatment regimens and techniques based upon them. This may well only deepen the internal MSOP allegiance to such concepts and treatment regimens, and may make it more difficult for outside pressure to be brought to bear to reform such flawed conceptual basics. So don't expect any real, substantial changes in 'the way things are' in MSOP in the foreseeable future.

And not to be forgotten, these new, degreed therapists have required a substantial upward increase in pay scale for those positions, making MSOP even much more expensive, particularly over its projected doubling of detainee occupancy by 2020.

---

1 *Ibid, pp. 61–62.*

2 *Ibid., p. 62, emphasis supplied.*

3 *Ibid, pp. 59, 60.*

4 *Ibid, p. 60.*

Finally, as the OLA Report noted, at p. 61, "clinicians may not want to work for MSOP because of its reputation for program instability and not releasing any clients" (more accurately, the avowed *intent* expressed in the still-in-effect executive order *never* to release anyone not judicially ordered released). So these newer, professional therapists may disproportionately became disillusioned and quit as time goes by, assuming no real change in the MSOP program or its outcome.

Claims of Theoretically Attainable Treatment 'Effectiveness'

Despite its own phenomenal failure, MSOP administrators argue for continuing Minnesota's scheme of committing sex offenders by asserting that sex offender treatment has been 'effective' elsewhere. Really? Let's look at the facts. The point to sex offender treatment is to reduce sex offense recidivism. Hence, statistical monitoring of such recidivism is the measure universally examined to judge the effectiveness of such treatment.

A 1997 statistical study performed by the Minnesota Department of Corrections at the request of the Minnesota Legislature found that, on average, sex offense recidivism among sex offenders who had not participated in sex offender treatment in prison was 11%. Comparably, among those sex offenders who did participate in such treatment, the average sex offense recidivism was 12%. This finding, of course, suggested that sex offender treatment, at least as then carried out by the Minnesota Dept. of Corrections, had no sex offense recidivism reducing effect at all, and could actually be argued to have marginally increased it.

Bearing in mind that sex offender treatment programs and techniques tend to copy from one another, attention should be paid to a more recent very-large sex offender sample study in the California prison system. Janice Marques, et al., in an article titled "Effects of a Relapse Prevention Program on Sexual Recidivism: Final Results from California's Sex Offender Treatment and Evaluation Project" (SOTEP)[1], comparatively studied three groups (those receiving two years of inpatient-style sex offender treatment while imprisoned; those choosing not to receive same; and those not receiving same other than through choice). That study has been praised for its ideal experimental design and strong research methods, as well as for using a long follow-up period, in addition to that huge sample size. That study found *no significant differences* between those three groups in their *rates of sexual and violent offending* over the follow-up period. It should be particularly

1 *Sexual Abuse: A Journal of Research and Treatment, Vol. 17, no. 1, pp. 79–107 Jan., 2005.*

noted that the type of treatment used in that two-year California sex offender treatment program was 'cognitive behavioral treatment' — exactly the same type as is used in MSOP currently with no success.

Evidently stung by both its own original findings and that California study by Marques, the Minnesota DOC chartered a study by its own sex offender treatment program director, Robin Goldman, of sex offenders who received treatment in Minnesota DOC facilities. This sample was smaller, but this study did also use a long follow-up period. This 9.3-year period connotes that this study involved those in treatment not long after the first Minnesota study reached its conclusion. In sharp contrast to the earlier Minnesota finding as to lack of effectiveness of sex offender treatment, this later study by Goldman concluded that sexual recidivism was 27% lower for sex offenders who entered such treatment than for those who did not participate in it. Arguments were made that this statistic was due to improvements to the DOC treatment program studied. However, because of the aforementioned temporal closeness of the treatment in the Goldman study to the first Minnesota results, the Goldman results may instead be a product of deliberate statistical selection. Hence, reliability may be lacking in the Goldman study, particularly as a chartered study by inside personnel.

Although acknowledging the Marques study in California, the OLA Report, at p. 55, by counterbalancing with the Goldman Minnesota DOC study (although silent on the DOC's own 1997 conclusion about sex offender treatment), merely states that "it is impossible to offer more definite conclusions about sex offender treatment's effect on recidivism". But it clarifies thus: "...There is no definitive research demonstrating the effectiveness of sex offender treatment in reducing recidivism". However, in almost the same breath, that OLA Report acknowledges that 'psychopaths' (deemed highest-risk offenders and over-represented in MSOP's inmate population) have been found to have an increased risk of reoffense following treatment.[1] Yet that OLA Report, at p. 25, acknowledges that 49% of MSOP detainees were judicially found to have "sexually psychopathic personalities". MSOP officials themselves concede the existence of this problem, and even have "a separate unit for clients with high psychopathy".

In sum, it is highly doubtful that MSOP can claim any measure of effectiveness in recidivism reduction, other than through the sheer preventive detention of keeping its detainees locked up. As will be seen elsewhere, intensive supervision of released sex offenders by corrections staff itself accomplishes that purpose at a small fraction

---

1 *Grant Duwe & Robin Goldman, "The Impact of Prison-Based Treatment on Sex Offender Recidivism: Evidence from Minnesota," Sexual Abuse: A Journal of Research and Treatment, Vol. 21, no. 3 (Sept., 2009), pp. 279–307.*

of the cost of imprisonment, and thus at a nearly infinitesimal percentage of the cost of detaining sex offenders in MSOP. Indeed, such post-release intensive supervision may well account for most of the recidivism reduction claimed by Goldman for Minnesota prison-based sex offender treatment. In this light, especially because MSOP does not have the confidence in its treatment to release more than one detainee to date of its approximately 600 detainees currently, it becomes clear that MSOP has no effectiveness at treatment, and that its rubric of 'treatment' is simply a pathetically thin disguise for a true nature of purely preventive detention.

Treatment? Or Just Failed Experimentation Repeated for 20 Years?

MSOP is not accredited by any agency outside of its own administrative 'parent', the Minnesota Dept. of Human Services. As will be seen throughout, infra, as to MSOP, that parent agency might more aptly be termed the 'Dept. of Inhumane Services'. The implication of near impossibility of gaining release from MSOP, within a surrounding sea of adversely exercised discretion and a shifting of such an enormous burden of proof to the offender to satisfy, is clear from the statement by MSOP itself, appearing at p. 21 of the OLA Report, requiring reduction of recidivism risk as to any given offender to "very low levels", and also from the single release to date (and only under strong political pressure for just such a token release). One may well ponder this: if in all the years of this commitment program, no one else has been able to satisfy this standard, then obviously all that so-called 'treatment' has not had any such 'significant impact' on the 'behavior and thoughts' of any offenders[1]. In other words, whatever the program is doing *can't be regarded as treatment at all*, but rather, at best, only experimentation, all of which the program itself implicitly deems to have been a running series of failures of singular aggregate proportion for at least the last 20 years.[2]

Consider the case, In re Kunshier[3], in which Mr. Kunshier complained that "he had no way to gain release from MSOP even though he successfully completed sex offender treatment". It appears that after he had done so, and while he awaited clearance for release to 'provisional discharge', MSOP officials replaced that former treatment

---

1 *Ibid.*

2 *Citing Howard Barbaree, Calvin Langton & Edward Peacock, "Sexual Offender Treatment for Psychopaths: Is It Harmful?", in Sexual Offender Treatment: Controversial Issues, Wm. Marshall, ed. (John Wiley & Sons, Ltd., West Sussex, G.B., 2006) at p. 159.*

3 *Consolidated with In re Lonergan, 811 N.W.2d 635 (Minn. Supr. 2012).*

regimen with an entirely new one. Although Mr. Kunshier pointed out that there was no clear and convincing evidence that the first treatment program he completed was unsuccessful, MSOP forced him to start all over again in the new, even-longer, replacement regimen. The Court backed up MSOP, and Mr. Kunshier still remains detained.

Indeed, in the early 1990s, when sex offender commitments in Minnesota began in earnest and MSOP was proposed as a formal agency, Dr. Michael Farnsworth, then a forensic psychiatrist at St. Peter Security Hospital (MSH), led opposition to that proposal and to substantial numbers of sex offender commitments, saying, among other reasons, that there is no proven technology to treat sex offenders. Interestingly, when state leaders forged ahead with that plan over Farnsworth's objections, he suddenly found himself assigned to design the MSOP treatment regimen. The treatment model then chosen was a cognitive-behavioral approach stressing 'relapse prevention'.[1]

Yet, even as recently as July 2008, a report by the U.S. Congressional Research Service concluded that "research indicates that there is not enough evidence to definitely prove that treatment for sex offenders works".[2] That same report noted that, through the fall of 2006, only 252 committed sex offenders had been discharged nationwide, and almost all of them only within the most recent few years. Experts say that this makes it statistically impossible to tell whether treatment of sex offenders in the commitment context works. Farnsworth adds that, in the nearly 20 years of MSOP existence, "There has not been a huge explosion in the knowledge or the efficiency of treatment".

However, more recently, MSOP clinical directors have shifted to a different treatment mode more akin to the 'brainwashing' of Cold War days. In this mode, MSOP declares a large number of cognitive beliefs verboten, as likely to lead to sex offending. Then they engage in intensive scrutiny of everything a treatment participant says and does for any seeming implications or indications that the participant has any such forbidden belief. As to each such (rightly or wrongly perceived) belief, MSOP treatment staff demand that the participant verbalize rejection of that belief and to demonstrate by his behaviors that he sincerely and firmly believes that rejection and adopts it as his own. This insistence is enforced by denying advancement in treatment to anyone who refuses or fails to relinquish any of the 'forbidden thoughts'. These are referred to as "thinking errors". Continued existence of forbidden thoughts is checked by polygraph testing.[3]

---

1 *Larry Oakes, "OK'd for Transfer, but Going Nowhere", Star Tribune, June 9, 2008, p. Al.*

2 *Quoted by Larry Oakes, ibid.*

3 *Larry Oakes, ibid.*

This should not be downplayed as banal. Effectively, this converts MSOP into a 're-education camp' as run by the Red Chinese for decades following communist takeover of that country in 1949. Those who satisfied their masters that they had truly changed their thoughts on salient subjects were released to be obeisant subjects of the communist totalitarian state. Others were detained — and eventually executed. 'Thought police' is an anathema to the American concept of rights of the individual. Even more bedrock to the right of free expression (which is recognized as extending even to prisoners) is the right to freedom of thought and of conscience. A very dangerous line has been crossed when one's captors can insist that one change one's thoughts and beliefs — and prove it — as a condition of release. It gets worse as this insistence on abandoning one's own thoughts and replacement by a 'party line' of articles of faith, a politically correct dogma, if you will, is projected into post-release years (assuming any number of MSOP detainees are ever released).

Example: Suppose a released and ultimately fully discharged sex offender demonstrates over many years that he is leading a crime-free lifestyle. In casual conversation or friendly correspondence, our former MSOP detainee makes a statement that he then has reconsidered his views, and has decided, as to any one of the myriad 'forbidden thoughts', that he now believes, *on a purely intellectual level*, that he was right all along initially about that particular 'forbidden thought'. What would stop an MSOP official, having had this brought to their attention, from petitioning for re-commitment, or referring to a county attorney for that purpose, of our long-released, and thoroughly law-abiding former detainee? The theory would be that, by re-adopting a thought that co-existed at a time our former detainee was sexually offending, our detainee was becoming 'dangerous', that is, exhibiting an elevated risk of sexual reoffense, even though nothing in his behavior supports that proposition.

A far-fetched and thin scenario, you say? OK, let's suppose that, over time in freedom, our former detainee — still completely law abiding — announces (either all at once or over time) that as a result of uncoerced thinking and observations of the world, he has decided that most — no, for argument's sake, all — of the many 'party line' doctrinal points insisted upon in treatment are incorrect or of seriously limited applicability.

In this scenario, there can be no doubt that, had our former detainee made that announcement while detained, he would still remain detained. And it seems quite apparent that, even after all those years of law-abiding freedom, the 'thought police' would find this latter-day renouncement of the MSOP dogma either so frightful or so repugnant that they *would* seek our boy's re-commitment.

Really? For what? — dangerous thoughts? At what point in this gentleman's life does he get back his rights to freedom of thought and conscience, and freedom of expression?

Elsewhere in this work, one MSOP detainee is quoted as making a metaphoric statement that, when confronted by someone who constantly insists he is a frog, that detainee will eventually voice agreement, just to get the insistent one to shut up about being a frog ... though it's plainly self-evident, at least to the detainee, that the insistent one is not a frog, and is probably delusional for thinking so. What this short parable means is that MSOP detainees can — and do — 'play along' with that 'party line', but do not remotely believe all or even just most of it.

In most cases, the 'planks' of that politically correct 'MSOP party platform' run contrary to the real-life lessons of the various experiences of the detainees, some of which experiences can be classed as aberrant (in the sense of highly unusual) and others not. To erase such lessons of truth, and replace them with contrary 'convenient fictions', is an impossibility. So an unyielding demand to that effect upon current detainees will only ensure that no one is ever released.

Think not? What if a given detainee even passes a polygraph exam as to the sincerity of belief in all of the 'MSOP party line', but for any myriad possible reasons, treatment staff believe that the detainee is somewhat likely to eventually re-adopt some of his former beliefs? It would seem to follow from the importance attached by MSOP to one's thoughts that our hypothetical detainee would likely find his release denied — indefinitely and repeatedly. Not for acts suggestive of propensity to reoffend, not even for mere speech, not even for 'thought crime', but merely for the likely prospect of *eventual* 'thought crime'. If this is the only way to prevent reoffense, sexual or otherwise, then we must re-think the attainability of a treatment outcome that can give any assurance of non-reoffense.

Bottom line: people — including sex offenders — will believe what their experience teaches them. Efforts to jam thoughts into people's heads to replace such natural beliefs and thoughts deemed by treatment staff to be 'dangerous' are, in the long run, doomed to failure. Meanwhile, the coercion and extortion applied in that effort are barbaric and draconian, and deprive one's most elemental human rights simply because one disagrees with one's captors. America cannot ever be about this. Think long and hard before standing on that steep and very slippery slope.

The fact is that all of this so-called 'treatment' has been nothing more than experimentation and has never been divulged to those committed at MSOP, in violation of their legal rights. Given this non-stop string of failures, it is fair to deem such repeated experimentation simply wild flailing-about without a clue. This calls into question whether even the most basic concepts adhered to as articles of faith by 'clinical' decision makers of MSOP are just plain wrong.

The outrageous unfairness should be immediately apparent. Condemning individuals thought to be 'risky' to a program which, for more than 20 years, has repeatedly failed in its mission, indicates a complete ignorance of how to achieve that mission. It thereby *prevents* those committed to MSOP from ever being able to make the extremely high standard of proving, in those same faulty concepts of MSOP administrators, that their recidivism risk hasn't just been reduced, but, through nearly impossible treatment completion (ignoring all other favorable influences and natural progression, such as sheer age), their recidivism risk has been reduced to "very low levels" — perhaps down to the general incidence of sex offense by members of the public without prior sex crime records.

A nearly impossible-to-satisfy standard is bad enough; providing a false 'map' of how to get to that goal, and then changing every few years to a different, but equally false 'map', is just sheer emotional torture. This, plus the routine demotion of committed individuals from advanced levels of attainment to lesser, or even beginner, levels certainly seems to amount to a 'punitive treatment environment', as cited in the Washington state case, Turay v. Seling, 108 F.Supp.2d 1148 (W.D. Washington) 2000), which resulted in a 13-year injunction against that parallel commitment program because of a similarly flawed treatment program. The aforementioned OLA Report, at p. 52, concedes about the MSOP program: "A court could consider failure to release offenders from civil commitment as evidence that inadequate treatment is being provided, or that the purpose of the program is punitive rather than rehabilitative".

Repeated Replacement of MSOP Treatment Program Contents Reveals That It Is Just a Series of Experiments

From 2003 through 2010, MSOP has experienced a sequence of three executive directors and four executive clinical directors. The OLA Report, p. 58, states: "Due to these many leadership changes, the content of the treatment program at MSOP facilities *has changed multiple times since 2003*. With each change in leadership and the treatment program, clinicians and clients have needed to learn the new program. Also, clients have had to be reassessed according to new program requirements. At times, clinicians have lacked supervision to help them make good clinical decisions. Because of changes in MSOP's leadership and the treatment program, the program has not been able to deliver consistent treatment to its residents."

This explanation implies that: (a) each succeeding clinical director has realized that what was passing as treatment to that point was ineffectual; and (b) that 'cognitive behavioral treatment', as practiced at MSOP, is not a unitary thing, but rather only a realm of possible, alternative approaches and techniques. That complete changes to program content have happened multiple times in such a short number of years points up that MSOP hasn't truly been delivering 'treatment'. This series of complete program overhauls shows that each new approach has been nothing more than just blindly throwing spaghetti against the wall to see what may actually stick. That has a name: rank experimentation.

High clinician turnover and chronic therapist vacancies, together with clinical supervisor positions that MSOP can't fill[1], confirm this conclusion of sheer experimentation, with which potential job candidates want no part.[2] Even within the latest 'edition' of the MSOP treatment program, it is clear that the treatment model is being divergently interpreted and applied by the various therapists.[3] This too is experimentation in action, signifying a lack of agreement by treatment staff as to a single 'best practice'.

Minnesota claims to have been inspired by the State of Washington's sex offender commitment legislation. Yet, after intense litigation culminating in the year 2000 in Turay v. Seling[4], Washington substantially reformed its sex offender commitment treatment problems. In that case, the ruling by the court refused to dissolve its earlier injunction and enforced per diem contempt fines on that commitment program for failing to effect constitutionally adequate mental health treatment for committed sex offenders. In so ruling, the court found that the commitment program had so substantially departed from professional minimum standards as to demonstrate that its decisions and practices were not based on professional judgment.

The constant 'remakes' of MSOP in Minnesota strongly suggest that same lapse from such professional standards. Rather than working toward release through treatment, MSOP appears obsessed with 'proving' the thesis (contrary to the judgment and experience of all other of the 20 'commitment jurisdictions', including their successful releases to date) that it is supposedly impossible to release sex offenders safely.

---

1 *OLA Report, pp. 59–60.*

2 *Ibid, p. 61.*

3 *Ibid., p. 60.*

4 *108 F.Supp.2d 1148 W.D. Wash. 2000.*

With such false beliefs as their banner, it appears that the entire clinical staff and clinical management of MSOP must be replaced with reasonable professionals before improvement can be seen in MSOP. Turay dealt with many of the same problems confronted in this work as to MSOP. It staggers the reasonable observer that, a dozen years later, MSOP claims to not be able to improve their 'batting average' of release through treatment above a single releasee. A house cleaning is warranted to free MSOP of its counterproductive, absolutist iconoclasts in clinical positions.

What on Earth Could Take That Long? The Limits of Treatment; When Enough Is Enough

In an excerpt in which the authors must have been contemplating MSOP, although speaking generally, Prentky, Janus, et al., "Sexually Violent Predators in the Courtroom" ... (etc.) at 12 Psychology, Public Policy, and Law 281, explain that, in such commitment facilities staff usually can't make up their minds about the goal. Should they try to treat detainees effectively to maximize the likelihood of release, or instead, do they regard their prime duty to be to keep detainees committed? Impossibly high release standards and endless treatment, combined with a demand for treatment 'completion', are applied to block release. Objecting to a lack of definite treatment goals and objectives that can be counted on to result in treatment completion, Prentky and Janus point out that treatment providers endlessly create treatment plans for each succeeding year, adding new tasks, such that the detainee never 'completes' treatment.[1]

This is reminiscent of the mythical tasks of Hercules, which would have continued to be assigned as long as Hercules would have continued to accept them. Only when he stopped accepting them did the situation change.

Before progressing through this section, it is worth noting that, in 'selling' the vastly expanded commitment of sex offenders via the then-proposed SDP (Sexually Dangerous Persons) Law, state officials assured legislators and the legal community that "an 'average patient' was expected to complete the 'intensive' treatment program in a 'minimum of 24 months'."[2] Call in fact *upheld* that legislation in part on reliance on this assurance. "Later, treatment officials described the length of treatment as at least four years ... (noting that most patients are unable to complete the program in the minimum period)."[3]

---

1 *Emphasis supplied.*

2 *Call v. Gomez, 535 N.W.2d 312, 319, n. 5 Minn. Supr. 1995.*

3 *E. Janus, "Closing Pandora's Box" (etc.), supra, at 34 Seton Hall L. Rev. 1238*

Since that amended assurance, the claimed minimum length of commitment-based treatment just keeps lengthening exponentially. The OLA Report, at p. 72, notes a recent statement by MSOP's executive clinical director that changing detainees' behaviors can take *many* years. This strongly suggests that the intent, ab initio, was to use commitments as a permanent detention scheme, but to disguise that intent with false assurances that since then have been gradually dropped, like a bad Halloween disguise falling away, piece by piece.

We have already noted that MSOP has *only one* provisional discharge (as yet unrevoked) to point to as 'success' out of more than 650 detainees currently. We have also noted that a large portion of these have remained detained in MSOP for 10 years or more to date. Of these especially, an unusually high percentage are over 50 years of age, with many in their 60s and beyond, representing an undeniably diminished threat of recidivism, as discussed supra.

Only a very small percentage (7%) of MSOP detainees are even in Phase 3 of the treatment program (OLA Report, p. 56), and only a handful of these are in the latter part of that phase closest to treatment completion. At the start of 2012, MSOP officials reported that they were looking at one detainee for possible release (beyond the sole detainee actually released to date). However, that claimed second release never materialized. Whether or not this claimed projected release was a sincere expectation or simply a baseless claim to defuse criticism of MSOP, what is clear is that MSOP does not claim that any more releases are in the offing. Indeed, in 2011, MSOP declared that no releases were anticipated for the *foreseeable future*. The fact that MSOP's projection of 1109 detainees in MSOP custody by 2020 is based on current rates of commitment, but with no releases confirms that MSOP has no expectation of releases. *It is not serious about treatment* as a path to release.

The way that MSOP conducts its treatment program confirms that it is not seriously attempting to advance any detainees toward release, but, to the contrary, is tacitly *thwarting* such reasonable progress toward release.

Consider the following: according to the OLA Report, pp. 55–56, the MSOP treatment program is divided into three successive phases. "In Phase 1, clients are expected to learn how to comply with facility rules and learn basic treatment concepts. In Phase 2, clients are expected to ... understand their patterns of sexual abuse. Phase 3 ... focuses on community reintegration ...".

However, percentages and numbers tell the story. That report, at p. 56, uses a pie chart to depict percentages of MSOP detainees in each phase. According to that chart, slightly over half of MSOP treatment-eligible detainees were still in Phase 1. This excludes those committed to MSOP, but who are either in the pre-treatment 'admissions' unit, and those who had been returned to prison, whether by choice (discussed elsewhere) or by involuntary parole revocation for 'technical' (non-crime) parole-rules violation. Hence, these percentages were calculated on the present-and-treatment-eligible balance (542 detainees, as of June, 2010). Hence, the 51% in Phase 1 comprised 275 detainees at that time. At the same time, 114 were in Phase 2 (21%), while only 7% (39 detainees) were in Phase 3. Another 21% (114) were refusing treatment.

Now ponder this: how long should it take to instruct detainees about 'facility rules' (and how to comply with them) and about 'basic treatment concepts' (i.e., Phase 1)? One month? Perhaps two months, if an unusually large portion of participants are exceptionally mentally sluggish? Yet the figure of 275 Phase 1 participants is about what MSOP claims are its total admissions in the last five years. This necessarily implies that, on balance, those detainees who participate in MSOP treatment are retained in Phase 1 for about 5 years, going over and over material that could have been mastered in less than 1/30th that amount of time. This fact alone should communicate unmistakably to anyone that MSOP 'treatment' is a joke — on its detainees.

By no means are MSOP treatment shortcomings and stumbling blocks limited to Phase 1, however. As a general matter, sex offender treatment in the Minnesota DOC, by comparison, consists of an average of 12 hours per week of therapy. Alpha Human Services (the only privately operated inpatient sex offender treatment provider in Minnesota) provides 20.5 hours per week of scheduled group therapy. However, MSOP-Moose Lake delivered only six hours of group therapy per week to its treatment participants in November 2010, with no individual therapy.[1] Informal communications received by the author from MSOP indicate that this has shrunk since then to only two hours per week, with two additional hours per week of self-taught 'psychoeducational modules', as of December 2012. Given that MSOP claims that many years of *intensive* group therapy are required to complete treatment, this low number of weekly hours of treatment would seem to doom all treatment participants of MSOP to permanent detention.

In addition, we have elsewhere discussed the suspicious phenomenon of unjustified, unexplained demotions from a higher phase or treatment module within a phase to a lower phase or module, and of similarly mysterious failures to advance a participant from one

---

1 *OLA Report, p. 62.*

module or phase to the next when all expectations of the lower phase or module have been met. This obviously thwarts advancement in treatment, and thus blocks eventual release. Other factors complained of as blocking treatment success include: (1) disrespectful, negative, punitive and untherapeutic attitudes on the part of some therapists and other MSOP staff toward treatment participants; and (2) MSOP culture, as led by staff, being counter-therapeutic. Thus, "... clients were sometimes treated with suspicion, their reasonable frustrations were considered treatment problems, and they were sometimes punished for behaviors that appeared to be normal", sometimes resulting in the aforementioned demotions or non-advancements, and therapists' demands for impossible perfection.[1] These factors too can make progress in treatment difficult.

MSOP quarterly treatment reviews typically fail to clearly specify "what the client needs to do to advance in treatment, especially when the client is meeting all their goals and doing well in treatment. Clinicians also do not always explain or discuss how they came to their conclusions about client progress.".[2] Without such guidance, MSOP treatment participants are often left foundering in uncharted seas in pitch-darkness, unable to find their way forward on their own.

We have also mentioned periodic participant testing by means of penile plethysmograph and other means of measuring one's sexual interests. We have already criticized reliance upon this testing as creating an impossible demand to 'stop being a deviate' in order to successfully complete treatment. These tests are also largely beside the point; it is not whether one experiences unusual sexual attractions that matters, but what one would or would not do about such attractions if released, that is the crucial question. We have also already discussed the inaccuracy of multiple-issue (utility) polygraph testing (as it is employed in MSOP) with unfair, unscientific 'false positive' outcomes that block honest, non-dangerous individuals from advancing in treatment.[3]

Finally, we have already alluded to the so-called 'matrix' of Dynamic Risk Factors and corresponding behavioral areas used by MSOP as a means of judging treatment progress. Unfortunately, these 'matrix' standards are largely undefined and certainly non-specific, and they allow for overly subjective evaluation by clinicians in MSOP.[4] In most cases, these 'matrix' standards have been employed to thwart treatment progress, rather than to promote it.

---

1 *OLA Report, p. 66.*

2 *Ibid., p. 73.*

3 *Cf: ibid., p. 76.*

4 *Ibid., p. 75.*

In sum, it appears that MSOP clinical staff have spent a great deal of effort inventing rationales for denying treatment advancement and completion to MSOP treatment participants. This again confirms that MSOP is not serious about facilitating releases through treatment.

The lack of sincere intent or any true attempt to achieve release through treatment for detainees is confirmed by the aforementioned insistence by MSOP officials on a 'zero-percent public safety guarantee', something no one with a record of past sex offenses can demonstrate to the satisfaction of MSOP, especially given MSOP's refusal to accept the reality of aging as an inherent diminution of percentage of probability of reoffense. In view of this rejection, MSOP does not really believe that any living sex offender can reduce his level of likelihood of reoffense to "very low levels". In the view of MSOP, the only way any sex offender can furnish a 'zero-percent public safety guarantee' is to die while still detained in an MSOP commitment facility.

To justify this impossible standard, MSOP's interminable treatment seeks to literally 'brainwash' its detainees, in an experimental attempt to 'remake' them as a kind of 'emotional Frankenstein re-creation'. This, of course, is not possible. Whether through brainwashing or otherwise, it is not actually possible to remake someone emotionally as someone else. Even were that possible, it would in effect be a kind of 'psyche murder' that would transgress every ethic and moral known to humanity. MSOP is acting out the ultimate confirmation of its conceptualization of its true role: permanent preventive detention until death.

We have already discussed the unattainability of the impossible MSOP goal of 'zero-percent' recidivism risk by any means other than such natural-life detention. We have also discussed the ineffectiveness of even the extreme 'brainwashing' approach to which MSOP has desperately resorted to literally 'remake' sex offenders, as to sexual orientation and attraction. MSOP has been astoundingly unrealistic and self-deluded about such a goal. Instead, had it set its sights lower, to simply *reduce* recidivism risk, many releases could already have been effected — as they have in other states, with *almost no* recidivism by releasees.

But, because MSOP knows that its efforts to remake its detainees have failed, and will remain doomed to failure, it is easy to understand from a bureaucratic perspective that, in an age of potential lawsuits by future victims, any therapist or treatment program administrator would be reluctant to appear to place a 'seal of approval' on any detainee by consenting to his release. However, the proper response to this seeming dilemma is simply to redefine release as not comprising any such assurance to the public, and to immunize the state and its employees from lawsuits by any future victims, in the same way that corrections officials around the country are so immunized.

Tort theory cannot be allowed to evolve into an inherent, implicit, enforceable guarantee of non-recidivism in any event; it is simply contrary to the inherent unpredictabilities of life. Nor, properly understood, is there any principle of morality that forbids releasing a detainee, merely on the supposition that he might commit a crime of a given type. By falsely erecting a virtually impossible standard of 'very low risk' of reoffense, MSOP officials have proceeded on the basis that both such tort and morality concerns bar releases under any less certain circumstance. Following this standard, it is certain that only a nominal number of MSOP detainees will ever be released, if that. Instead, the concept should be that of *manageable* risk. That is, comparatively, corrections departments around the country — including the 30 states *without* sex offender commitment laws — regularly release sex offenders, including those with extensive prior sex offense records. As to those thought to present a high risk of sexual reoffense, corrections officials simply *manage* that risk by invoking a discretionary regimen of requirements, prohibitions, monitoring, and surveillance (in Minnesota, known as 'intensive supervised release').

Coupled with laws already in place, drastically increasing criminal sentences for sex crimes for recidivists (often, to natural-life terms), this program of 'intensive supervision' has both eliminated recidivism outright and, in other instances, has interdicted attempts at sexual reoffense before such crimes actually occur. Beyond this, the only concern sex offender commitment laws and their treatment programs should need to address is a given sex offender who demonstrates or admits that his drive to commit sex crimes is irresistibly compulsive. This must be sharply distinguished from mere indications of any given 'deviant' sexual attraction. Only that very small subclass of those committed who declare or undeniably evince such irresistible compulsion would have any significant probability of sexual reoffense beyond what such intensive supervision would be almost certain to prevent. This subclass of irresistibly compulsive reoffense is the only proper subject of commitment. All others can and should instead be managed through well established and highly successful correctional management and penological deterrence.

MSOP Improper 'Litmus Test' Reliance on Polygraph Tests and Plethysmography

MSOP refers a given detainee under consideration for either level-advancement or demotion to a visiting polygraphist. Any detainee declared to be deceptive in any regard by the results of that polygraph test will be subjected to adverse action (whether denying advancement or imposing a demotion to a lower treatment level).[1]

However, this type of polygraph testing is almost invariably 'multiple-issue utility testing', which the American Polygraph Association regards as an unprofessional misuse of polygraphy.

Noted polygraph expert Kenneth Blackstone, in an article, "BNA Insights, Sex Offenders: Post-Adjudication Polygraph: A Discussion of the Science and the Law",[2] declares that the 'dragnet' manner of such polygraph misuse is *no more accurate than pure chance* (50-50%). Blackstone notes that such "utility tests, such as the ones popular in sex offender management, *actually invite errors*". Thus, a sex offender can easily be mis-assessed by a polygraphist as lying, when in fact he is telling the truth. According to Blackstone, the appalling reality is that the 'sex offender industry' has embraced multiple-issue utility polygraph testing; 19 of the 20 states with sex offender commitment programs make use of this flawed, unreliable testing.

Where release, advancement, and demotion decisions inherently affect the course of the rest of the detainee's life, such unscientific reliance on such unreliable testing is unconscionable as nothing more than a modern-day 'witch finder's tool'.

In addition, MSOP makes considerable use of plethysmography (for the uninitiated, a penile 'erection detector') and also of the Able assessment of sexual interest. While both of these tests also have accuracy or reliability problems and are subject to operator manipulation of test results, the real issue with these is that, even if accurate, such test results focus on the wrong thing. Basically, for instance, a committed pedosexual or pedophile whose test results reflect such sexual orientation can never be released, because that sexual orientation is permanent. This is not treatment, but permanent condemnation. Of course, the real question, obviously passed over by such testing, is whether, if released, a given pedosexual or pedophile can avoid recidivating.

These inaccurate and irrelevant tests must be abandoned.

The Well Justified Frustration of MSOP Detainees Participating in 'Treatment'

Seventy-nine percent of MSOP detainees residing in MSOP's facilities were in treatment as of 2010. Of this participating group, however, 64.5% were only in Phase 1 of the three phases of treatment.[3] Only 8.86% were

---

1 *OLA Report, pp. 60, 76.*

2 *Criminal Law Reporter, Vol. 90, No. 9, pp. 306–08 2012.*

3 *OLA Report, p. 56.*

in Phase 3, and the remaining 26.64% were in Phase 2. Proportionately, this means that over two-thirds of the treatment participating detainees are in Phase 1, notwithstanding many years of treatment in some cases. This percentage is nearly two and a half times the percentage in Phase 2 and over seven times the number in Phase 3.

That OLA Report, at p. 64, itself decries this exceedingly frustrating situation:

> "Phase One of the program does not focus directly on the behaviors that led to offenders' commitments. Rather, Phase One is focused on *preparing clients for treatment* by asking clients to *demonstrate that they can follow rules* and *learn how to participate in treatment groups*. Phase One treatment does not explore the reason for offenders' sexual offending or help offenders develop tools to prevent offending.
>
> "Some clients may be 'stuck' in Phase One because the program has not been sufficiently staffed or because the environment at Moose Lake has not promoted positive treatment participation. *Many clients who are in Phase One have been at an MSOP facility for years and have participated in a lot of sex offender-specific treatment at MSOP previously. Some of these clients have expressed frustration that they are no longer in treatment specifically focused on their sexual offenses.*"[1]

One thing is immediately clear from this quote. Phase 1 isn't really sex offender treatment at all. Footnote 25 on that page states: "MSOP administration noted that addressing behaviors that interfere with treatment is standard in the early stages of contemporary sex offender treatment programs". However, MSOP does not point to any other such program where addressing such interfering behaviors is the subject of any 'pre-treatment' phase of any substantial duration, let alone to any other program where such a pre-treatment phase stretches on for years, and to which treatment participants are constantly being demoted back to from Phases 2 and 3.

Clearly, it should not take long to orient participants into how to follow rules or to participate in group therapy or to test them to ascertain that they have learned those lessons and are willing to apply them. These functions cannot reasonably be argued to take longer than one month at most. In the case of participants who have been demoted back to Phase 1 for any reason other than treatment-disrupting behaviors, Phase 1 participation should be skipped altogether.

---

1 *Emphases supplied.*

We have already seen that replacements or changes in treatment curricula have forced all or most treatment participating detainees back to Phase 1 strictly as a 'holding pattern' until such revised treatment can be resumed. However, currently, no such 'treatment overhaul' excuse exists. It can only be concluded now that prolonged retention of detainees in Phase 1 is a deliberate stalling device — often of year-upon-year duration — to intentionally slow the rate at which detainees can complete the program and thereby become eligible for release.

More generally, we have already noted detainee complaints that:

1 some MSOP staff have shown disrespectful, negative, punitive, and untherapeutic attitudes toward detainees, including treatment participants;

2 the culture at MSOP facilities is counter-therapeutic; and

3 clients are sometimes treated with suspicion, their reasonable frustrations dismissed as treatment problems, and even their entirely normal behaviors punished.

Additionally, at least in the past, client behaviors have received such inordinate focus that any infraction, however slight, could result in denied advancement or in demotion to a lower phase. The OLA Report, on p. 66, states: "The program still struggles with staff who are overly suspicious of clients or who expect impossible perfection. This can make progress in treatment difficult". Effectively, this is another means by which progress toward release is stymied by unwarranted staff action.

Most of all, however, MSOP detainees — both treatment participants and 'refuseniks' — are frustrated and hopeless about the extremely remote possibility of release. Consider this: even in the 1991–2003 era before the Alfonso Rodriguez case, one-third of the present detainee population of MSOP was already committed.[1] This means that this one-third have been locked up purely under commitment alone for nine to 21 years, with only a single release to date. No course of conceivable treatment of any kind can take anywhere close to that period of time. This alone telegraphs that commitment is not really about treatment, but instead just permanent preventive detention. Confirming this, over one-third of MSOP detainees are over 50 years of age, a stage of life of undeniably waning sexual interest. As discussed elsewhere, sexual recidivism beyond the age of 50 drops off precipitously, with almost no one recidivating in their 60s, and absolutely no known cases of recidivism from age 70 on. Yet 10% of MSOP detainees are in their 60s, and an additional 4% are in their 70s or 80s.[2] Who has *ever* recidivated in their 80s? Don't you think that such an exceptional

---

1 *Ibid p. 5.*

2 *Ibid, p. 6.*

crime would make the news? Have you ever read or heard of one? The fact that MSOP does not release even these oldest senior citizens smacks soundly of pure add-on retribution for their past crimes, rather than for any real 'risk' of future recidivism if released. MSOP administrators should be embarrassed.

MSOP, in addition to conceptually basing treatment on 'cognitive-behavioral therapy', subscribes to a set of treatment principles known as 'risk, need, and responsivity'.[1] "Sex offender treatment literature generally suggests that treatment should address areas which are linked to reoffending for each individual (the need principle)."[2] Yet, astoundingly, MSOP does not keep a database on its detainees' psychological diagnoses, test scores to predict likelihood of recidivism, or any other factors considered in their civil commitment proceedings. If treatment truly is for the purpose of reducing risk of each committed sex offender to levels below those for commitment (as they must be under the treatment-completion standard, discussed supra), how can treatment be carried out without knowing what to address individually, that is, the factors found to be of concern by the committing court. To disregard that information clearly shows up the *fiction* of 'treatment' and release as being the goal.

Just as bad, detainee progress in treatment has often been poorly documented — or not documented at all — in the detainee's file, and paperwork necessary to advance a detainee to the next phase has often been overlooked, leaving the detainee waiting for a long period until the oversight is discovered. OLA investigators also discovered instances of missing quarterly and annual reviews of detainees' respective treatment progress in the three most recent years examined. And in general, detainee treatment files since 2008 tended to contain far less detail than those from previous years.[3]

Indeed, records are downright chaotic, and often completely incorrect, as illustrated by Barber v. Jesson[4]. When Mr. Barber sought release, the appeal panel considering his petition relied on inaccurate information that had persisted and, indeed, periodically reappeared in his file. First, an erroneous 2008 diagnosis of alcoholism was removed in February, 2012. However, it mysteriously reappeared as part of a Sexual Violence Risk Assessment the following June and, despite renewed objection, also showed up in the Special Review Board Evaluation Report in July, 2010. Independently, in November, 2010, an Annual Treatment Assessment reported that Barber scored

---

1 *Ibid, p 57.*

2 *Ibid, p. 72.*

3 *Ibid, p. 66.*

4 *2012 Minn. App. Unpub. LEXIS 526 Minn. App. 2012.*

29 on the Hare Psychopathy Checklist–Revised. That score would indicate a high degree of psychopathic traits. But the preceding June, that same Assessment (supra) had determined Barber's score as actually only 24, reflecting a considerably reduced psychopathic tendency. The change that appeared by that following November, was simply handwritten in, by an unknown person, with no explanation or basis.

MSOP testing procedures are equally chaotic and incompetent. Barber also reports that Mr. Barber was rated using ACUTE-2007, an RAI "inappropriate to use on people who are institutionalized".[1] Had Mr. Barber instead been rated using the Static-99R, Mr. Barber would have been assessed as in the low moderate range for sexual reoffending, reported the court.[2]

Moreover, while in theory MSOP treatment plans are individualized and are supposed to set meaningful goals, in current practice they do not provide the level of detail of past plans. "... It is not always clear ... what the client needs to do to advance in treatment, especially when the client is meeting all their goals and doing well in treatment. Clinicians also do not always explain or discuss how they came to their conclusions about client progress."[3]

> "... Annual reviews ... often rely heavily on summary statements without providing specific details regarding why a client advanced (or not) and how he was meeting his treatment expectations."[4]

Clearly, without the foregoing data and without detailed assessments of needs and progress, both therapists and detainees in treatment are proceeding without a map.

Since 2009, MSOP has relied on a 'treatment matrix' to assess detainees' needs and progress in treatment. Yet treatment 'matrix' standards are somewhat undefined or only ill-defined, and are overly subjective. Many therapists report that the matrix is not being uniformly applied and that standards for interpreting the matrix are lacking, allowing a wide range from impossible-perfection standards to excessively lenient standards, from one therapist to the next.[5] A mere glance at some of the factors used in various 'behavioral areas' confirms this subjective vagueness: "negative social influences"; "poor self-regulation"; "general hostility"; and "antisocial attitudes and behavior".

1 *Ibid.*

2 *Ibid.*

3 *Ibid, p. 73.*

4 *Ibid, p. 74.*

5 *Ibid, p. 75.*

Typical of objections by MSOP treatment participants in that commitment facility are these:

1 Repetitive changes of the entire treatment regimen in MSOP creates the feeling in treatment participants of being 'human guinea pigs' in what has amounted to endless, repeatedly failed experimentation, rather than treatment.

2 Treatment advancement criteria lack real, ascertainable goals . This is felt to be a deliberate shortcoming, enabling treatment staff to advance a given treatment participant only when they subjectively 'feel like it.'

3 Participants often feel like they are being coerced or extorted into agreeing with the truth and the applicability of particulars of treatment 'dogma' that treatment participants actually disagree with or deem inapplicable to their personal circumstances. Verbalizing such divergent views results in punitive refusal of treatment advancement or even in demotion.

4 Similarly, treatment participants are not allowed to voice criticism of the treatment regimen or of actions by treatment staff. Doing so results in identical denial of treatment advancement or in demotion.

In MSOP, in order to qualify for release, detainees must complete treatment. Notably, this includes satisfying the standard of demonstrating that "treatment has had a significant impact on their behavior and thoughts". In practice, this has amounted to a requirement that detainees demonstrate that they have reduced "their recidivism risk to very low levels".[1] Until early 2012, MSOP had not released any of its committed detainees. Thus far in 2012, only one has been released (to provisional discharge status — similar to 'intensive supervised release' after prison for uncommitted sex offenders), and only one other is under consideration. According to the MSOP's executive director, no further releases are contemplated in the "foreseeable future". In other words, this sole release (and possibly one other) is merely to show that MSOP is *capable* of releasing detainees. However, lacking the will to do so, this is meaningless to its frustrated detainees.

MSOP puts the blame back on the rest of the detainees themselves for not having been able to satisfy the foregoing, nearly impossible standard. However, ponder this: if no other detainees (out of more than 600 presently) have been able to prove that, through treatment, their recidivism risk has been reduced to very low levels, then obviously, all that 'treatment' has not had any such prescribed 'significant impact' on detainees' 'behavior and thoughts'. In other words, whatever MSOP

---

1 *Ibid, p. 21.*

is doing really isn't treatment at all. To fail to successfully treat some, perhaps even as many as half, of those committed *might* be concluded (after a careful, one-by-one audit — nonexistent to date) to have been due to individual resistance to treatment or to other extenuating circumstances. But, deducting those not in treatment, MSOP has been providing what it calls 'treatment' for years to approximately 428 detainees on average (see 'refuseniks' subsection, infra). Failing to successfully complete treatment of any of those hundreds, save one, or possibly two, reveals that the so-called treatment model in use isn't treatment at all.

Even MSOP's own therapists concede that the MSOP-Moose Lake facility comprises a "clogged drain" as to potential release. However, the current executive clinical director states that, in her view, no Moose Lake detainees were 'ready' to be advanced to Phase 3 (conducted at the MSOP-St. Peter, MN, facility). Defending this conclusion, she adds that "changing clients' behavior can take many years".[1] Even were this a valid statement, most MSOP detainees in treatment have in fact already been in treatment for at least several years, and quite a few of them for 10 to 20 years. If this is not sufficient for that executive clinical director, it suggests three possibilities:

1 it is not possible to change any detainee's behaviors within their remaining lifespans;

2 the treatment concept and/or its methods in use in MSOP is an abject theoretical and/or practical failure; or

3 it is time for a different executive clinical director with new ideas and less Herculean standards for detainees.

Possibility (1) is not likely, given regular releases of committed sex offenders in other states, including Wisconsin, right next door. In fact, Wisconsin currently releases as many sex offenders annually from its commitment facility as it commits. Most probably, both possibilities (2) and (3) must be dealt with before Minnesota can achieve anything that can be called 'treatment success'.

In sum, given all the foregoing, the frustrations expressed by many MSOP detainees, as cited often in the OLA Report, are amply justified and entirely understandable. What is less understandable is why those detainees have not risen up in organized protest, or even civilly disobedient demonstrations, in reaction to the myriad obstacles and machinations to thwart their every effort in pursuit of 'treatment completion' and release. Given the overall, cumulative enormity of their frustrations, this may occur in the near future.

---

1 *Ibid, p. 72.*

The 'Refuseniks' Speak Silent Volumes about the Worthlessness of MSOP Treatment and the Hopelessness of Release

MSOP admits that "21%" of its detainees who live in its facilities (Moose Lake or St. Peter, MN) decline to participate in treatment.[1] The total population it uses for this calculation (542) excludes detainees in the admission unit (not yet eligible for treatment) and also those held in prisons or local jails. Actually, however, these last are additional 'refuseniks', and are 55 in number.[2] These are detainees under sex offender commitment who deliberately chose revocation of their parole — in many cases, of several years remaining duration, in order to be in prison, over being in the MSOP facilities.[3] "They described living at Moose Lake as so stressful under the new administration that [they] have sought revocation of their [DOC] supervision so that they may return to correctional facilities where they at least saw people being released."[4]

Adding this 55 to the 542 total cited by MSOP yields an overall treatment-eligible pool of 597 (as of January, 2011). MSOP did not specify the *number* of on-site refuseniks. However, 21% of 542 equals 114. Adding to that 114 the 55 who returned to prison equals 169 total refuseniks. Dividing this 169 by the overall treatment-eligible pool of 597 yields the *actual* percentage of treatment-eligible refuseniks: 28.3% — nearly 3 out of 10 — who by their actions have demonstrated the belief that MSOP treatment, perhaps the very concepts on which it is based, is worthless junk-science that holds no promise for MSOP detainees.

Now pause to reflect that MSOP personnel make it emphatically clear that no one who does not participate in treatment — and thus does not satisfactorily complete it — will ever be released. When nearly 3 out of 10 MSOP detainees still refuse to participate in treatment, it implies two things with equally emphatic clarity.

1 All of these refuseniks have concluded that release through treatment participation is hopelessly unattainable and not worth trying (and perhaps also loaded with such discomfort, displeasure and sacrifice as to be a substantial disincentive).

2 An unknowable, but probably substantial portion of those participating in treatment actually agree with the refuseniks as to hopelessness or, at best, extreme unlikelihood of

1 *OLA Report, p. 56.*

2 *Ibid, p. x.*

3 *Ibid, p. 71.*

4 *Ibid.*

release through treatment completion as things are currently administered in MSOP, and who likewise experience the sacrifices and the unpleasantness of MSOP 'treatment' with secret resentment, but are simply afraid to say so, or even to merely let MSOP therapists or administrators suspect that they feel that way, out of fear of reprisals (such as the aforementioned demotions). Members of this 'treatment' portion continue in treatment only in hope that one day governing laws will change, allowing such release on a lesser standard — one still requiring, or at least strongly favoring those who participate in treatment. This circumstance, combined with a sense by treatment-participating detainees that "some staff hold disrespectful, negative, punitive, and untherapeutic attitudes toward clients"; that the "culture of the facilities is counter-therapeutic"; that clients' "reasonable frustrations are considered treatment problems"; that clients are "sometimes punished for behavior that appears normal"; and that "any infraction could result in a client failing to progress or being sent backwards in treatment" (demotion)[1] makes it an absolute wonder of human patience that many more MSOP detainees have not dropped out of treatment. To some degree, at least, that mystery is clarified by the fact that MSOP penalizes refuseniks by only allowing them to work a small fraction of the hours per week for pay that treatment participants are allowed to work.

The Increasingly Incarcerative Nature of MSOP Facilities and Operation

A long-time linchpin of judicial decisions rejecting constitutional challenges to sex offender commitment upon prison release is that, cumulative to findings of non-punitive intent, the actual facilities and operation of commitment facilities are non-punitive as well. This appears to be changing nationwide, as more and more states are resorting to correctional settings or are constructing prison-like facilities and operating them identically, or very nearly identically to prisons. This trend is fully apparent in Minnesota's MSOP facility at Moose Lake, where all but a few committed sex offenders are detained. This was recognized almost right away: "Make no mistake. The medical facilities designated in the statute are the equivalent of medium to maximum security prisons.".[2]

1 *OLA Report, p. 66. s*

2 *In re Linehan, 544 N.W.2d 308 (Minn. App. 1996; "Linehan II"), Randall, J. dissenting, at footnote 1.*

Physical Layout and General Conditions

The class action complaint by MSOP detainees[1] serves as a comprehensive compendium of the layout and detainee living conditions at the MSOP Moose Lake commitment facility. Consider these descriptive excerpts:

> "The MSOP facility at Moose Lake is laid out exactly like state prisons with cell units facing into a central courtyard where [detainees] may be observed from one central station. MSOP staff wear police-style uniforms. The newly designed and constructed living unit, Complex One, is designed just like a correctional facility. The Legislative Auditor Report [OLA Report] confirmed that is was not designed with therapeutic goals in mind.[2]
>
> "Despite the well documented concerns regarding the difficulty of fostering a therapeutic environment in the current facility at Moose Lake, MSOP is currently planning an expansion that will create a second building identical to Complex One.
>
> "Mail and kitchen facilities at the Moose Lake facility have not been expanded since the program was originally started. Therefore, a facility that was designed for 130 patients is now required to serve over 400 patients. Those limited facilities have resulted in inadequate meal and mail service for [detainees]."
>
> *Karsjens, Paragrs. 106–108*

Most MSOP Moose Lake detainees are currently housed in Complex One. The Karsjens complaint has this to say in description of cell conditions in that building:

> "When Complex One was constructed, the MSOP obtained waivers from the Minnesota Department of Health so it would not have to comply with statutorily required living standards for state hospitals. The waivers allowed the MSOP facility at Moose Lake to have things like the springless beds, smaller cells with inadequate space between beds, inoperable windows in cells, and a more prison-like setting as opposed to a home-like environment.
>
> "This resulted in the current cells [detainees] reside in. [Detainees] are double-bunked in 9.5 *x* 15-foot wet

---

1 *Titled: Karsjens, et a. v. Jesson, et al., U.S. Dist. Ct. Case No. 11-cv-3659-DWF-JJK (Dist. of Minn); hereinafter 'Karsjens'.*

2 *OLA Report) p. 68.*

cells, consisting of two metal bed frames with springless mattresses that are only 30 inches apart, small stainless steel desks, and a stainless steel toilet and sink combination unit fixed into the cell.

"Cell doors are metal and only have a small viewing window. The two windows in each cell are only five inches wide. The only privacy when using the toilet is a movable screen. The only storage [detainees] are allowed are three storage lockers that must fit under the bed."

Karsjens, Paras. 111–113

There are no therapists' offices in Complex One. Unlike therapists for the relatively few detainees housed in the facility's older living units, therapists for detainees in treatment who live in Complex One have offices outside of any living unit in what is known as the 'bullpen'. The OLA Report, on p. 67, notes that "Despite acknowledging that the large units in Complex One are less than ideal for creating therapeutic environments, MSOP is currently planning an expansion which would create a second building identical to Complex One".

The Plan to Expand the Prison Model

That's right; between Complex One and the projected, identical Complex Two, that's 800 beds, total. MSOP projects that its population of detainees will jump to roughly 1100 by 2020. This is nearly double the 2010 total, which in turn was nearly quadruple the total in 2000.[1] But the real tale lies in the actual numbers behind the increases: From 30 detainees in 1990 to 149 in 2000 (an increase of 119); from 149 in 2000 to 575 in 2010 (an increase of 426); and from 575 in 2010 to 1109 (projected) in 2020 (an increase of 534).

Accommodating Continuation of the 'Commitment Binge'

Clearly, this implies that prosecutors intend to continue the 'commitment binge' that they have been on in Minnesota ever since the notorious Alfonso Rodriguez case in 2003, as fed by a torrent since then of referrals by the DOC for commitment (contrast: about 26 per year up to 2003; about 157 per year thereafter). [FOOTNOTE: Ibid, p. 5] In sum, Minnesota is on a commitment tear that it seems it cannot (or will not) shake off, despite deep drops in sex offender recidivism. Even in 2003, all those referrals were a generalized overreaction to a single case that embarrassed the DOC. (Rodriguez freely told numerous people in prison, including staff, that he intended a sexual assault upon release. Apparently, no one took him at his word.)

---

1 *Ibid, p. 4.*

But in light of drops in: (a) sex crimes in general; and (b) recidivism by sex offenders in particular, both revealed by statistics announced since then, a massive commitment campaign such as Minnesota's is unwarranted.

'Drafting Detainees' to Lower per Diem Costs

One criticism of MSOP is its high operating cost per detainee per diem. The largest component of that cost, surprisingly, is for security staffing. Security staff required to monitor the new Complex One and (projected) Complex Two units is minimal, due to open sight-lines in their design. Therefore, MSOP believes that additional detainees can be housed in those new units at substantially lower *marginal* per diem costs. This will "bring down the *overall* average per diem costs".[1]

Therefore, crass though it is, a large part of the motivation to 'draft' the next 534 sex offenders for commitment is merely to lower that per diem cost overall, stifling the 'cost criticism'. It is, of course, unconscionable to commit someone, potentially for the rest of their life, as a cost-reduction maneuver.

Prison-Like, Drastically Heightened Regimentation and Deepening Austerity

Separately, safety and security concerns have largely dominated the manner of operations in the MSOP Moose Lake facility since 2008, resulting in many changes to a more austere, prison-like set of rules and restrictions.

Detainees, who formerly were allowed to order food from outside vendors, were forbidden to do so from then on, except for quarterly instances only from a single vendor and only from a six-item (average) selection list, comprising 'franchise food'.

Although detainees were formerly allowed a reasonable amount of personal possessions and papers, from 2008 on they have been limited to one small plastic tub of all property — *half* of what is allowed in Minnesota's prisons.

Detainee movement outside of living units, which previously was restrained only by curfew and a prison-like need to conduct counts, was limited from then on to certain pre-designated times each day and by way of specific pass otherwise, an arrangement known in maximum security prisons as 'restricted movement' — again, just like prison. Detainees, who previously could leave their cells at night, are now locked in them overnight (a minimum of ten hours total

1 *Ibid., p. 12.*

per day)[1]. This is equal to the most restrictive Minnesota prisons, and is not even required in certain living units in two Minnesota medium-custody prisons.[2] Even worse than in prison, detainees cannot even shake hands with each other, much less with staff.[3] And some security officers (called 'security counselors') have recently documented irrelevant behaviors of detainees as if they presented treatment issues and have become overly concerned about minor violations by detainees.

Other policy changes in and after 2008 include punishment or abuse of detainees through threats, restricted visitation, censored mail, monitored telephone calls, unreasonable searches, and discipline without due process.[4] Most policies and procedures implemented since 2008 have been *adopted directly from DOC parallel documents*. Examples of these include: Use of Force; Office of Special Investigations; Intelligence Information Gathering; Evidence Policy; Behavioral Expectation Reports (BERs); Client Grievances: Client Request Policy; Visiting Behavioral Expectations; Mail Policy; and Property Policy. Nearly all of these new policies and procedures were enacted purely for staff convenience and for uniformity with prison policies, for the ease of security personnel experienced with prison procedure.

Instead, each of these new policies goes beyond what is necessary for treating MSOP detainees in a therapeutic manner, based on professional judgment in a safe environment. None of these new restrictions was deemed necessary before 2008 to maintain control or security for the facility, nor have there been any incidents that plausibly could have prompted such new restrictions. These new restrictions and changes have created a hostile environment encouraging a sense of hopelessness, powerlessness, and fear among MSOP detainees, including treatment participants.[5]

Essentially, the overall impact of institution of these disciplinary rules has been to reduce all MSOP detainees (although not committed as or for punishment) to the status of prison inmates in a maximum security prison, thereby eliminating or reducing their legal rights as committed 'patients' under Minn. Stat. Chapter 253B, and their rights under both federal and state constitutions. Some of these new restrictions are equal to parallel prison rules; others are effectively worse than comparative aspects of prison life.

---

1 *Karsjens, Para. 79.*

2 *OLA Report, pp. 67—68.*

3 *Karsjens, Para. 104(u).*

4 *Karsjens, Para. 69.*

5 *Ibid, Paras. 70–71.*

Among these new MSOP rules of the 'prison-equivalent' kind are the following:

- allowing staff to punish detainees by locking them in their cells;
- taking away the right for detainees to visit each others' cells;
- denying detainees the right to share food and other items with others;
- denying detainees the right to wear certain clothes, such as hats, bandanas, and muscle shirts, including within their own living units;
- allowing staff to punish detainees by denying them access to the yard or to the gym;
- restricting the time that detainees are allowed access to the yard;
- denying detainees access to hobbies;
- permitting staff to punish detainees by denying them employment;
- restricting what can be purchased by detainees from the detainee store.

Among MSOP rules that are more restrictive, adverse, or harsh than comparative aspects of prison life are these:

- punishing detainees by denying them access to group therapy;
- intentionally, unnecessarily delaying delivery of mail to detainees;
- unreasonably restricting access to, and conduct during visitation;
- restricting detainees' access to a law library and to a regular library;
- denying detainees' access to recreational activities and exercise;
- denying detainees educational programming;
- denying detainees meaningful employment opportunities;
- punishing detainees by removing furniture;
- executing 'security checks' every 30 minutes by knocking loudly on each detainee's cell door (including during hours of sleep);
- taking away the basic life skills of allowing detainees to manage their personal financial affairs;
- taking away the right to drug and alcohol treatment for detainees;
- denying detainees the right to shake hands with other detainees.

Karsjens, Para. 104,
g. MSOP Discipline Process:
Worse Than Prison

If MSOP staff believe a detainee has violated a rule, they issue a 'redirect' or a 'major' Behavioral Expectation Report (BER), equivalent to a prison disciplinary 'incident report'. A 'redirect' is a request from MSOP staff to a detainee to alter or cease a specified minor rule-violating behavior. This is analogous to a prison-based 'direct order'. A redirect is supposed to be removed from the detainee's record after 45 days; however, often, this does not happen. If the offending behavior persists or recurs, staff may then issue a minor rule BER. The Behavioral Expectations Handbook (i.e., disciplinary rule book) is not clear on what constitutes a 'minor' or a 'major' rule violation and what the disciplinary consequences are for different violations.

There is *no hearing* or other fact-finding procedure for a redirect. After receiving a BER, a detainee can only request review of the BER itself (not the redirect) and the restriction(s) imposed for the BER. Contrast this to prison, wherein a major rule violation affords a hearing to the prisoner *before* imposition of punishment. Also, note that, for a BER based on a minor rule violation, even the issuance of the BER does not create or allow a latter-day challenge to the original redirect. The BER review panel consists of employees from various MSOP departments, including clinical, security, and programming. This panel is not impartial, disinterested, or objective, and this review-hearing process is a sham.[1]

At a BER review hearing, a detainee is not allowed to: face his accuser(s); cross-examine witnesses; or present evidence. Nor is the detainee ever given a copy of the incident report or other written memo of evidence used against him. A detainee can *only* appeal an adverse decision by the review panel to the MSOP Facility Director. However, because the Facility Director implements all such policies and procedures complained of in any given appeal, the appeal is inherently not impartial.[2]

A special instance of discipline unique to MSOP exists when treatment staff are displeased with any matter involving treatment as to a given detainee. At the request of treatment staff, Vocational Services staff will either reduce the number of weekly hours the detainee is allowed to work and be paid for, or completely remove the detainee from authorization to work altogether. Conversely, receiving a BER causes at least a six-month delay in progression in treatment.[3]

In addition to other punishments typified by the above listings, a 'High Security Area' (HSA), equivalent to solitary confinement in prison, is used for disciplinary confinement in MSOP. Unlike

1 *Ibid, para. 96.*

2 *Ibid., paras. 97–98.*

3 *Ibid., paras. 99–100.*

segregation disciplinary sentences in prison, however, in MSOP, a detainee remains in HSA until MSOP staff declares that the detainee has 'regained behavioral control'. However, in reality, detainees are kept in HSA far longer than necessary as a purely punitive measure, rather than a behavioral control measure.[1]

Brutal and Unwarranted Searches — Worse Than Prison

Anyone doubting the unmitigated brutality of the search behavior of MSOP security staff should consult Serna v. Goodno.[2] That case recounts an episode at MSOP Moose Lake facility in which a cell phone was suspected of having been smuggled into the facility. After a search of the premises came up empty-handed, security staff stripped every detainee nude in turn and peered into the forced-open rectum of each of the approximately 550 detainees then held, on the unlikely thought that an unknown detainee might have forced it into his rectum to avoid its discovery.

There was no certainty that a contraband cell phone was even within the facility at all, and there was no reason to suspect that any particular detainee possessed one. No cell phone was found in this incident of mass-brutality. This was the forbidden 'general search' of 4th Amendment infamy. Even in prison, such a physically invasive search of an entire prison population, or even merely of a whole subdivision (e.g., all prisoners in a given living unit) would never be tolerated, especially when founded on mere general suspicion.

The general theme of MSOP searches as being unwarranted and unreasonable, and more egregious than in prisons, is best captured by the following excerpt from Karsjens, pp. 33–35:

- "[MSOP staff] perform unwarranted and unreasonable searches of [detainees'] persons, property, and living quarters at MSOP.
- "Currently, [detainees] are subject to unwarranted pat searches of the body, unclothed body searches, and body cavity searches without reasonable suspicion being established. [Detainees] may be pat searched or wand searched at any time for no reason, including whenever leaving the craft room in recreation, the visiting area or vocational work areas.
- In the past, [detainees] were not subject to strip searches. [Detainees] are now subject to strip searches upon entry to the HSA, regardless of the incident that led to being placed in the

1 *Ibid., paras. 101–102.*

2 *567 F.3d 944, 2009 U.S. App. LEXIS 11767 (8th Cir. 2009).*

HSA. When a [detainee] refuses to comply with a strip search, the facility staff will forcibly cut off his clothing and physically inspect his groin area and buttocks.

- [Detainees] are also subject to strip searches any time they leave or re-enter the secure perimeter of the MSOP facility. For example, if they are suffering from a medical emergency and need to go to the hospital, the [detainee] will be strip searched prior to being allowed to get in a waiting ambulance. The [detainee] is then strip searched again when they return to the secure MSOP facility, even though two MSOP security guards accompany [detainees] the entire time they are outside the secure facility.
- [Detainees] are also subject to regular random cell searches. These cell searches are used as a punitive exertion of authority on [detainees]. [Detainees] are not allowed to observe the searches or be present during their performance. No meaningful process exists to oppose the searches or appeal the resulting arbitrary confiscation of [detainees'] property.
- In addition to pretextual random searches, [detainees] are subject to daily 'window checks' of their cell. [MSOP staff] claim the purpose of these searches is to physically inspect windows in the [detainees'] cells. The reinforced glass windows are roughly five inches wide and recessed into the wall over a foot. The windows do not open. Although the stated reason for the window checks is prevention of escape, it is not possible for a person to fit through the window opening even if the reinforced glass could be broken. The true function of the window checks is to allow guards to enter the cells of the [detainees]and perform regular, unwarranted searches of the cells.
- The following policies, procedures, and practices related to searches performed by (MSOP staff) are also unreasonable:
    - the policy and practice of routinely searching the contents of [detainees'] incoming and outgoing mail;
    - the policy and practice of opening and reviewing [detainees'] mail that has been clearly marked as legal correspondence;
    - performing strip searches on [detainees] after visitations, despite the excessive monitoring and conduct regulations during visitations;
    - strip searching and shackling [detainees] during transportation outside the secure perimeter by MSOP personnel;
    - conducting random, unreasonable, and unwarranted searches of [detainees'] quarters, property, and persons;

- monitoring [detainees'] telephone calls;
- constant monitoring of [detainees'] every action and conversation;
- requiring staff person(s) to be present during visits between medical provider(s) and [detainees];
- monitoring [detainees] when they are speaking with clergy or other religious volunteers;
- forcing [detainees] to buy from approved vendors only, even though staff check all incoming mail; and
- allowing staff to shake down [detainees'] cells at any time.

Restraints on Detainee Movement and Physical Restraint

Another aspect of MSOP detention that has become as severe as protocols in a maximum-security prison concerns restrictions on detainee movement within MSOP and physical restraints placed on detainees on authorized departures from an MSOP facility. As above, the ensuing excerpt from Karsjens, at pp. 35–36, succinctly captures these restrictions:

- "In the past, (detainees) were allowed to leave the facility with a staff escort and without physical restraints. [Detainees] could move freely about the compound and socialize with other [detainees] at MSOP. [Detainees] were not locked in their rooms at night. [Detainees] could shop at local stores, cook food on stoves and barbecues, run their own businesses, carry cash, and conduct personal banking.
- "Since Mr. Benson took over MSOP in 2008, the restrictions on movement at the MSOP facilities are identical to a maximum security correctional facility.
- "When [detainees] leave the secure facility they are placed in handcuffs, leg irons and a black box, complete with waist-chain. They are then pushed in a wheel chair to the transport vehicle where they are placed in a small cage inside the van. They are subject to these same restraints when they suffer a medical emergency and need to leave the secure facility via ambulance.
- "[Detainees] cannot ever move freely around the facility. The only time they can move around an area as they wish is when they are locked on their designated living unit.
- "The physical restraint policy is impermissibly applied across the board to [detainees]. No consideration is given to the individualized security risk that a [detainee] poses."

Inadequate Medical Treatment

Even worse than prisons, SOP does not provide adequate medical treatment to its detainees. The aforementioned general prison provisioner, 'Minncor' (with no pharmaceutical branch or druggist on staff), is designated by MSOP as its exclusive provider of prescription medications and over-the-counter remedies and health aids. This exclusive-provider relationship has resulted, and continues to result in, extreme, unnecessary, and potentially life-threatening delay in providing necessary medication to MSOP detainees. No pharmacy or drug dispensary is located within MSOP.

MSOP staff do not provide necessary insulin and other diabetic management care to any detainees who suffer from diabetes. MSOP staff do not seek professional medical assistance outside of MSOP's own Health Services Office for conditions such as salmonella and hammer toes. Such medical care as has been provided by MSOP Health Services for those conditions has resulted in the affected detainees suffering lasting negative effects.[1]

Restrictions on, and Procedures as to, Detainees' Personal Property

MSOP restrictions on detainees' personal property are as restrictive as those in maximum security prisons. Its procedures for dealing with detainee personal property are worse than in any prison and are utterly lacking in the basics of due process.

These points are aptly described in Karsjens, pp. 37–38:

- "[Detainees] may no longer possess personal computers,. laptop computers, or computer software or storage of any kind. (Detainees) may not access printers, copiers, scanners, or the Internet. This further isolates (detainees) as they may not pursue educational opportunities, engage with the outside world, or communicate with friends and family.
- "(Detainees) are forced, at their own expense, to mail property that MSOP deems contraband outside the facility, or the property will be destroyed by staff.
- "If [detainees] possess property that is considered contraband, such as books and movies that are not on the approved media list, that property is confiscated. [Detainees] may then submit a request to appeal the denial of their property, but such requests take MSOP ten business days to handle. By the time that request has been processed, the property has been

1 *Karsjens, paras. 130-131.*

destroyed. [Detainees] must submit at least two requests before they may file a grievance, which is well beyond the 10-day period. The process to appeal the confiscation and destruction of property is not only overly burdensome, it is futile.

- "[Detainees'] personal computers were removed from the MSOP in 2008 after Mr. Benson started his tenure. A 'patient network' was established with four computers per 96 detainees to perform word processing and other simple tasks. The MSOP seized all removable media such as floppy disks and CD-ROMs and have instructed [detainees] that they will have to print their electronic files instead of allowing them to save files on electronic media to send to courts, attorneys, or family. This restriction is very burdensome on [detainees] because their only storage space is the three lockers under their bed.
- "[Detainees] have been denied and restricted from using or accessing the internet even though no individual reasonable suspicion has ever been established to warrant the restriction. The MSOP already possesses the commercial software necessary to monitor an internet server, which is currently online for employees of the MSOP.
- "Completely preventing [detainees] from accessing the internet further isolates them from the world because they are not able to pursue online education or employment opportunities or even communicate with friends and family via email."

Restrictions on Visitation

Another realm of MSOP operation that has lapsed into comparability with maximum-security prison operation is visitation.

Again, Karsjens, pp. 38–39, succinctly summarizes thus:

- "[Detainees] used to be afforded liberal visitation policies, with visiting hours daily from 1–9p.m. Visitors were allowed to prepare food or order food to be delivered for consumption with [detainees]. Contact between visitors and a [detainee] was broadly permissible — hand-holding, hugging, and holding children were all accepted. Visitors could drop off gifts and groceries on their visits with [detainees].
- "Currently, visitation is limited to Wednesdays through Sundays from 12:30p.m. to 8:30p.m. Visitors must now be pre-approved for visitation, submit to a criminal background check and submit to a pat search. Contact between [detainees] and a

visitor is limited to one hug at the beginning and end of each visit. Smoking is not permitted during visitation and no food is allowed during visits. [Detainees] are strip searched after visitation. MSOP routinely denies access to visitors and limits the size of a [detainee's] visiting list as well as the number of visitors at one time.

- "The current visitation practices greatly discourage visitation and serve to further isolate [detainees] and hinder therapeutic progress."

Education and Employment Opportunities and Payroll Accounting Are Worse Than in Prison

Karsjens, pp. 39–40, explains as follows:

- "[Detainees'] vocational work assignments are limited to menial labor. [Detainees] must perform janitorial maintenance work on their living unit to progress in treatment or receive vocational placement. Many do not have access to facility jobs which would allow the [detainee] to be more employable upon re-entering society, such as plumbing, electrical, HVAC or any other vocational programs which would afford them meaningful job skills.
- "Regardless of a [detainee's] previous college degree or age, he must maintain certain educational qualifications to hold a vocational work assignment or advance in treatment.
- "The Legislative Auditor Report agrees with [detainees'] assertions that employment and education opportunities at MSOP are lacking, finding that 'there are limited work opportunities for clients' and that 'most of Moose Lake clients' time is unstructured' (OLA Report at p. 65). Although the amount of time that a [detainee] may work is limited by their progress in treatment, the upper limit of time working is 24 hours in a two-week period. 'Few, if any clients are scheduled the maximum amount of work hours' (ibid).
- "Vocational programming jobs at the MSOP pay minimum wage, however, [detainees] are only given half that amount as wages by MSOP. They are not provided an accounting of the remainder of their wages.
- "The need for employment opportunities is especially pressing given the fact that [detainees] are billed over $100,000 a year for their treatment. Those bills accrue until the [detainee] is released from MSOP."

Inadequate Diet, Poor Food Handling, Spoiled and Poor-Quality Food

MSOP provision of meals to detainees borders on a horror show, as Karsjen, pp. 40–41 describes:

- "The diet for [detainees] must provide, at a minimum, the Recommended Daily Dietary Allowances established by the National Academy of Sciences. In developing such menus, MSOP must utilize the moderate food cost plan of the United States Department of Agriculture.
- "MSOP cannot spend less per [detainee] for raw food, including donated food, than the most recent per-person costs of the Moderate Cost Food Plan for the Northern Range of the United States, as compiled by the United States Department of Agriculture, for appropriate groupings of [detainees], discounted for any savings which might result from institutional procurement of such food.
- "The MSOP food contractor CWF continually shortens meals or simply does not deliver what is on the menu. Meals are poorly prepared and in some cases handled without due care, which has led to illness. Food portions are rationed out at a lesser degree than the menu states due to the practice of equating food volume with weight. The food [MSOP staff] provide to [detainees] is of extremely poor quality and includes by-product meat and old fruits and vegetables."

Restrictions on Communication and Access to Publications

At pp. 41–42, Karsjens discusses this topic of conditions as bad, or worse than prison existence.

- "MSOP charges [detainees] exorbitant rates for using telephones. Currently, [detainees] are charged approximately 32 to 39 cents a minute to use the phone. The MSOP phone system is the only phone system [detainees] are allowed to use.
- "[Detainees] are not allowed to use 800 numbers to conduct business.
- "Calling cards are prohibited. [Detainees] are very limited in the number of phone calls they are allowed to make.
- "The extremely high rates [detainees] are charged serves no therapeutic or security purpose.
- "[MSOP staff] limit which magazines and newspapers [detainees] can read. They also censor and remove certain articles and sections of the newspapers that are given to [detainees] to read.

- "(MSOP staff) also have an unofficial policy of keeping [detainees] who have filed lawsuits against MSOP or MSOP personnel separate from other [detainees] who have not filed lawsuits."

Religious Restrictions

Lastly, Karsjens, p. 42, outlined this prison-like aspect:

- "[MSOP staff] monitor [detainees] when they speak to clergy and religious volunteers, even though they have been screened by MSOP staff upon entry to the facility. They also monitor [detainees] during religious services.
- "[MSOP staff] do not provide [detainees] kosher or halal meals. [Detainees] cannot wear yarmulkes, kufis, or religious medallions and pendants unless they are in their cells or at a religious service.
- "[Detainees] are only allowed five religious items in their personal property, and [MSOP staff] limit the types of religious items [detainees] may have.
- "[MSOP staff] only allow [detainees] to have religious feasts once a year, despite the fact that [detainees] have offered to pay for those feasts."

Double Jeopardy

Courts in other states deem such prison-like conditions as converting the nature of sex offender commitment to punitive confinement, thus opening the door to double jeopardy, ex post facto, and other claims for release.

A Washington case, Young v. Weston[1], was brought by a committed sex offender who objected to conditions of committed confinement that were more restrictive than those imposed on non-sex-offender committed individuals, and even more restrictive than conditions imposed on state prisoners. Noting that the commitment facility was sited within the perimeter of a prison compound, and that the facility relied on the Dept. of Corrections for a host of essential services, the court in that case held that such alleged facts, if proved, would establish the punitive nature of his confinement, entitling him to relief on his double jeopardy and ex post facto claims.

While not grounds for release, a California case, Hydrick v. Hunter[2], ruled that committed sex offenders' rights to privacy were violated where their commitment facility did not allow for privacy when showering, sleeping, using toilets, or participating in therapy sessions.

---

1 *176 F.3d 1196 (9th Cir. 1999).*

2 *449 F.3d 978 (9th Cir. 2006).*

Elsewhere, it has been generally held that involuntarily committed sex offenders, just as all others involuntarily committed, have greater rights regarding conditions of their confinement under the 14th Amendment than imprisoned criminals do under the 8th Amendment. The former are entitled to more considerate treatment in conditions of confinement than are the latter.[1]

Thus, under such precedent, it appears that MSOP is vulnerable to litigation. Indeed, fulfilling this apprehension, the aforementioned federal class action (Karsjens) has been filed attacking the foregoing conditions. That lawsuit remains pending as of this writing. It deserves close monitoring.

Overall, such recent changes since 2008 as complained of in Karsjens have been to the detriment of therapy. Such restrictive measures were put into effect without adequate consideration of their impact on the therapeutic environment. Those new rules and policies, according to MSOP detainees, have strongly contributed to an 'us versus them' attitude between detainees and staff.[2] In general, daily life in MSOP-Moose Lake is now effectively identical to that in Minnesota prisons of a medium-to-maximum-custody level. This alone is sufficient to cause MSOP to be judicially struck down.

Busting Minnesota's Impossibly Restrictive Standard for Release from Sex Offender Commitment

The OLA Report, p. 20, states that, unlike other states having commitment laws, Minnesota lacks "a required periodic report to the courts regarding each sex offender's continuing need to be committed. Most states require an annual report to be sent to the courts on each committed sex offender as to whether he continues to meet the commitment standard. Some states require mandatory court hearings, while others may only hold a hearing if necessary. In some states, the state is required to re-prove the commitment case in court periodically. Minnesota and Massachusetts appear to be the only two states where an annual report to the courts is not required."

Most states having sex offender commitment laws have provisions calling for ending a given sex offender's commitment whenever he no longer meets the commitment standard. This may occur through treatment or, if nothing else, will be achieved as the sex offender in question increases in age, with inherent corresponding statistical drops in recidivism (discussed elsewhere in this work).

---

1 *Terrance v. Northville Regional Psychiatric Hosp., 286 F.3d 834 (6th Cir. 2002).*

2 *OLA Report, pp. 68, 70.*

In contrast, Minnesota has a statutory release standard that is far more restrictive — some say nearly impossible to satisfy the 'treatment completion standard'. Only North Dakota is known to share this exacting standard. Not surprisingly, North Dakota has had only a few releases to date.[1] The fact that it has any suggests that North Dakota applies that standard less harshly than does Minnesota.

Releases from sex offender commitment are usually to a restricted status known as 'provisional discharge'. Final discharge from commitment comes only after a substantial period, usually several years. Releases from sex offender commitment, as discussed in this work, are to such restricted status, whether called 'provisional discharge' or some other name. It is unknown, but unlikely, whether anyone released in North Dakota to such status has completed that period and thereby received a final discharge. The only existing Minnesota person at present currently remains on provisional discharge, with no plan to make that discharge final in the foreseeable future.

Release standards are a product both of the state law and of state agency policies and practices. An important factor in Minnesota is an executive order by former Governor Pawlenty, preventing any releases from MSOP's sex offender commitment facilities, except if ordered by a court or 'required by law'. This executive order remains in effect to date. Until very recently, it was taken by the respective MSOP facility administrators to impose an absolute ban on releases.

Thus, responsive to that edict and other political pressures, 'completion of treatment' in Minnesota has been stymied by repetitive, uncalled for demotions of those MSOP detainees in the higher phases of treatment, whether for trivial shortcomings or upon rank pretext. This prevents anyone from 'completing' treatment, so that the question of release is never reached. According to an official explanation by the state itself, in Minnesota, to "complete the treatment program" requires that a detainee not just complete all treatment phases (each with its own many 'modules') but also "... demonstrate that treatment has had a significant impact on [his] behavior and thoughts. In other words, detainees must reduce their recidivism risk to very low levels."[2]

Rydberg v. Goodno, 689 N.W.2d 310 (Minn. App. 2004), states: "MSOP was developed and implemented with the intent of releasing 'even the most violent sexual offenders' into the community after successful completion of the MSOP program."

Yet obviously, that is not happening.

---

1 *Ibid.*

2 *OLA Report, p. 21.*

According to a Star Tribune article, as of 2008, 24 sex offenders committed to MSOP had left MSOP in the only way they could — they all died. Morbid humor among guards and counselors characterized such deaths as the inmate having completed treatment. This lack of releases has increased the likelihood that MSOP will ultimately be declared unconstitutional as simply being supplemental incarceration and that judges will order the release of all of its detainees.[1]

Actually, as a footnote, there is a bit more to it. A later article cleared this up. "... Only two have won provisional discharge. One of those, Ray Hubbard, was pulled back into a treatment lockup because a psychiatrist thought he might reoffend. He died shortly thereafter."[2]

Some significant background facts: Ray Hubbard was an old man by the time of his release. He had been locked up in MSOP (and its predecessor program, ITPSA) for more than a decade, originally as a condition of probation. He was committed when his probation expired by an unsatisfied county attorney purely as a means to continue to hold him. His release was brief. He did not commit any crime, nor was he caught preparing to. At best, the psychiatrist who triggered his renewed detention in MSOP was just nervous.

However, the realpolitik of that seizure and placement of poor old Ray back in lockup was that it happened in the midst of the mass-commitment frenzy that followed Alfonso Rodriguez' crime and arrest. It is more likely to surmise that, in that frenzy, it occurred to someone that Hubbard's released status might pose a media-scandal risk.

The second releasee to whom that 2012 article referred was released in January, 2012. That release followed the scathing report on MSOP authored by Legislative Auditor James Nobles and released in 2011.[3] That report strongly criticized the longstanding lack of any releases (beyond Hubbard's brief release) by MSOP, as evidence that it was utterly failing in its mission of treatment toward the end of releases without sex-crime recidivism.

That report called for action by the 2012 Legislature when it convened (can you guess?) in January, 2012. What's more, after many civil rights lawsuits were filed and pending in federal court, that court was already in motion by the end of 2011 to appoint attorneys to consolidate at least several of those suits into a class action of impressive merit (about which, incidentally, that August, 2012 article,

---

1 *Ibid.*

2 *Larry Oakes, "Minnesota Must Change Sex Offender Program, Judge Orders", Star Tribune, August 17, 2012, p. Al. Emphases supplied.*

3 *OLA Report, cited supra.*

supra). Undoubtedly. MSOP itself was alerted to this by the state's defensive attorneys in those suits, probably in that same time frame.

Thus, it is highly likely that the second release was an effort by MSOP officials to mitigate what was then apparent as an oncoming storm of criticism of MSOP in public, and to head off possible legislative or judicial actions. Conversely, it is fair to conclude as highly probable that, in the absence of these developments, the second release would never have occurred. Many others were as entirely well prepared for release, if not more so, than the one released. This was strictly a nominal release, not a change in policy. Even the bona fides of MSOP in choosing that particular detainee to release are subject to adamant questioning. He had a record of multiple sex offenses over time, involving children. Many other detainees had records far less extensive than his. Unlike many other qualified detainees, he was not old and hence not in that 'greatly diminished recidivism' category. If there was any valid ground for Hubbard's release revocation, based on such apprehensiveness, the sheer nature of the second releasee's background would justify an equal level of apprehensiveness, and hence offer a rationale for revocation of his release too, any time MSOP so chooses. A good bet would be that this will happen, just as soon as the 'heat dies down' from the current spotlight on MSOP's failure.

Now let's get technical. Under Minnesota's commitment statutes, two forms of release exist: provisional discharge and final discharge. For clarity, let's start with final discharge first.

> "A civilly committed sex offender may be fully discharged only after a determination is made by SRB (Special Review Board) and SCAP (Supreme Court Appeal Panel) that the person 'is capable of making an acceptable adjustment to open society, is no longer dangerous to the public, and is no longer in need of inpatient treatment and supervision' (Minn. Stat. Sec. 253B.185, subd. 18). In making a determination regarding discharge, SCAP and SRB must consider whether 'specific conditions exist to provide a reasonable degree of protection to the public and to assist the patient in adjusting to the community'. If those conditions do not exist, the discharge cannot be granted. A 1995 Minnesota Supreme Court case established that solely proving that a committed person no longer meets the commitment standard is not sufficient to justify discharge of that individual.
>
> *Call v. Gomez, 535 N.W.2d 312 (Minn. 1995), Ibid, p. 87*

It is important to distinguish provisional discharge from final discharge. Physical release from an MSOP facility is intended to be effected by a ‘provisional discharge’. The word ‘discharge’ is somewhat misleading, since one ‘provisionally discharged’ remains under the authority of the Dept. of Human Services under extremely restrictive regulations, in the same manner as a non-committed sex offender released from prison remains on ‘conditional release’ for either five or ten years thereafter. Indeed, the Legislature recently confirmed this explicitly, requiring a ten-year term of conditional release for anyone released from MSOP.

In contrast, in theory, a ‘final discharge’ of a committed sex offender occurs when the commitment itself is legally dissolved by either operation of law or by administrative and judicial action (as spelled out, supra). Given that new legislation requiring ‘conditional release’, ‘final discharge’ cannot now occur for a minimum of ten years post-release from MSOP.

The aforesaid Call v. Gomez holding has been applied since then to provisional discharges as well. Specifically, MSOP itself will not support any detainee’s petition for provisional discharge unless he has first completed the MSOP treatment program. The prevailing standard of demonstrating that treatment has had a significant impact on one’s behavior and thoughts, and its corollary-in-practice that one must reduce one’s recidivism risk to ‘very low levels’ has already been discussed as being a near impossibility to prove.

However, despite such tough-sounding language, the factors spelled out by the statute itself[1] to be considered in determining whether a committed person may be provisionally discharged are somewhat more hopeful:

“1 whether the patient’s course of treatment and present mental status indicate that there is no longer a need for treatment and supervision in the patient’s current treatment setting; and

“2 whether the conditions of the provisional discharge plan will provide a reasonable degree of protection to the public and will enable the patient to adjust successfully to the community.”

However, because MSOP itself must develop a release plan, it can block release by simply declining to do so.[2]

Moreover, the SRB relies on MSOP treatment team reports and an MSOP risk assessment in making their recommendation to the SCAP. The OLA Report, on p. 88, states: “Clients who appeal cases to SCAP have an opportunity to have an outside expert review their treatment status and current risk as well. However, both SRB and SCAP probably rely greatly on MSOP’s assessments of their clients.”

In the more than twenty years of MSOP operation (as of February, 2012), “only two MSOP [detainees] had ever been placed on any kind

---

1 *Minn. Stat. Sec. 253B.185, subd. 12.*

2 *OLA Report, pp. 86–87.*

of provisional discharge. One of them had his provisional discharge revoked after violating its conditions, and the other was only recently granted provisional discharge."[1] In contrast, as of 2006, among the other states with sex offender commitment laws, 251 of those committed had been *finally* discharged, and another 154 were by then already on provisional discharge.[2]

In an effort to explain why only one ongoing provisional release has been affected from MSOP to date, therapists said they felt that 'public pressure' was being exerted upon the SRB and on judges on the SCAP to be 'extraordinarily conservative' in release decisions. However, because MSOP is not even supporting detainee requests for release or developing release plans needed, this set of statements is pure 'buck-passing'. It is possible, of course, that in addition to MSOP's own extraordinarily conservative decision-making on release, there may be certain small special interest groups within the public attempting to categorically lobby SRB members and SCAP judges to never grant release petitions. However, it is never good public policy to give in to such self-appointed vigilante 'lynch mobs'. Moreover, politically, in the modern age of extreme criminal sentences for sex offenders, there is no longer any political 'wind' in the sails, from which to threaten SCAP judges with 'unelection' in retaliation for such release decisions. Such small extremist groups have long since spent all their political ammunition. Extremists for whom nothing will ever be enough to assuage their unmerited, unslaked, personal rage must at some point be politely thanked and then tacitly left behind.

Of the twenty states with sex offender commitment, only three (including Minnesota) do not release offenders once they no longer meet the statutory commitment criteria.[3] This makes Minnesota considerably more vulnerable than the other 17 states to a constitutional challenge to its commitment regime. This is true especially because the standard in Minnesota for commitment as a 'sexually dangerous person' is amazingly easy for a prosecutor to satisfy. Conversely, then, it is more difficult for a detainee to 'prove the negative', i.e., that he no longer meets that commitment standard. But, in Minnesota, as has already been explained, supra, even proving that is not sufficient to gain release from MSOP.

In point of statistical fact, treatment is not the only means by which one's risk of recidivism is lowered. Sheer increased age alone is by far the largest reducing factor in sex offense recidivism.[4]

---

1 *Karsjens, supra, p. 44, para. 164.*

2 *Ibid, para. 165.*

3 *Ibid, p. 89.*

4 *See section above, on this point, focusing on the meta-analysis by Wollert.*

Now recall that, in order to be committed as a 'sexually dangerous person' in Minnesota, a person must: (1) have engaged in a course of harmful conduct; (2) suffer from a current disorder or dysfunction; and (3) be unable to adequately control his or her behavior, such that the person is highly likely to commit additional harmful sexual acts. Obviously, the first element (past acts of harmful sexual conduct) is not a changeable (dynamic) fact. But the second and third elements are dynamic. Yet Minnesota's current release standard requires treatment completion, as if such completion (or even merely participation) is the only means of alleviating the 'disorder of dysfunction' of the second element and of offering 'adequate control' of sexual behavior in the third element. However, this is the factual fallacy.

> "Some clients may no longer be considered 'highly likely' to commit additional acts of sexual harm. For example, some clients were committed prior to development of actuarial risk assessment tools or after scoring norms on actuarial tools were changed. Courts often rely on these tools to help them determine whether or not someone is highly likely to commit additional sexual harm. Prior to the development of actuarial tools, courts had to rely more heavily on experts' clinical judgment, which research has shown to be the least reliable predictor of risk (citing Karl Hanson, Risk Assessment, Ass'n. for the Treatment of Sexual Abusers, Beaverton, OR, 2000). If assessed with current actuarial tools, some of these clients could no longer be found to be high risk. Scoring norms have also changed on some of these tools. Some clients at MSOP facilities may no longer be considered high risk if scored under new scoring norms based on the newest research."
>
> *OLA Report, p. 89*

The footnote at the end of that passage is of considerable, illustrative importance:

> "38: In particular, the developers of the Static-99, a widely used tool to assess static risk, recently changed the scoring norms *to account for offender age* in calculating risk. New research on this tool also indicates that the tool may not accurately predict risk without taking into account the offender's dynamic risk factors."[1]

Advancing age moves any given detainee, age 40 up, from a younger, higher-risk cohort to a lower-risk, older cohort, inherently

1 *Emphasis supplied.*

meaning less risk of reoffense through increased age alone, regardless whether that detainee ever participated in treatment in MSOP — or anywhere else.

> "A 2006 study of states' release processes found that when a treatment program has a policy of not recommending release until treatment is completed (as is the case in Minnesota) and the program must make decisions regarding provisional releases, provisional releases are unlikely."
>
> *Ibid, p. 90, citing Dennis Doren, "The Model for Considering Release of Civilly committed Sexual Offenders" in The Sexual Predator: Law and Public Policy; Clinical Practice, Anita Schlank, ed. (New Jersey, 2006)*

A comparison to sex offender commitment releases just across the border in Wisconsin is startling. Unlike Minnesota law, a sex offender committed in Wisconsin must be released if risk of reoffense later fans below the commitment standard. Minnesota's standard of an acceptable adjustment to society results in release only where a detainee has essentially a zero probability of reoffense.

Until the year 2000, Wisconsin, like Minnesota, had insisted upon treatment completion to qualify for release. But from then on, Wisconsin changed its policy to one of safe manageability of an offender's risk in the community. This policy change caused Wisconsin's release rate to double. As of the close of 2003, none of Wisconsin's releasees had sexually reoffended. [1]

Consider also: In re Young, 86 P.3d 810 (Wash. App. 2004), which held that a 61-year-old committed sex offender presented a *prima facie* case for release on the sheer fact of his age, showing statistically therefrom that his probability of recidivating was nil. Washington, in contrast to Minnesota, does not require treatment completion[2], but only that a detainee show that he no longer meets the commitment standard itself (including the constitutionally required 'high likelihood' of reoffense). A detainee can show, alternatively to treatment completion, either that: (1) he "no longer suffers from a mental abnormality or personality disorder"; or (2) if he still does, that abnormality or disorder "would not likely cause the prisoner to engage in predatory acts of sexual violence if conditionally released ... or unconditionally discharged".[3] At a bare minimum, Minnesota should amend its commitment law to allow this mechanism and this showing for release, following the lead of In re Young. Among other points of

---

1 *E. Janus, "Closing Pandora's Box", at 34 Seton Hall L. Rev. 1245.*

2 *Ibid., p. 812.*

3 *Ibid., p. 811.*

objection, there is no excuse for continuing to lock up senior citizens and keeping them locked up long after the fires of passion have died.

Because of these facts, the Minnesota release standard appears to be extremely vulnerable to a due process challenge. Intuitively, had the Minnesota Legislature thought an even lower standard of commitment than in the SDP Act could withstand a constitutional challenge, it would have enacted it. Hence, the SDP Act probably represents the high-water mark of sex offender commitment laws.

Hence, Minnesota's more extreme release standard probably violates due process.

As the last quote, supra, demonstrates, the due process violation, rather than being based on the facts of any given detainee's commitment or his treatment during commitment (or the lack thereof), or his age, for instance, is more fundamentally grounded in institutional bias against release, as reflected by Minnesota's release standard itself, by various pronouncements by MSOP as to its conservative release policy, and by Doren's findings of the unlikelihood of provisional releases in Minnesota and the other two states like it.

Essentially, the due process violation arises from the fact that, had a given offender not been committed before, he could not, on current facts and actuarial risks, be committed today. Yet, in the context of the two 'dynamic' elements for commitment under the SDP Act, that same offender cannot be freed today from an earlier commitment under the MSOP standard for release:

> "... A client's progress in the treatment program continues to be a factor in considering a reduction in custody, even if the client no longer has a mental disorder or is no longer highly likely to commit additional acts of sexual harm."
>
> *Ibid., p. 89*

That is a present denial of due process.

Now recall that MSOP itself prepares a risk assessment for SCAP. This reveals that MSOP does have a 'risk assessment department'.[1] Adding insult to injury in MSOP disregarding that in a given case, the commitment standard is no longer met, the existence of this department and preparation of such risk assessments implies that MSOP is *well aware* of when a given detainee, through age or any other dynamic factor, no longer meets the commitment standard of high risk; yet they withhold this vital information from the detainee and from everyone else.

1 *Ibid., p. 91.*

A useful comparison is presented by State v. McCuiston[1]. That case involved a committed sex offender's challenge to the State of Washington's statute governing release from such commitment. Under that statute, the sex offender was limited to presenting evidence of either a permanent physiological change or a treatment-based mental change, as a means to show that he had changed and no longer fit the definition of a sexually violent predator. However, the court ruled in the sex offender's favor, agreeing that there was a multitude of ways in which the sex offender could show that he was no longer a sexually violent predator. By limiting the type of relevant evidence to physiological changes or treatment-based change, that statute effectively permitted the continued detention of someone who was no longer mentally ill or dangerous. Therefore, held the court, that statute was no longer tailored to the state's compelling interest, hence violating due process.

Because Minnesota's release statute similarly requires completion of treatment, and a demonstration of change through treatment, it appears to be vulnerable to the very same challenge.

That's part of what the currently pending Karsjens class action indeed does challenge. As the Oakes article of August 17, 2012, updates about that case:

> "Chief U.S. Magistrate Judge Arthur Boylan ... ordered [the] state Human Services Commissioner to convene a task force ... to recommend (1) options less restrictive than the state's prison-like treatment centers and to suggest (2) changes in how offenders are selected for civil commitment, as well as (3) how they might earn release from the program ...
>
> "Former State Sen. Don Betzold, co-sponsor of the 1994 Sexually Dangerous persons Act ... said the courts have repeatedly upheld the law as constitutional because judges believed the confinement was for treatment ...
>
> "However, even Betzold ... said the lack of releases ... invites the conclusion that the program's only purpose is confinement."

Unfortunately, the Karsjens class action does not ask for an end to Minnesota's scheme of sex offender commitment. Unless and until that happens, the MSOP prison-like facility will continue in operation, the number of those detained within it will continue to grow, and the whole machinery of lengthy, if not permanent, preventive detention masquerading as treatment will continue to grind on. Presumably,

---

1 238 P.3d 1147 (Wash. 2010).

because this book followed the filing of that class action by quite some time, the reason those attorneys chose not to seek that end to commitment was that they were simply unaware of all the facts mentioned herein comprising sex offender commitment, especially as practiced in Minnesota.

MSOP Is a Deliberate Bureaucratic Boondoggle, Not Intended to Release Anyone

The annual costs to operate MSOP now top $76 million, or approximately $328 per day per detainee ($120,000 per year each).[1] Note that the foregoing figures do not include the costs of attorneys and expert witnesses in the commitment proceedings themselves, estimated at $100,000 per commitment (ignoring general court costs of such proceedings).

MSOP claims that "additional residents can be accommodated at a lower marginal cost ..."[2] Because MSOP plans to use this to blunt legislative criticism of its cost, it is clear that, to the contrary of wanting to release detainees, it wants to incarcerate far more in its two facilities. Although MSOP claims that it is all about providing treatment, only 11% of its budget and staff are allocated to that purpose. Four times as much of its budget and nearly six times the number of staff (61%) are devoted to security — approximately 436 security staff, approaching 1:1 with the number of detainees. In contrast, of its 714 full-time-equivalent employees, only 78 MSOP employees are involved in treatment in any way.[3]

Compared to MSOP, the per diem rate at the Minnesota Security Hospital is almost twice as high. Other DHS residential facilities have higher per diem rates yet: Anoka-Metro Regional Treatment Center (over 3 times as high), all the way up to child and adolescent behavioral health services (nearly five times as high). All of these higher per diems are chalked up to far higher professional treatment staffing ratios to residents. This also reflects that MSOP is not truly serious about treatment.

In contrast to the $120,000 annual cost of MSOP per detainee, the 2011 MSOP Report itself (on page 12) admits that, even using inflated figures at the top end of the cost range, total costs of "intensive supervised release" (ISR — think maximum-security parole, including house arrest), including mandatory post-prison-release treatment of sex offenders, amount to only $24,200 per year at most. Note that the

---

1 *E. Janus, "Closing Pandora's Box ...", supra, at p. 1251 — as of 2010.*

2 *OLA Report, p. 12.*

3 *Ibid., p. 13.*

$120,000 annual cost for that same sex offender in MSOP does not include amortization of the huge total cost of the court proceeding to commit that detainee.

Judges are starting to get the 'big picture' about MSOP, i.e., that treatment to actually effect releases is simply not the aim of MSOP or its political backers. From MSOP's perspective, permanent detention of all committed sex offenders is simply their lifetime career plan for full employment. Consider In re Johnson[1]. That case upheld Mr. Johnson's commitment to MSOP, but out of seven justices, three filed differing opinions ('concurring' only in the result). Of these, the opinion of Justice Page is particularly telling about the motivation and intent of MSOP and its superiors. Page wrote:

> "I disagree with the court's reliance on 'rehabilitating the mentally ill', In re Linehan[2], as an 'exceptionally strong state interest' ... here ... In light of the recent report released by the Office of the Legislative Auditor [(OLA) (Evaluation Report: Civil Commitment of Sex Offenders 2011)], it is disingenuous to claim that the State has a strong interest in rehabilitating sexually dangerous persons ... The State's disinterest in rehabilitation is reinforced by the fact that 'no sex offender has ever been discharged from MSOP'.[3]
>
> "... I cannot agree that Minnesota views the rehabilitation of sexually dangerous persons as an 'exceptionally strong interest' ...".

At footnote 3 to that last paragraph, Justice Page clarified his meaning even more sharply:

> "I do not argue, as the court asserts, that the State's interest is minimized because it has not accomplished its objective. Rather, the OLA's report suggests, and I conclude, that the State's interest is minimized because *the State's actions indicate that the State is not interested in rehabilitation.*"[4]

If actions, then, speak louder than words, let's consider the foregoing to derive MSOP's true interest and the State's true intent.

Apart from being a boondoggle and a waste, MSOP has simply been a political football. In 2003, after the Alfonso Rodriguez incident (supra), Minnesota's then Attorney General and gubernatorial

1 *800 N.W.2d 134 (Minn. Supr. 2011).*

2 *Linehan IV, 594 N.W.2d 867, 872 (Minn. 1999).*

3 *Ibid, at 19.*

4 *Emphasis supplied.*

candidate Mike Hatch accused the administration of then Governor Tim Pawlenty of planning releases to save money. Governor Pawlenty then issued the still-extant executive order (described supra) barring releases from MSOP except under court order. This public exchange caused Dr. Michael Farnsworth, the psychiatrist who helped design the MSOP program, to quit his post as MSOP director, protesting that MSOP was "mired in politics".[1]

Courts have held elsewhere that involuntary confinement for the status of having a mental illness or disorder, unless accompanied by adequate treatment, constitutes imposition of cruel and unusual punishment.[2] The question, of course, is — what comprises 'adequate treatment'? Courts have long (too long, really) given sex offender commitment programs great leeway. However, where, as in Minnesota, the long record of lack of releases and of nearly constant revision of treatment regimen (which conveniently thwarts treatment completion), and of equally convenient discovery of last-minute excuses to revoke the completions of those who have actually attained them, and demotion of treatment participants (in some cases drastically) — again conveniently has, in the aggregate, deprived nearly everyone of being deemed ready for release.

Such leeway is undeserved.

MSOP is a sheer boondoggle, using human beings as the never-ending grist for their self-perpetuating bureaucratic mill. This must cease!

---

1 *Larry Oakes, "Locked in Limbo", Star Tribune, June 8, 2008, p. Al.*

2 *See: People v. Feagley, 121 Cal. Rptr. 509, 535 P.2d 373 (Cal. 1983).*

Chapter 10

The Wild Rhetoric Of MSOP

"You Need Treatment; You'll Never Be Risk Free. So We're Never Going To Release You."

The classic example of permanent commitment: the application of the 'criminogenic needs' doctrine to pedophiles — "Just stop being a pedophile and we'll let you go!".

A classic illustration of things claimed to require total elimination before one can be deemed safe to release pertains to pedophiles, to whom MSOP is referring by the code-phrase 'sexual deviancy'. MSOP argues in support of commitment that being a pedophile presents 'criminogenic needs'; that the pedophile 'needs' treatment, regardless of his insistence on not needing same, or any more of same, or commitment (probably natural life) to MSOP; and that pedophilic attractions, plus two instances of same, inherently presents such likelihood of reoffense that commitment is necessary, so that treatment can talk the offender out of being a pedophile. Of course, based on this rhetoric, our pedophile is committed for that purpose.

However, no matter how socially loathed and feared in our society pedophilia may be as a sexual attraction, the fact remains that attraction or orientation is what it is — not a 'treatable' personality, emotional, or sexual malady, which will go away with sufficient treatment. There is no 'cure' for the pedophilic orientation, any more than there is a 'cure' for your own orientation, whatever it may be. Yet the 'deviant sexual interests' or 'sexually deviant interests' targets in MSOP Report to Legislature[1] certainly implies that a pedophile would have to prove that he no longer has pedophilic attractions, in order to satisfy 'meaningful change' and be released.

Recall from the OLA Report, p. 76, that, to advance in treatment, one must pass a penile plethysmograph (PPL) and the 'Abel assessment of sexual interest'. Hence, since a pedophile will always have that attraction, he is forever pre-ordained to fail treatment. Our pedophile, indeed, all pedophiles, will remain locked up until death in MSOP, if MSOP has anything to say about it.

Without intending to get personal, let's assume you are heterosexual. Will *any* number of years in the most intense 'treatment'

---

1 *January, 2011, p. 31.*

— even 'brainwashing' — ever end your heterosexuality, or convert it to, say, homosexuality? Why then would anyone expect otherwise of pedosexuality? But, of course, attractions do not equal actions. By locking all pedophiles up permanently, MSOP presumes the contrary, and acts upon that presumption. This is the very heart — and dark indeed — of preventive detention.

MSOP's Rhetorical Web: The 'Zero-Percent Public Safety Guarantee'

Confirming this, that MSOP Report[1] cites "ensuring that a Level III sex offender *never* recidivates sexual harm" is the goal of MSOP. Zero percent equals death while committed.

The rhetorical means by which MSOP justifies this is the dual-headed standard of release requiring both completion of treatment and "demonstrated meaningful change". What is 'meaningful change', per the MSOP view? MSOP does not say outright, but the actual standard of 'meaningful change' can be deduced by noting the MSOP Report's explanation of why commitment is necessary even for those who have already 'successfully completed treatment' elsewhere: "Successful treatment reduces risk, but does not eliminate it. In some cases, the reductions achieved through treatment, when weighed against the case as a whole, remain insufficient to guarantee public safety, thus suggesting the need for a higher intensity treatment within a secure setting." (i.e., MSOP commitment).[2]

Of course, the only 'guarantee' of 'public safety' would be if the probability of recidivism were reduced to *zero* percent. *No treatment known to humanity makes any claim to be able to achieve such — or anything close to it.* This includes other states' commitment programs, which aim for lesser, arguably achievable goals. Minnesota's MSOP stands *alone* in insisting upon such an *absolute guarantee* of public safety before releasing any given detainee.

Parenthetically, the MSOP Report[3] declares that the commitment programs of other states "have survived legal challenges because they are designed to provide treatment that has the potential for individuals meaningfully participating in them to reduce their risks sufficiently to be released back into the community". But by demanding the 'zero-percent public safety guarantee', MSOP is not within the contemplation of such judicial decisions elsewhere.

---

1 *"Options for Managing the Growth and Cost of (MSOP): Facility Study", p. 43.*

2 *Ibid, p. 20.*

3 *Ibid, p. 24.*

MSOP's Illusory Promise of Releases

As if to belie this, the MSOP Report[1] declares: "Treatment systems in Minnesota have the *potential to further reduce the need for civil commitments* and to help support the appropriate release of *some* civilly committed individuals when they have made sufficient progress to warrant transition to society from MSOP. In either case, these strategies result in increased reliance on community-based treatment to manage higher-risk sexual offenders than has been the case to this point", adding, farther down that same page, "The clinical and legal basis for MSOP is that the program will release individuals who *successfully complete* treatment and there are *several* clients who are *close to earning provisional discharge.*"[2]

In response, first, the material preceding this quote shows that 'sufficient progress' means that same 'zero-percent public safety guarantee'. Second, even when *that impossible standard* may ever be attained, only 'some' detainees who thus qualify will be released. Third, given that the MSOP Report is dated January, 2011, and that only one detainee has been released since then, the veracity of the claim that 'several' were then 'close to provisional discharge' is open to strenuous question. In the two years since then, no others of this supposed cadre have been released. If this is the definition of 'close' in MSOP-speak, then no appreciable change through internal MSOP action can actually be expected. Such MSOP statements are merely puffery without serious intent of reform.

The tale of Mike Meyer (not the detainee released in 2012) illustrates the tantalizing, but utterly illusory nature of MSOP's promises of release. As of 2008, Meyer had been locked up for 13 years in MSOP. After the first nine of those years, Meyer had completed all required MSOP treatment phases, and also had constructed an 18-page Predischarge Plan, which, among other things, listed Meyer's strategies for not reoffending.[3] Yet, to date (start of 2013), Mike Meyer remains locked up in MSOP. So too do all other MSOP detainees, many of whom occupy the same circumstance as Meyer does.

Among the 18 states with roughly similar sex offender commitment programs, only MSOP (extant as such for 18 years presently, longer than all but one other such state) and three other (but far newer) commitment programs have released *none* of their detainees. Part of what separates MSOP from other, comparable states is that those states rest release decisions in their courts.

---

1 *p. 21.*

2 *Emphases supplied.*

3 *Larry Oakes, "OK'd for Transfer, but Going Nowhere", Star Tribune, June 9, 2008, p. Al.*

Minnesota, until 2008, left that decision to the Commissioner of Human Services (a political appointee). Legislation in that year placed that decision with a review board. However, that board's members are in turn appointed by that same commissioner. This means that the release decision is still made by political appointees under the indirect superior political power (including replacement of any such appointee).[1] In a gubernatorial administration resolutely opposed to MSOP releases, as was the Pawlenty Administration in 2008, it is completely understandable that those politically subordinate board members *never* approved a single release.

In the ensuing administration of Governor Mark Dayton, notwithstanding press releases from the Governor's Office expressing concern about MSOP's burgeoning growth and cost, the political appointees filling that board still have authorized only that single sex offender's release in 2012. Explaining this, Larry Oakes observes: "Because no one can guarantee an offender won't rape or molest again, the safest course for political appointees has been to keep offenders locked up regardless of how their treatment has progressed". The political nature sex offender commitment has thus effectively barred the exit door, making release impossible regardless of perfect compliance with every treatment demand made upon any MSOP detainee. All promises by MSOP of the possibility of release by completing their treatment regimen and convincing treatment staff of 'meaningful change', as they demand, are utterly illusory for this reason of political considerations as well.

Q.E.D[2].: MSOP Is a Permanent Detention Scheme

Even the State of Minnesota's own courts have begun saying that Minnesota's sex offender commitment program is permanent detention by another name. The Minnesota Court of Appeals, in In re Tolbert, 2008 WL 3898457, at *5 (Minn. App. 2008), stated that the district court in that case had made a finding that MSOP is not actually a treatment program, but only a detention facility. In Tolbert, Olmstead County District Judge Kevin Lund stated: "Since no patient has ever been discharged ... the [MSOP] is not a treatment program, and [MSOP] facilities are not treatment facilities. These facilities are nothing more than detention facilities". For this reason, Judge Lund refused to commit rapist Robert Tolbert. However, although appellate courts are supposed to give such trial courts' findings binding effect, in Tolbert, the Court of Appeals swept *that* finding away, calling it "nothing more than dicta". Hardly. Such appellate decisions reduce

1 *Larry Oakes, ibid.*

2 *Quod erat demonstrandum (that has been demonstrated).*

respect for law and illustrate that sex offender commitment is a politically mandated outcome in any such case. Judge Lind's decision had ordered that Tolbert be freed. The Court of Appeals dissolved that order and committed Tolbert anyway.[1]

Other states have taken notice of Minnesota's misuse of commitment as a device to detain sex offenders otherwise about to be released. The Vermont Legislative Council, in 2005, issued a report concluding that Minnesota "is essentially warehousing sex offenders in mental health facilities at a cost far higher than that to incarcerate them in prison ...".

Since 2007, MSOP has declared this mission statement: "To promote public safety by providing a safe and secure environment in which civilly committed sex offenders are offered the opportunity to participate in high-quality treatment programs to enhance the success of their reentry into society."[2]

Recalling the lack of releases to date (save one in 2012), and MSOP's own projection that assumes *no significant number of releases during at least the next ten years*, the closing line about 're-entry into society' is a sheer lie. Given the truth about inadequate and ever-shifting treatment approaches in MSOP, the only truth to the phrase, 'high-quality treatment programs' is that 'programs' has been in the plural — sequentially, each one requiring participants to start over. This is the 'bad joke version' of the never-ending series of tasks assigned to Hercules.

Of course, in the case of any pedosexual (the accurate term, stripping away its faux 'medicalization'), MSOP itself will always say, in excusing its failure to release same, even after a decade or more of its treatment, that the detainee continues to have pedophilic attractions, and therefore presents some level of risk of reoffense — and hence, does not possess a 'guarantee' of public safety. All of the foregoing confirms the previous point, not so directly stated, however, until now: *MSOP is simply a thinly disguised, artificially treatment-justified permanent (natural life) preventive detention scheme.*

In testimony to a state legislative committee, Prof. Eric Janus, president of William Mitchell College of Law, argued that the civil commitment of criminals is a 'Pandora's box' that could reach beyond sex offenders.

> "'We as a society will be locking up people for years, based not on a crime that they committed ... but because they pose a risk, and we think they might (someday) commit some undefined, unspecified crime."'
>
> *L. Oakes, ibid.*

---

1 *Larry Oakes, "Locked in Limbo", Star Tribune, June 8, 2008. p. Al.*

2 *L. Oakes, ibid.*

Professor Janus authored the book, *Failure to Protect — America's Sexual Predator Laws and the Rise of the Preventive State*, expanding on this point.

MSOP Staff as a Nest of Absolutist Fanatics

MSOP's theory of extremely intense, all-consuming, and endless sex offender treatment is shared by virtually no one else. Further, even if sex offender therapists elsewhere in the state would be willing to adopt MSOP's treatment methods, the cost of such residential treatment would be extremely prohibitive. It is clear that no 'commitment graduates' would have any resources to pay for same. Moreover, because of the intensity of this day treatment that MSOP proposes, employment of former MSOP detainees would seem impossible, foreclosing even this small contributing source to partly defray that cost. Instead, it is implicit in this MSOP proposal that government would have to pick up the entire tab for this network of regional 'treatment houses' sanctioned by MSOP, at a huge aggregate cost, perhaps rivaling MSOP's current per-diem cost.

This obviously reduces the incentive to demand commitment releases (given such high per-diem ex-detainee costs). Again, it is difficult to believe that MSOP is serious about this suggestion — rather, once again, it is another variant of the argument that 'these guys are too dangerous to release'. Except, of course, that that assertion is simply false.

In sum as to this section, MSOP is a form of thinly disguised preventive detention. And worse, it is exhibiting that classic symptom of all bloated bureaucracy: constant persuasion efforts to justify its continued, and even expanded, size and mission. In other words, it is preventive detention seeking to be deemed governmentally and socially institutional. It must be stopped, or historically rooted and still honored concepts of individual liberty in this country will die a slow and ugly death.

MSOP Conveniently Ignores What Always Worked Before Commitment

Note carefully that the claim that release would result in 'higher risk sex offenders' than before being managed through community-based treatment is simply false. Before the start of the insane ramp-up of commitments in Minnesota (even if this is calculated as commencing in 1992, as the MSOP Report itself claims), community resources were always used. This includes not only community treatment, but also especially Intensive Supervised Release (ISR), which actually pre-dated that 1992 ramp-up by one year. Very shortly thereafter, 'conditional release' (effectively, a long-term version of ISR) was also implemented.

It should be noted that, in all that time, only one spectacular instance of recidivism occurred (Alfonso Rodriguez), in an isolated corner of the state where full ISR resources were not yet deployed. Thus, both before and during the commitment ramp-up to its current status, community resources have been used, and, in the case of ISR or conditional relase, recidivism has been successfully prevented.

Consider this: as of mid-1994, almost two thirds of Minnesota's adult, felony-level sex offenders under either probation or parole were assigned specially trained agents specifically for the purpose of supervising released sex offenders. Many of the other third, including 'Level III' sex offenders released from prison, were assigned to ISR agents, who supervise certain high-risk offenders (mostly sex offenders) released from prison. State law allows the Commissioner of Corrections to keep sex offenders on ISR for up to their full term of supervised or conditional release. Offenders under ISR have frequent contacts with their agents (including home visits more often than once per week). In fact, during the first of four sequential phases of ISR, the required minimum is four face-to-face contacts per week.

During the first phase of ISR, a sex offender is subject to strict house arrest, except for work hours. Throughout the rest of ISR, a daily curfew applies. Electronic surveillance is optional during all ISR phases. In addition, a host of 'special conditions' can be applied to sex offenders on any form of post-prison supervised release, at agent discretion, subject to Department of Corrections guidelines. These include, for instance, all forms of sex offender treatment and related programs; prohibitions on: living in a building where children are present, possession of sexually explicit materials, owning or operating a computer allowing internet access or otherwise accessing the internet, contact with minors; and being within specified distance of schools, parks, etc. Other requirements include obtaining permission to take a given job and to move to a new residence, and submitting to polygraph examination.[1]

Also, many sex offenders are assigned upon release to reside in a halfway house, providing security as to comings and goings of its residents. Sex offenders account for 74% of those on any form of supervised release living at these facilities.[2]

Minnesota law has required 'community notification' regarding sex offenders released from prison since 1996. The law requires widespread notification for 'Level III' sex offenders (those deemed most likely to reoffend), plus lesser notification measures for lower-level sex offenders.[3]

---

1 *Ibid, p. 57.*

2 *Ibid, p. 95.*

3 *State of Minnesota, Office of Legislative Auditor, "Community Supervision of Sex Offenders", January, 2005, pp. x, 39, 42.*

Minnesota State Senator Linda Berglin observed in an interview that most Minnesota sex offenders live successfully in the community, adding that some of those committed to MSOP could have been doing so as well, had they not been committed.[1]

As a significant comparison, Wisconsin also has a sex offender commitment law, as noted above. That commitment program had already discharged 14 sex offenders after what was deemed successful treatment. In addition, 19 others won release in court, based on legal challenges or risk reassessments. Of all 33 of these releasees, only two reoffended sexually (roughly 6%), a recidivism rate far below all predictions by those that advocate sex offender commitment.[2] This means that these men were *never* the 'recidivating machines' they were cast as, to justify their commitment. Doubtlessly, the same is true in Minnesota's MSOP.

Self-Defeating Statistics

MSOP's own statistics matching treatment to lowered recidivism actually show a lack of need for commitment, and the impossibility of MSOP attaining its stated goal of releasees with a zero-percent probability of reoffense.

Although this pair of points has been mentioned in passing, statistics offered in the MSOP Report[3] require a closer inspection. Among those statistics are these comparisons of note:

1 The cited Duwe & Goldman 2010 article found a 19.5% average (base rate) recidivism rate among sex offenders who did not complete sex offender treatment in prison, as opposed to a 13.4% recidivism rate for those who did so. Taking these statistics as valid and as establishing what they purport to (albeit strictly arguendo), this comparison actually stands for the proposition that treatment completion in a prison-based (and hence, probably more intensive) treatment program of considerable duration only reduces recidivism *somewhat*; it does not extinguish it. Indeed, among 'completers', there apparently still was roughly 69% of the non-completer's rate of recidivism (13.4/19.5%). Note that "... the DOC prioritizes treatment to those sex offenders who are assessed as moderate to high risk to reoffend."[4]

2 Because no other sex offender treatment program on the planet is either as intense or as over-the-top in length as MSOP, there are no statistics that would support MSOP's claim that 'more

1 *L. Oakes, "Locked in Limbo", supra, p. Al.*

2 *L. Oakes, ibid.*

3 *p. 11.*

4 *Ibid, p. 115.*

is better'. Indeed, another comparison of note on page 11 is between completers and non-completers of *community-based* 'outpatient' sex offender treatment programs — obviously, much 'lighter' treatment. In that comparison, recidivism was *reduced by a larger percentage* (59% of the comparative rate for non-completers still recidivated after completion). So actually, these figures really suggest that there is a *'fall-off'*, not an increase, of *recidivism-reducing impact*, as treatment programs become more intense and longer.

3 Because this is so, MSOP is neither needed nor helpful, beyond the impact of prison-based and community-based treatment programs. These figures, strongly suggest that 'more is not better' when it comes to sex offender treatment, and that prison-based (as opposed to community-based) treatment does not reduce recidivism by as much as community based treatment. Thus they point up the impossibility of any treatment program, particularly a very long, very intense treatment program like MSOP, actually attaining nil or negligible recidivism rates. That is an illusory, unattainable goal, and it must be relinquished.

Toxic Treatment

MSOP's 'treatment' Is alarmingly toxic and likely to cause worsening of participants' likelihood of recidivism.

1 In this light, MSOP's strategy of exactly these two attributes may be quite self-defeating. Indeed, elsewhere[1], the MSOP Report acknowledges that treatment can have 'boomerang' effects, actually worsening later tendencies to recidivism. "... treatment participation can either significantly reduce *or increase* an individual's risk status".[2] MSOP *asserts* that this may be due to failure in treatment, but concedes that it has no statistics upon which to base that conjecture.

2 It is, consistent with the comparisons supra, alternatively just as likely, if not more likely, that beleaguering sex offenders with too much treatment not only immures them to its intended effect, but even worse, can engender a cynical sense of being indoctrinated with propaganda, increasingly suspected of being distorted or utterly false. This in turn can lead to a 'falsus in uno' effect, in which the validity of entire treatment concepts, long acccpted by a given participant, can be cast into internal doubt, and perhaps even silently come to be rejected outright.

1 *Ibid, p. 20.*

2 *Emphasis supplied.*

3 Also, this sense of having been deceived can add a permanent distrust of therapists, and the whole program, as sources of such information. In the subsequent report by the Office of the Legislative Auditor (March, 2011), the twin MSOP frequent phenomena of refusal-to-grant module or level advancement to, and of demotion between levels or modules for, most MSOP treatment participants (many repeatedly) were discussed.

4 Taking the MSOP explanation of this at face value, at the very least, it bespeaks a kind of long-term treatment 'burnout' that makes utility of further treatment a matter of unmistakably diminishing returns. The foregoing explanation of a growing 'breach of faith' by treatment participants as the years of treatment stretch on fits this observation of 'burnout' like a proverbial glove. Moreover, the author's correspondence with MSOP treatment participants confirms the reality of this gradual 'treatment apostasy' phenomenon.

5 This being so, such long-term participants not only eventually become disillusioned with the 'world view' of sexuality delivered through treatment, but also become angry that promises of qualification for release by 'playing ball' with MSOP treatment are gradually revealed to be more and more illusory and even fraudulent.

6 In this context, one may well ask if, among other adverse outcomes, MSOP may actually be unwittingly prompting worsened likelihood of recidivism in their treatment population through this endless, intense treatment with no likely end-point or release. One may actually state this through only modest literary license as actually creating the recidivating monsters they feared and sought to tame, on an incorrect assumption that they were such monsters to begin with.

MSOP's Demand for an Exorbitant Network of MSOP-Style, Locked 'Treatment Houses', Before Considering Any Releases

Ah, but at p. 38 of that MSOP Report, it finally emerges where this false claim of 'community treatment and supervision never before' as to high-risk sex offenders was heading: "The State of Minnesota must develop alternatives to MSOP that *maintain public safety*. The current options for community-based treatment programs for the highest-risk sexual offenders are limited. Advanced training and ongoing monitoring is needed to ensure appropriate standards of care. *Once there is a 'track' in the community to appropriately support and monitor offenders*, be they in reintegration, *MSOP cost and census will go down.*".[1] This is a clever but specious argument that MSOP cannot currently (and not for quite some years) release anyone, because no community programming is currently 'safe enough'. Firstly, MSOP is obviously overlooking the formidable ISR/CR resources the DOC has amassed in the last twenty years, including overlapping layers of low-caseload field agents monitoring and surveilling their charges daily and (at least electronically) 24/7.

Because commitments are almost invariably directed at those about to be released from prison exactly to these arch-restrictive and highly enforced monitoring and surveillance regimes (not to mention the synergistic effect of intensive community notification), it is ludicrous for MSOP to claim that it alone stands the gaff. The Minnesota DOC asserts that no one to date has perpetrated a recidivistic sex crime while under these programs (now a minimum of ten years' duration). If that's not 'safe enough' ... what is?

Most importantly, MSOP is blatantly implying by this quote that, regardless of 'treatment success' and proof of 'meaningful change', it does not intend to release anyone until Minnesota has a series of locked 'inpatient' houses (à la Alpha House, Minneapolis) that use a treatment regimen and operational procedures approved by MSOP itself (for which read, endless treatment).

The MSOP Report Stoops to Inaccuracy, Distortion and Baseless Conclusions to Justify Its Perpetuation and Expansion

The overall aim and tenor of that 2011 MSOP Report was a persuasion campaign toward obtaining legislative funding for yet another major expansion of the MSOP Moose Lake, MN, facility — in that case, a requested additional 400 beds. In making this request, the MSOP Report cites the recent annual pace of sex offender commitments, as if such commitments comprise an inexorable given.[2] Of course, it is not. If anything, all of the foregoing sections of this work state a compelling case for ending such commitments altogether. Yet nowhere does the MSOP Report mention the option of non-growth of MSOP's detainee population, whether through releases or reduced or ended commitments.

That report also uses inflated figures for the comparative costs of in-home-and GPS-monitoring, to add to other costs of intensive supervision (ISR) and outpatient treatment of released sex offenders, as if to suggest that the cost differential between commitment and

1 *Emphases supplied.*

2 *Ibid., pp 17, 51.*

such ISR isn't that much.[1] In point of fact, however, even using those inflated figures at the top end of the ISR cost range, those costs total only $24,000 per year, as opposed to the annual cost of commitment, per inmate (i.e., post-commitment detention, ignoring all costs of such commitment proceedings and other costs categories specified) of $120,000.

In the following sections[2], that report argues that committed individuals needed to be committed, on the claim that MSOP is the only way to provide sufficient treatment to prevent those committed from recidivating. This is a baldly baseless assertion at work, not requiring an elaborate response here. In previous sections, this work has demonstrated beyond serious question that completely adequate alternative ways of sex offense recidivism prevention are in place, such that there is simply no need for MSOP. To the contrary, the MSOP Report continues a long-asserted, but totally baseless theme that, but for commitment and MSOP, recidivism among those detained would be a 100% forgone conclusion. That itself is the 'big lie'.

In a change of tack, that report[3] discusses sex abuse prevention efforts in Minnesota, suggesting that MSOP has a place in prevention of molestations[4]. In that section, the report also cites Cordelia Anderson and other political activists in the anti-rape, anti-molestation, anti-domestic abuse alliance, implying that those political forces back civil commitment of sex offenders, as if *daring* the Legislature to take any action that would even merely lessen the rate of commitment, much less to cause anyone to be released. Thus, it is no wonder that the Legislative Auditor felt compelled to rejoin all of these cheap tricks of political manipulation by way of his own report[5].

Finally, that report[6] slides into its real pitch by offering a number of competing options, each of which would *add at least 200 beds* to MSOP bedspace. This, of course, deliberately ignores the other options of capping MSOP occupancy, curtailing commitments, requiring releases, putting a time limit (as Washington) on commitment term, or simply ending commitment of sex offenders altogether.

In response to other specific passages in that MSOP Report, first note that, on page 9, it *crows* about the fact that it offers "the *longest treatment durations*", apparently as a goal in and of itself.[7] In contrast,

---

1 *Ibid., Table 1.1, p. 12.*

2 *pp. 15–18.*

3 *At pp. 40 et seq.*

4 *By preventive detention, it implies — see p. 43.*

5 *OLA Report, cited passim.*

6 *pp. 50 et seq.*

7 *Ibid, p. 9.*

on p. 14 the report notes on that treatment length in the SOTP program of sex offender treatment in MCF-Lino Lakes and MCF-Rush City is a mere 20 months. Nowhere does the report truly explain this disparity or justify it, other than suggesting that those committed, purely because of that commitment, present supposedly such a certain probability of recidivism that long-term detention is necessitated.

Additional assertions in that MSOP Report are also worthy of close critical examination.

Assertion: Capacity (bed space) of MSOP facilities currently totals 747[1]

Fact: True, however, current detainee total occupancy amounts to only 600 (as of January, 2011)[2], leaving substantial room for additional detainees before running out of bed space (without expansion).

Assertion: "The past year has seen a decrease in both referrals and commitments."[3]

Fact: It is unclear whether this refers to 2009 or 2010. Either way, by MSOP's own account, since the civil commitment process "may take several years"[4], it is extremely hard to understand how MSOP could have had final commitment figures in January, 2011, for 2010 or even for 2009. Even as to the period 2004–07, its report concedes that 11% of those commitment petitions then remained 'under review'. The MSOP Report includes no figure for 2009 or 2010 referrals. At p. 21, however, it does cite 567 referrals in the four-year period, 2004–07. This calculates to an average of 142 per year in that period. The OLA Report differs, citing on p. 28 an average in that period plus the next year (2008) of 157 referrals per year. It does cite a referral figure for 2009: 114. However, prior to the 'balloon' of referrals in December, 2003, ushering in the current period of sustained higher referrals, commitments comprised a higher portion (61%) of the lesser number (28) of offenders referred.[5] In contrast, the OLA Report cites 42% as the portion of offenders referred in 2004–08 and thus far (as commenced in 2009) are far higher than pre-2003 numbers. Further, the respective numbers for 2004–08, as shown[6] exhibit a statistical 'random walk', rather than a clear downward trend. Consequently, applying 42% to that average (157), a more likely forecast, barring any conjectural future downward trend, would be 66 commitments per year, not the 50 predicted by MSOP.

1 *Moose Lake: 550, plus St. Peter: 197 (p. 12).*

2 *Moose Lake: 450; St. Peter: 150.*

3 *Ibid., p. 16.*

4 *Ibid, p. 21.*

5 *Ibid, p. 27.*

6 *Ibid, p. 30, fig. 2.1.*

Assertion: "It is not uncommon for successful completion of treatment for the most motivated civilly committed client to take an average of eight years."[1]

Fact: The cited source, Appendix B to the Treatment section of that report, does not include data on releases in any state. So this assertion cannot be verified. Moreover, although that report calls such commitment releases in other states 'few', that characterization is numerically inaccurate. Of the 19 other states with sex offender commitment laws, New York and Texas must be excluded in this connection, as partly or wholly based on non-institutional commitments. Pennsylvania's tiny commitment program should also be excluded, as exclusively for juveniles.[2]

Other states' releases, as a percentage of those committed, vary between 8% and 17%[3]. Taking the median between these (12.5%) and applying that to the national total currently under commitment (over 4,000), then a figure substantially over 500 more correctly estimates the number of releasees from sex offender commitment nationwide to date. This is far from a 'few' releases.

Taking this further as is relevant to MSOP, even using the '8-year' figure, roughly one third of MSOP detainees have been in MSOP that long. Is MSOP saying that none of that one third (about 200 detainees) have been sufficiently motivated to complete treatment by now? Wouldn't that be 'uncommon', given the MSOP 80% ratio of treatment participants? Or instead, is the actual truth that MSOP keeps demoting participants to lower levels or modules within them, and keeps declining to promote them to the next module or level, all in the well-orchestrated plan to prevent any participants from 'successfully completing' treatment?

Assertion: A panel of judges should be appointed to preside in all sex offender commitment cases, in order to allow such judges to develop an 'expertise' and to receive the same 'pertinent updates from the field of risk assessment'.[4]

Fact: This appeal to 'expertise' is nothing more than an invitation to judges to play at 'armchair psychology' while individuals' lifetime liberty hangs in the balance. It trivializes the deadly-earnest nature of the case. Such 'armchair psychology' in the area of impressions about sex offenders has been a pure cavalcade of horrific misinformation and utterly false (and malicious) propaganda calculated to create not just bias, but extreme fear and loathing of sex

---

1 *MSOP Report, p. 34.*

2 *OLA Report, pp. 16–17.*

3 *Ibid, p. 17.*

4 *MSOP Report, pp. 37–38.*

offenders. The truth is that, although judges protest (and perhaps sincerely so) that they are either immune to all that, or can set it aside, in reality, it creeps into their decisions on a subconscious, visceral level, which then is covered over with glib rationalizations. Both trial level judgments of commitment and appellate opinions upholding them are rife with such rationalizations already. Only rationalizations, for instance, could justify commitment of ripe old men who no longer have any serious interest in sex, and who have even less physical ability to do anything about it even if they did.

Another truth is that all information weighed by a judge in a commitment case should enter his awareness only through the admission process as to evidence and testimony. Even to allow so-called 'judicial notice' in such a field as so-called forensic study of behaviors of sex offenders (inherently a would-be seer-like guessing game of prediction of what an individual may or may not do in the future) invites terrible errors of science, asserted with high, but utterly incorrect, confidence in the supposed certainty of the conclusion stated. None of the 'information' in that field can be considered as 'hard science' gospel truth; all of it is highly controversial. Matters are proclaimed one day and are de-dunked the next. Much of the field appears driven by the urge (or paid assignment) to find some scientifically plausible basis upon which to justify commitment of at least some subsets among sex offenders, if not reasons-to-commit applicable to all sex offenders. Matters pronounced as new, firm scientific conclusion are often soon examined more closely and denounced as 'junk science'.

In response to the specific proposal to 'disseminate' to such judges 'updates' on sex offender risk assessment, the question immediately arises: who decides what is 'valid' science and disseminates it — MSOP, perhaps? Clearly, that appears to be the intent behind this proposal.[1] It is a ploy to pure indoctrination of judges, end-running that evidentiary process by sanction of an overarching judicial administration, allowing injection of bias under the rubric of judicially accepted, noticeable 'facts'. The fact is: if judges from Mars (and hence, utterly removed from all of this bias-masquerading-as-science) were available, any sex offender facing a commitment petition would be well advised to seek recusal and replacement by said Martian. The suggestion of establishing such a panel goes diametrically in the opposite direction. Indeed, in counties that assign a specific judge (or set of judges) to hear such commitment petitions, the commitment respondent should seek recusal or removal from all judges therein, on a due process claim

1 *Ibid.*

of unconscious, experiential bias. Where such specialized panels exist, judges on them invariably rack up much higher percentages of commitment judgments than do 'non-panel' judges.

Assertion: The DOC referred sex offenders for commitment in only 45 counties in 2008.

Fact: Appendix A (pp. 39–40) to the "Civil Commitment Process" section of that report, which purports to show this, is woefully incomplete, listing only 45 counties and only 32 of 151 commitments that year.

Conclusion asserted: "Civil commitment programs for sexual offenders are [a] necessary tool in an effective, comprehensive statewide management strategy."

Fact: No, it is not. As described, DOC management of released sex offenders, across the most recent 20 years, has become unbelievably restrictive and presently includes many mandatory directives, notably community-based treatment for all sex offenders who did not receive or accept treatment in prison, and including community-based aftercare for all who did. Monitoring of released sex offenders (because they are on either ISR or conditional release for a minimum of the first 10 years post-release) is intense and is in operation 24/7. Surveillance occurs at least daily, and often many times daily.

It is extremely difficult to believe that, given this network of close management, any sex offender would even be able to plan to commit a sex offense, without such plan being detected. Even impromptu, sheer-impulse sexual assault would hardly be possible, given monitoring of whereabouts, restriction of movement at most hours of day and night, and the aforementioned surveillance. Offenders wear GPS-tracking anklets, operate GPS-equipped vehicles registered with their agents, and are intensely watched by beat cops aware of their residence. Other measures far too numerous to mention here are also in place, not to mention public notification and the self-appointed, spying vigilantes it engenders.

If all of this is not 'safe enough', nothing could be. With only extremely rare exception, released sex offenders do not fit the stereotype embodied by Alfonso Rodriguez or Joseph Duncan. Commitment is inherently unfair, in that psychological science cannot identify the 'Rodriguezes' or the 'Duncans' (as rare as they mercifully are). Because of this, hundreds (soon to be more than 1,000) in Minnesota alone are locked up under the suspicion that somewhere among them lurks such a walking horror movie. Yet even the intense forensic assessments in MSOP itself cannot ferret out who (if anyone there) fits this mold.

Meanwhile, somewhere in the free world, such a monster, with no criminal record yet, awaits an opportunity for immeasurable psychopathy in action.

All of the 'shotgun-guessing' in the world taking place in commitment cases daily accomplishes only this 'hundreds-to-one' 'repeat-incarceration', through sheer repulsion, hysteria, and the most unbelievably baseless, deliberately biased junk-science ever to disgrace the principle of academic research in a courtroom.

Twenty years from now, calmer heads will shake in disbelief, wondering what in the world possessed legislators, jurists, and the public at large to so radically lose their collective reason and proportion over one topic so obsessively. This really must cease, before all of law devolves into sheer ad hominem accusation and unrestrained emotionality.

Chapter 11
Unconstitutional Bill of Attainder

The Minnesota Sex Offender Commitment Program, under both of its alternative supporting statutes, constitutes an unconstitutional 'Bill Of Attainder' against sex offenders thereby described.

Numerous constitutional challenges to various sex offender commitment laws around the country have been stiff-armed aside by courts. One claim apparently universally overlooked is that at least some such laws, by virtue of their facial extremism and by the manner in which they are applied and in which commitment is administered, amount to punitive 'bills of attainder'. Both the federal and state governments are prohibited by side-by-side sections in the U.S. Constitution (Article I, Sections 9 and 10) from legislating 'bills of attainder'. Attainder, historically speaking, in pre-revolutionary times, referred to bills authorizing summary execution on sight of one (or more than one) named or identified by description in the bill. It was, for lack of a closer term, 'legalized murder'.

Typically, those against whom it was wielded were declared to be enemies of the state, or pirates, or chronic criminals of one kind or another. At its worst, one could be subjected to attainder simply for criticizing the monarch or the government or any of its laws. A lesser form, a 'bill of pains and penalties', did not call for execution, but typically called for indeterminate imprisonment in some dungeon, or confiscation of all of one's property, or banishment. Very early in American case law, it was held that such 'pains and penalties' were implicitly included in the bar on 'bills of attainder'.[1]

The currently prevailing, case law-based definition of whether a legislative act comprises a bill of attainder consists of two elements:

1 whether the act either specifically names a person or group or identifies same by sufficiently specific description; and

2 whether the act inflicts penalties within the meaning of the bill of attainder prohibition.[2]

It is true that a third 'pseudo-element' is often tacked onto this formulation, to-wit: "... without provision of the protections of a

1 *See discussion in Drehman v. Stifle, 75 U.S. 595, 19 L.Ed. 508 (1870).*

2 *See: Nixon v. Adm'r of General Services, 433 U.S. 425, 473 (1977).*

judicial trial".[1] However, the mere grant of the formality of a trial does not suffice to avoid the status of the underlying legislative act as a bill of attainder.

Rather, the focus of this third element is that the act must not deprive an accused of the protection afforded by judicial process.[2] Hence, where the nature of the legislative act is to pronounce upon the 'guilt' of the party, it deprives that party of the meaningful protection of a trial.[3] In such circumstance, the 'trial' that follows becomes purely perfunctory and, as we have seen from decisions reviewed supra, often downright Kafkaesque.

It is, held[4] the unfairness of trial by a large body, peculiarly susceptible to popular clamor, that underlies the attainder prohibition. Certainly, such popular clamor, and the legislative pandering that catered to it, reflects the 1994 Minnesota Legislative Special Session, convened for the sole purpose of enacting Minnesota's SDP law and revising and renaming its SPP law.

As to those laws, the legislature defined a class by past conduct.[5] In so defining the classes established by the new SDP law and the revised SPP law, the Minnesota legislature effectively decided the issue of preventive detention (under rubric of 'commitment') before the trial of any individual thus included in either defined class.

We have already seen this through the preceding examination of the farce of commitment trials, based only on such past records and acts of the individual, supplemented only by the rankest 'junk science' opinions of hired-gun psychologists acting as character assassins.

This combination utterly negates the protections of a trial, and leaves it entirely in the 'discretion' of a judge as to whether to render the individual over to natural-life preventive detention, cloaked only in the thinnest gossamer veil of supposed release through treatment. To be sure: that, and Arbeit Macht Frei.

It is not necessary that there be a legislative announcement of punishment as an aim in order to constitute a bill of attainder. Moreover, the protection of the Bill of Attainder Clause is quite broad, not only barring deprivations of liberty and of property, but also of

---

1 *See, e.g.: State v. Whitaker, 700 S.E.2d 215 (N.C. 2010).*

2 *State v. Swartz, 601 N.W. 2d 348 (Iowa 1999).*

3 *Longmoor v. Nilsen, 285 F.Supp.2d 132 (D. Conn. 2003).*

4 *Keyishian v. Board of Regents, 255 F.Supp. 981 (W.D. N.Y. 1966).*

5 *See, e.g.: Berry v. Lucas County Bd. of Comm'rs, 2010 WL 480981 (N.D. Ohio 2010) (described in terms of conduct that, because it is past conduct, operates only as a designation of particular persons); WMX Technologies, Inc. v. Gasconade County, Mo. 105 F.3d 1195 (8th Cir. 1997) (ditto); Lee v. City of Villa Rica, 449 S.E.2d 295 (Ga. 1994).*

political and civil rights, such as the rights to vote, to equal treatment by law, and to practice professions, operate a business, hold public office, advocate political causes (etc.).[1] Another point is that whether punishment is inflicted by a law is impacted by whether a person affected by the law can escape its application by modifying present or future conduct.[2]

> "SVP laws make an extraordinary moral and constitutional claim: We permit our government — despite its democratic values — to pick out a small group of people and treat them in a way that we would never allow ourselves to be treated. We allow this group — and only this group — to be locked up to prevent unspecified crimes that they might (or might not) commit at some unspecified time in the future. These laws violate a fundamental premise of our constitutional system: as a general matter, the State can take away a person's physical liberty only if he or she is charged with a specific crime, and convicted of that crime according to a set of strict procedural protections. As Justice Jackson stated in Williamson v. United States, 'Imprisonment to protect society from predicted but unconsummated offenses is so unprecedented in this country and so fraught with danger of excesses and injustice that I am loath to resort to it'."
>
> *Eric S. Janus, "Closing Pandora's Box: Sexual Predators and the Politics of Sexual Violence"*[3]

Joel A. Sherwin, writing in "Are Bills of Attainder the New Currency? Challenging the Constitutionality of Sex Offender Regulations That Inflict Punishment Without the Safeguard of a Judicial Trial"[4], sets forth the case that sex offenders can satisfy the foregoing specificity requirement by analogizing their situation to past groups that have succeeded in invoking the attainder bar. Because the details of this analysis are chiefly of interest only to lawyers, they will not be discussed here.

Suffice it to say that a sex offender described in a commitment statute by characteristics that merely define a given sub-group of sex offenders, and because commitment does not turn on any present criminal offense, but rather only on an asserted 'tendency' (high

---

1 *Cummings v. Missouri, 71 U.S. 277 (1867).*

2 *Cummings, supra; cf.: American Communications Ass'n. v. Douds, 339 U.S. 382 (1950).*

3 *34 Seton Hall L. Rev. 1233 (2003-04).*

4 *37 Pepperdine Law Rev. 1301 (2009-10), at pp. 1331–33.*

likelihood) of *future* offenses, and because, at the time of commitment, there is nothing any sex offender can do to 'undo' any past sex offense, it is clear that such sex offender laws are *singling out* certain sub-groups of sex offenders for their *characteristics*, not as a means of *prohibiting* present or future offenses, and it is also clear that the included sex offenders cannot 'escape' or otherwise avoid that classification-by-description by refraining from doing, or by doing, any particular thing.

Indeed, a sex offender commitment trial is replete with evidence of certain traits (including behaviors-as-traits) that either comprise or support one or more descriptive elements for the classification subject to commitment. The whole trial is a matter of group characteristics, personally applied. The bottom line, according to this cogent argument, is that sub-classes of sex offenders specified in sex offender commitment laws comprise descriptive categorization as a basis for the infliction of commitment, thereby fulfilling the 'specificity requirement' of group identification.

The other element of a bill of attainder is the infliction of some penal measure upon those meeting the specific identification or categorical description. As Sherwin points out, "The punitive nature of a legislative enactment can be found according to one of three tests: historical, functional, or motivational".[1]

Taking the last test first[2], Sherwin observes that "the motivational test is an inquiry into the legislative record (including legislative committee hearings and debates) to see if there is evidence of a legislative intent to punish". In this connection, Sherwin noted "the importance of the surrounding context and circumstances to the analysis of punitive intent of the legislative act at issue". Referring back to footnote 114 (ibid., p. 1320), Sherwin quotes Nixon v. Adm'r of General Services[3], for "one of the major concerns that prompted the prohibition against bills of attainder: 'the fear that the legislature, in seeking to pander to an inflamed popular constituency, will find it expedient openly to assume the mantle of judge — or worse still, lynch mob'."

Most sex offender commitment laws in the country were enacted in reaction to some particularly heinous sex crime, or to the release, or looming release, of some sex offender with an especially horrendous or disgusting record of sex crimes. In that context, the 'popular constituency' of the state in question was considerably inflamed by incessant, incendiary media coverage of the crime or offender being singled out. There can be no question that the general mood of the

1 *Ibid., p. 1333).*

2 *Ibid, footnote 190.*

3 *433 U.S. 425, 480 (1977).*

populace in that furor is fairly summarized as a rageful lashing out — truly as close as the law allows to the veritable 'lynch mob' mentality feared in the Nixon case.

To all appearances, the state legislature thereupon acted with stunning, extremely uncharacteristic speed, either passing a sex offender act as a freestanding proposal or as part of an ensemble of draconian measures imposing other restrictions on non-committed sex offenders as well. This aspect of great haste, in such a highly charged emotional context, itself supports the notion of a legislative aim to punish sex offenders (beyond the sentences that they are serving or have completed). "SVP laws were developed to address a pressing political and public safety imperative, incapacitating potentially dangerous sex offenders beyond the legally mandated end of their criminal sentence,"[1] adding, at p. 380, "... Treatment may be a right of those committed, but it is not a justification for commitment. The principal objective is to protect society, not to rehabilitate."

More to the point, committee hearings and (especially floor debates, most especially when being televised live or later, are typically replete with vile vituperation against sex offenders in general and certain kinds of them, and of individual sex offenders. Further, as to sex offender commitment proposals specifically, legislators typically opine to the necessity to 'get sex offenders off the streets' in general, and to keep them locked up permanently.[2]

Usually, very little is discussed by legislators in those fora about providing therapy to sex offenders, much less about doing so with an eye to minimizing length of stay of individuals in committed status. To the contrary as to later judicial decisions applying makeweight considerations to support the constitutionality of sex offender commitment, legislators don't even discuss, much less focus on commitment as a means of rehabilitation. The aim is pure incapacitation (about which more, infra, as a punishment aim).

Suffice to say that, for anyone willing to spend the time to investigate legislators' pronouncements in consideration of sex offender commitment, overt statements and implications of such aims to thereby punish sex offenders, or at least the object sub-class of sex offenders, will invariably be found in substantial numbers and evincing high states of extro-punitive emotionality — or at least, convincingly acting the part.

---

1 *Accord: R. Prentky, E. Janus, et al., "Sexually Violent Predators in the Courtroom: Science on Trial", Psychology, Public Policy, and Law, Vol. 12, p. 357 at 358 (2006).*

2 *Cf.: 1994 Minn. Laws, Chapter 636, Art. 8, Section 20, citing the need for 'confinement' of sex offenders beyond their sentences through the vehicle of civil commitment.*

This last possibility opens the door to an alternative view. Consider that, in *advance*, certain legislators or their political backers *engineered* the *appearance* of spontaneous news coverage — which just 'happened' to be highly synchronous and orchestrated in appearance, with very carefully crafted inflammatory propaganda. Consider the further possibility that the commitment proposal was itself not spontaneous and speedy, but in fact bore the appearance of surprising levels of 'constitutional bullet-proofing', and of careful tailoring to avoid any unintended discharges from commitment.

In other words, consider that such commitment legislation was privately deliberated and conspired for months, particularly for maximum effect as self-serving political theater. Does this mean it's not punitive in character? Au contraire, such advance careful deliberation connotes *exactly such punitivity*. Moreover, such punishment is the most egregiously abusive kind: not in response to any present crime, but solely as preventive detention.

Not to mention that, between such advance conniving and the permanent lock-up imposed, such legislation is pure Machiavellian evil at work, victimizing the politically defenseless for political career gain. Will the American public continue to be duped by such crass political yanking of its 'emotional chain'? That remains to be seen.

Eric S. Janus & Robert A. Prentky, "Forensic Use of Actuarial Risk Assessment with Sex Offenders"[1], states "SVP laws ... are morally and constitutionally suspect: by locking people up for long periods of time in order to prevent future crimes, SVP laws challenge deeply held notions of justice and ethics". Being, one is tempted to think, more charitable to such legislators than is warranted, Sherwin concludes on this point more cautiously as follows.

> "... Sex offenders incite the passions and outrage of the public. For legislators in highly publicized areas of law, 'the promulgation of criminal laws affords an irresistible chance to align themselves with the victims of crime and against the criminal element, [which is] a compelling political symmetry accentuated in modern times by the soundbite imagery of the media'."
>
> *Quoting Wayne A. Logan, "Democratic Despotism and Constitutional Constraint ...", 12 Wm. & Mary Bill of Rights Jour. 439, 495 (2004)*

In such an emotionally charged environment, there is political pressure on legislators to support sex offender bills despite the constitutional questions raised; they don't want to be viewed by their

1 *40 Am. Crim. Law Rev. 1443 — "Janus & Prentky" (2004) at p. 1447.*

constituency as 'soft', or by their colleagues or peers as sympathetic toward sex offenders. Therefore, the motivational test would likely be satisfied because such evidence reaches the concerns that Chic tact seeks to protect against

To apprehend preventive detention as the real legislative intent behind Minnesota's SDP law and the simultaneous re-writing of the newly renamed SPP law, consider these observations by Judge Randall, dissenting in Linehan II (not mentioning the attainder prohibition, but stumbling upon it in substance).

> "The legislative history of SDP, including the open debates and the recommendations and writings from staff, tell us that the overwhelming urge to pass this new version of PP/SDP statute was a direct response to *concerns about public safety. The statute was needed to ensure the continued incarceration of Dennis Linehan.* At times the word 'treatment' was mentioned, but always in passing, before *the real issue, continued confinement for reasons of public safety and deterrence*, was again the focus ...
>
> "The only honest inference is that the decks are intentionally stacked against anyone who is tagged with the prospective label 'SDP'. For reasons of public safety and deterrence, they are going to a secure locked facility, after they have served all the time they owe the state in secured locked facilities. I can no longer accept the argument that PP/SDP is about remediation and medical treatment. If medical treatment were part of the prosecution's game plan, they would bring the PP/SDP charge as soon as possible after the inmate's conviction and initial incarceration. The state has every right at that point to invoke the PP/SDP statute. In recent years they appear to deliberately choose not to invoke the statute at the onset of the person's time in prison ...
>
> "Instead, what the state does here is intentional. They wait until the target defendant is down to several months before expiration, then they invoke the PP/SDP statute, *so that the civil commitment will be used to ensure safe confinement after release* ...
>
> "Virtually the clearest argument that PP/SDP is for punishment and confinement, and not for treatment, is that we devised a civil commitment statute only for sex offenders. If sexual offenders are truly deserving of medical treatment, then why not all other felons who

> commit dangerous acts? [No] attempt is made to commit them against their will to a hospital. Respondent alludes to this reasoning, and argues that sexual offenders are dangerous in a way different from those who commit these other offenses ...
>
> "That reasoning, however, is not constitutionally significant. Instead, it proves the point. *Psychopathic personalities are the subject of preventive detention.* The state simply chooses this one class of people, to the exclusion of other classes of felons, to involuntarily commit to protect the public from any further possibility of harm — *read preventive detention.* The allusions to treatment are a guise to justify the detention ... The medical personnel at the security hospital are clear that *confinement is the guiding force*, not medical treatment."
>
> *In re Mattson, No. C5-95-452, 1995 Minn. App. LEXIS 805, unpub. op. at 2-4 (Minn. App., June 20, 1995). Linehan II, at 544 N.W.2d 322, 324-26.*[1]

Fifteen years later (2011), Judge Randall again lashed out even more emphatically, and just as eloquently, against Minnesota's sex offender commitment program.

> "The deeper issue, and the only real issue, is what we do with a system in which we warehouse these people for the rest of their lives because, out of ignorance and fear, we are afraid to do anything different. The executive, legislative, and judicial branches all 'kick the can down the road' and hope that it is someone else's problem some day when we are not up for election ... I am troubled by the reality that the psychopathic personality statute, if we are to be honest, is being used only for preventive detention. As Justice Wahl warned, 'The rigor and methodical efficiency with which the Psychopathic Personality Statute is being enforced is *creating a system of wholesale preventive detention*, a concept foreign to our jurisprudence'[2].
>
> "... In Linehan, I correctly predicted that the case was just one more step in a *continuing round to sidestep the Bill of Rights* and keep people *committed* under the SPP Commitment Act or the SDP Act (codified as Minn. Stat. 253B.01-253B.24 (2010)) in a secured facility, not for a crime, but *simply because we do not want* to let them out (Linehan 544 N.W.2d at 325).

1 *Emphases supplied.*

2 *In re Blodgett, 510 N.W.2d 910, 918 (Minn. 1994)' (Wahl, J., dissenting.*

"Finally, in 1999, I wrote a special concurrence in Joelson v. O'Keefe, 594 N.W.2d 905, 913 (Minn. App. 1999) ... In those three opinions, all 12 to 16 years ago, I said, along with Justice Wahl, what those who follow the system know: *There is no 'system of justice' in our present schematic of civil commitments ...*

"I concur separately again today because, in the recent past, this issue has broken into the open and is now in the public domain. The officials and administrative people in the Minnesota Department of Human Services (DHS), which administers SPP and SDP under the format laid down by the Minnesota Legislature, have gone public in an attempt to educate the public about the potential release of some of the detainees from the Moose Lake State Hospital and the St. Peter State Hospital. If they are released, it will be under strict terms of 'civil probation', which involves halfway houses, monitoring, medical exams, and the other means at the state's disposal to monitor and control released patients.

"Those prudent officials 'in the know' are doing this because they realize that with Minnesota's miserable track record, or 100% track record, pick your poison, of never releasing anybody, the entire scheme is due to dissolve under a load of constitutional bricks and the weight of the U.S. Constitution's Bill of Rights.

"I have said it before, but it is worth going through again, *we are not talking about criminal defendants.* The people committed had previously been convicted of sex offenses and previously served every single hour of every single day that they owed the State of Minnesota (criminally). Then, as all criminals who have served all their time, they should be released to serve an amount of time equivalent to one-third of their sentence on rigorous supervised release (it generally starts with ISR, meaning intensive supervised release) — see Minn. Stat. 244.05 (2010). Every serious crime in this state, including second-degree murder, manslaughter, kidnapping, aggravated robbery, aggravated assault producing substantial bodily harm, first-degree controlled substance crime and first-degree burglary and arson, and others equal to, or more serious than, many sex crimes, have a release date or 'an out date'. For none of these serious crimes do we wait until they are about to be discharged from prison, and then 'civilly commit them' for an indefinite period, which means for the rest of their lives. Not doing it for those crimes, but only sex crimes, is hypocritical — no other word for it.

"The 'law-and-order crowd' and the 'get-tough-on-crime crowd' have argued that sex crimes are different. No, they are not. They are serious crimes (ironically, with some less serious than the above-enumerated non-sex felonies). It is argued that those who commit sex crimes are 'sick' and have to be 'treated and cured' before they can be released. Would that logic were the case. We do not civilly commit other 'sick' people, such as kleptomaniacs, repetitive drunk-driver offenders, habitual check forgers, habitual illicit drug users and drug sellers, home burglars, thieves, second-story men and 'cat burglars', meaning, in various forms, people who are addicted to other people's money. We give them a fair trial, a fair appeal if they want one, then a reasonable and determinate sentence consisting of two-thirds behind bars and one-third on supervised release, and then we release them on probation with terms as necessary to give them a chance for rehabilitation and recovery ...

"I said in Mattson, 16 years ago: 'Preventive detention bears an eerie resemblance to the old Stalinist Russia winter resort for political dissidents at a gulag archipelago. It bears a resemblance to our own *Farewell to Manzanar*'. This is not to say that I am unaware that conditions in 1942 were different than conditions today. The Japanese Relocation Act was the considered decision of those in power during World War II. At least it was honest, not disguised as 'remedial treatment'. It was acknowledged to be pure preventive detention, preventive detention of a singled-out class of people, not for what they had done, but for what they might do. We look back on it now and learn. If history teaches us anything, it is that the past does not mandate the present. But history teaches that the past dictates that we give the past thoughtful consideration when seeking guidance for the present."

*Mattson, 1995 Minn. App. LEXIS 805, 1995 WL 365374, at *5. In re Bryant, 2011 Minn. App. Unpub. LEXIS 287 (Minn. App. 2011).*

In a second concurrence in Bryant, Judge Stauber agreed with Judge Randall's protest, adding that "only a very few (committed sex offenders) are being considered for possible provisional, but supervised release. Hundreds are essentially warehoused at public expense *after* long prison sentences, under the guise of 'treatment'.

Have we created a class of criminals who are never to be released from incarceration (and both the St. Peter and MSOP-Moose Lake facilities could be characterized as incarceration)? ..." *(Ibid)*.

It should not escape note that, since the decision panels of judges on the Minnesota Court of Appeals are assigned by threes, a double concurrence is rare, connoting agreement only in the outcome, not in the legal reasoning of the lead opinion. Mr. Bryant's commitment was affirmed, albeit only because of the exceedingly grudging concession by Judges Stauber and Randal that the present lay of Minnesota's relevant statutes forced that result. However, by their dual reference to 'preventive detention', both of these judges came as close as they could to declaring Minnesota's commitment of sex offenders unconstitutional, without doing so outright. As protests go, this was extremely forceful. The winds of change are finally blowing.

As to the alternative 'historical' test of attainder, Sherwin again quotes from Nixon, supra, at p. 473, about the abiding historical concern with "deprivations and disabilities so disproportionately severe and so inappropriate to non-punitive needs that they unquestionably ... fall within the proscription of [the Bill of Attainder Clause]".[1] Sherwin cites the comparatively lesser punishments of a ban on practising a profession and banishment as long-recognized attainder 'punishment'.[2] Of course, in a very real sense, both the intent and effect of sex offender commitment laws include a banishment — from not just one community, or even one state, but from all non-incarcerated environments everywhere. More profoundly, obviously, save only for a retroactive death penalty for sex offenses, it is impossible to name a more severe deprivation than that of one's liberty for, in all probability, the rest of that individual's life. While usually termed 'imprisonment', detention or confinement, regardless whether as a formal criminal penalty, is a classic 'punishment', for attainder purposes.[3]

We have already seen in other sections that the controls and restrictions foisted upon sex offenders by corrections departments as a condition of their release from prison are wholly adequate to prevent recidivism during the balance of their sentences. In the meantime, any given sex offender would certainly have the opportunity either to demonstrate a willingness and ability to refrain from sexual recidivism or to reveal a contrary intent or inability.

---

1 *Accord, e.g.: New York State Trawlers Assn. v. Jorling, 764 F.Supp. 24 (E.D. N.Y. 1991); Fasi v. Cayetano, 752 F.Supp. 942 (D. Haw. 1990).*

2 *See, e.g.: Cooper v. Henslee, 522 S.W.2d 391 (Ark. 1975); Rhode Island Depositors Economic Protection Corp. v. Brown, 659 A.2d 95 (R.I. 1995).*

3 *See: Consolidated Edison Co. of New York, Inc. v. Pataki, 292 F.3d 338 (2d Cir. 2002); Hogan v. Dept. of Children and Families, 964 A.2d 1213 (Conn. 2009).*

Were sex offender laws written in such a way as to evaluate a sex offender only at the end of such a term of supervised release, based on such adverse behavioral evidence, a plausible argument might be made that commitment is appropriate, rather than 'inappropriate to non-punitive needs', so as to avoid the attainder effect of 'punishment'. But as they are actually written, such commitment laws are invoked just before, and for the express purpose of thwarting, a sex offender's prison release, thus preventing the offender from having any opportunity to prove himself in the community under extremely tight controls and monitoring, as non-recidivistically oriented.

Moreover, we have also already seen that *community*-based sex offender treatment has been found to be effective and safe, particularly in conjunction with such 'short-reined' correctional supervision. In contrast, by self-profession by its own therapists and overseeing officials, treatment in sex offender commitment programs such as MSOP in Minnesota has been conceded to have so little, if any, positive effect that committed offenders undergoing such treatment are still deemed by those same staff themselves to still be too dangerous to release — and they so declare even as to senior-citizen detainees, and even a decade and more after commitment. This, without need for any fancy explication, self-evidently demonstrates that sex offender commitment is 'disproportionately severe' as to the end of community safety to be served, and is utterly 'inappropriate' to that end, or to the end of 'rehabilitation' of sex offenders through treatment. Sex offender commitment serves only one goal: lifetime preventive detention with no meaningful likelihood of release — ever. This is, in the most profound sense, a 'retroactive death sentence' — only with the execution of the detained sex offender forestalled until natural causes in the decrepitation of old age take their inevitable toll — long after any plausible need for 'prevention' has long since lapsed from those same vicissitudes of passing out of middle age. Sherwin is right: sex offender commitment fits right in with the historical atrocities of bills of attainders.

Finally, Sherwin notes at p. 1335 that the alternative 'functional' test, *almost* as a repeat of the 'motivational' test, involves an initial finding of some non-punitive purpose of the legislation under scrutiny. But even though a legislature intends the mechanism to be civil, the act must still not be so punitive in effect as to transform an intended civil remedy into a penalty. One can disprove non-punitive purpose by showing "a significant imbalance between the magnitude of the burden imposed compared" to that purported purpose, or by showing that "less burdensome alternatives" are available.[1]

---

1 *Foretich v. United States, 351 F.3d 1198, 1221 (D.C. CIr. 2003).*

Sherwin, at footnote 208[1], states that sex offender statutes "are not carefully tailored or narrow enough to be effective ... The courts' discussion of less burdensome alternatives further strengthens the proposition that the bill of attainder analysis is more stringent, resembling a higher level of scrutiny, than that of a normal rational basis review that other constitutional challenges have been held to in the sex offender context".

At this point, note that 'punishment', for attainder purposes, "may include inflicting deprivation on some blameworthy or tainted individual in order to prevent his future misconduct".[2] Obviously, this is exactly the claimed intent of sex offender commitment legislation. Nixon makes clear that the accepted means of legitimate regulation of conduct is to punish the future conduct when it occurs, whether through criminal law or civil penalties for such misconduct (e.g. statutory-damages judgments).[3]

To same effect, see: Kansas v. Hendricks[4], "Punishment serves several purposes: retributive, rehabilitative, deterrent — and preventative. One of the reasons society imprisons those convicted of crimes is to keep them from inflicting future harm, but that does not make imprisonment any the less punishment".[5] At 379–380, that dissent in Hendricks argued that a law with the aim of incapacitation might be found punitive if the confinement did not reasonably fit a medically-oriented treatment objective. Alternatively, as in Hendricks, a sanction might be labeled punitive if the state cites treatment as a reason for confinement, but requires commitment and treatment only after completion of a jail term.[6] Indeed, "... commentators have noted that 'from an individual rights perspective, the most troubling scenario is the evolution of a model that uses public health and safety rhetoric to justify procedures that are in essence punishment and detention'." Andre Yang, "Historical Criminal Punishments, Punitive Aims, and Un-'Civil' Post-Custody Sanctions on Sex Offenders"[7].

---

1 *Ibid., p. 1335.*

2 *Nixon, 433 U.S. at 476, n. 40.*

3 *Accord: United States v. Brown, 381 U.S. 437 (1965) (noting, albeit overlooked in more recent decisions, that 'punishment' serves purposes of rehabilitation and of prevention (through incarceration as personal incapacitation), as well as recently acknowledged purposes of retribution and deterrence).*

4 *521 U.S. 346, 379 (1997) (Breyer, Stevens, Souter & Ginsburg, dissenting), quoting United States v. Brown, id., at 458.*

5 *Accord: Hugo Adam Bedeau, "Punishment", The Standard Encyclopedia of Philosophy, P2 (Edward N. Zalta, ed., 2005), avail. at: http://plato.stanford.edu/archives/fa112005/entries/punishment.*

6 *Citing Allen, 478 U.S. at 369.*

7 *75 Univ. of Cincinnati Law Rev. 1299, 1320 (Spring, 2007), quoting: Logan, Jurisprudence of Punishment, at p. 1263, n. 18.*

As to Minnesota sex offender commitment in particular, consider these additional., specific indicia of punishment-in-effect:

- Minnesota has a statute requiring a sex offender in the custody of the Commissioner of Corrections who gets committed to first complete his prison sentence before transfer to the MSOP commitment facility (contrary to one committed for mental illness during a prison term).[1]
- Confinement in MSOP has been held secure enough to qualify for 'jail credit' in sentencing.[2]
- MSOP operates parallel programs both in the state prison system and also under the aegis of the Dept. of Human Services, supporting the argument that the DHS side of MSOP is the equivalent of correctional confinement.[3]
- The lack of discharges of sex offenders committed as SPP/SDP from MSOP demonstrates the true preventive-detention nature of such 'commitment'.
- The still-extant executive order by former Gov. Pawlenty barring MSOP releasees unless judicially ordered confirms the intent to keep sex offenders in commitment, regardless of completion of treatment, as preventive detention.
- Even a sex offender who has already just satisfactorily completed prison-based treatment can be, and often is, committed, suggesting the real goal of preventive detention regardless.[4]

Except in the emergency of world war, never has the U.S. Supreme Court allowed detention of an individual to survive an attainder challenge. To do so would disembowel the protection offered by that constitutional clause. History is replete with examples of ruthless monarchs and totalitarian governments, each of which can be argued to have aimed to prevent future crimes or other misconduct by use of attainder or "pains and penalties". Hence, the "legitimate regulation of conduct" cannot be deemed to include a purpose of prevention of misconduct by preventive detention.

Indeed, in Specht v. Patterson[5], the Supreme Court already ruled that the sexual psychopath commitment provision of the Colorado sex offender statute is criminal punishment (albeit without a bill of attainder claim before the court), even though that law was designed not so much as retribution as it was to keep individuals from inflicting further harm.

---

1 *See: Joelson v. O'Keefe, 594 N.W,2d 905, 911-12 (Minn. App. 1999).*

2 *Cf.: In re Green, 2007 WL 1532156 at *6 (Minn. App. 2007).*

3 *Cf.: In re Ponicki, 2009 WL 3818390 at *4 (Minn. App. 2009).*

4 *See, e.g.: In re Braaten, 2006 WL 247 4274 at * 4–7 (Minn. App. 2006).*

5 *386 U.S. 605, 18 L.Ed.2d 326, 87 S.Ct. 1209 (1967).*

Given the discussion (foregoing and elsewhere herein) of successful, adequate use of intensive supervised release provisions over substantial time periods, and of the success of post-release sex offender treatment, particularly in that intense-supervision context, it is clear that 'less burdensome alternatives' exist to the total burden of commitment detention, very likely for life, or at least all of its productive years.

Moreover, we have also already seen elsewhere herein that, despite the claims of actuarial risk assessment practitioners, true recidivism statistics show average 'base rate' sex-crime recidivism to be so low as to be nearly statistically insignificant. Even recidivism rates for previous recidivists are overwhelmed by the impact, if nothing else, of simply attaining middle-age and, ultimately, senior-citizen status.

Slicing the statistical 'pie' in ever-increasingly artful ways to find some combination of descriptors arguably applicable to a given individual, to artificially inflate the predicted probability of that individual's likelihood of recidivism, ignores the whole person at present, and worse, treats him like a statue, forever frozen in time with certain traits that doom him to such recidivism.

Folks, real life ain't that way. By our very nature, humans are not only changeable, we are constantly changing, even when we don't want to and when we are unaware of such personal change. Even firm intent to recidivate can, and usually does melt away over time as individuals experience and witness numerous events, learn of myriad things, and have discourse with any number of other individuals. Life is full of advance repentance of such temptations to evil deeds, whether petty or enormous. As surely as each one of us has experienced some such abandoned temptation, it is unfair to treat others as incapable of such abandonment of temptation. To commit someone to lifetime detention engages exactly that presumption, and then puts the seal of judicial judgment, not upon the deed, but upon the man. Nothing more accurately or completely depicts the nature of attainder than this.

Meanwhile, since the claimed, larger goal of such commitment statutes is to prevent sex crimes, those laws are an utter failure. The large category of sex crimes committed by those who have not yet been charged or convicted remains rampant, as countless news items attest. Unsolved rapes by unknown strangers still occur, and molestations by every category of individual, from parents to teachers to priests to athletic coaches, etc., continue.

Meanwhile, untold tens of millions of dollars are spent to commit each committed person and to keep him committed. Do you think this an exaggeration? Ponder for a minute these aggregate categories of expenses:

(a) initial expenses in commitment proceedings of: the prosecutorial side; the public-expense defense side; and judicial and court administration costs (complete with hugely expensive opposing experts, usually two to three-deep per side);

(b) many ensuing years of expensive treatment, housing, security, medical care (including for those beyond age 60, at much higher annual costs), and administrative costs;

(c) more rounds of additional legal costs of habeas corpus challenges to commitment;

(d) assessment and legal costs of statutory release proceedings (potentially several per inmate, when unsuccessful);

(e) defense of lawsuits by detainees for psychological malpractice, medical negligence, poor conditions of confinement, mistreatment by staff, etc.; and

(f) huge construction costs for new buildings required by expansion to accommodate more commitments.

Janus & Prentky[1], summarize these enormous costs thus: "Sexually Violent Person programs are exceedingly expensive, and growing populations of committed sex offenders will require an increasingly disproportionate share of treatment and prevention dollars ... SVP programs divert scarce funds ... from other, potentially more effective, sexual violence prevention strategies". Thus, by reason of such huge costs, that much less can be spent on sex-crime prevention programs and even on detection and apprehension of offenders. Effectively, this is rather like closely monitoring the back door of a large public venue while leaving the front door open and unattended.

So if the aim of sex offender commitment legislation is seen as more than sheer preventive detention of certain categories of sex offenders, individually, it fails at that larger goal of sex-crime prevention by inaccurate, unwise misallocation of monetary resources. As Sherwin concludes: "It would be hard to imagine that legislation that continued to inflict deprivations on people would remain immune from a bill of attainder challenge once the legislative purpose relied upon when putting it forth was shown to be ineffective".[2]

In the case of Minnesota's sex offender commitment legislation, a collective provision applicable to commitment under either of those two laws now requires that anyone released from MSOP must serve ten years thereafter on 'conditional release', just the same as every sex

1 *Supra, at p. 1447.*

2 *Ibid, p. 1336.*

offender released from prison must serve that same conditional release period, as part of the sentence itself for their sex crime(s). Indeed, the requirement for that term of conditional release as to commitment release *defines itself* by reference to the same requirement in the sex offender sentencing statute.

This means, quite flatly, that at least this part of the MSOP commitment scheme in Minnesota is expressly *penal*, due to the unquestionably punitive character of that ten-year term of 'conditional release'. In turn, that punitive character swings wide the door to raising a bill of attainder claim and, indeed, even a double jeopardy claim, against those Minnesota commitment statutes. Note that double jeopardy requires punitive character, in the sense of *criminal* penalties, whereas attainder requires only 'penal' character, a much broader term including, e.g., loss of employment.

A separate point from violation of the Bill of Attainder Clauses, but one closely related to it, is that such sex offender commitment laws also present a violation of substantive due process as 'status offense' laws. In this regard, analogously consider In re Gault[1]. Gault involved a juvenile in a 'delinquency' proceeding. Gault held that, regardless that such proceedings are not 'criminal' in nature, the right against self-incrimination applied therein. The Supreme Court observed that such proceedings "may lead to commitment to a state institution ... For this purpose, at least, commitment is a deprivation of liberty. It is incarceration against one's will, whether it is called 'criminal' or 'civil'."

The same considerations apply to sex offender commitments. Indeed, in some states, and in the case of the federal government, commitment facilities are actually located within prisons and are operated under the aegis of the prison administration outright. Other states, like Minnesota, while physically separating prisons and such sex offender commitment facilities, operate the latter either exactly the same as, or in ways materially indistinguishable from, prisons. All of this supports the view that, effectively, all rights applicable in 'criminal cases' must likewise extend as well to commitment cases.

Among these are the concepts that no one should be punished for a sheer 'status offense', and that vague provisions in such statutes, because they result in deprivations of liberty, must be held to the most rigorous standard of clarity and specificity, and that proof of the statutory elements required to commit must be by proof beyond a reasonable doubt.

---

1 387 U.S. 1, 87 S.Ct. 1428, 18 L.Ed.2d 527 (1967).

In sum, a very strong argument can be made that sex offender commitment legislation comprises a bill of attainder as to the classes thereby made subject to so-called civil commitment as preventive detention. It is hoped that, in the near future, courts will have the impartiality and the courage to acknowledge the basic human rights of sex offenders necessary to so rule, and thereby strike down such legislation.

However, if not, recall from the outset of this work, the cautionary tale of Mr. Sullivan in Great Britain. Europeans, at least, recognize such rights. By their refusal to honor our laws, such as extradition, because of sex offender commitment as a categorical peril facing every sex offender in this country, they highlight our embarrassing misuse of law in this way. Therefore, without waiting for courts to drop that axe, we should repeal such laws, and pursue the overarching goal of reducing or even eliminating sex crimes in this country by far more sensible and cost-effective means that affect all potential sex offenders, not merely some small sliver of those imprisoned for past sex offenses.

It's time to take a lesson from history.

In 1807, speaking against a proposal to allow then-President Jefferson to preventively detain certain individuals, Representative Randolph of Virginia (otherwise a political ally of Jefferson) spoke these words in Congress in opposition to that proposal:

> "... Attacks on the liberty of the people are ... made always in the persons of the vile and the worthless. But when precedent is once established in the case of bad men, who like pioneers go before to smoothe the way, good men tremble for their safety."
>
> *16 Annals of Congress 538 (1807)*

Michael L. Corrado, "Sex Offenders, Unlawful Combatants, and Preventive Detention"[1], applying this quote to the modern case of 'sexual predators' under the U.S. Supreme Court ruling in Kansas v Hendricks, supra, said this:

> "They were indeed the 'vile and the worthless' of Representative Randolph's speech, and they smoothed the way for the first indefinite detention of sane individuals ever explicitly approved by the [U.S. Supreme] Court for the purpose of preventing future harm.
>
> "It is true that for the most part those detained under the Kansas statute are persons who have been convicted of a crime, but by the time their detention begins, they

1 *84 North Carolina Law Rev. 77 at 114–15.*

> will have served their criminal sentences, and under other circumstances would be entitled to go free. *Their continued confinement is not based on what they have done, but on what they might do in the future. It is pure preventive detention, and it is for an indefinite period of time ...*".[1]

Corrado makes the point that, under the precedent of Hendricks, any individuals or groups thought 'dangerous' can now be indefinitely detained as just such additional instances of preventive detention. Overlooked though it may be, such preventive detention violates the prohibition on 'bills of attainder'. To prevent this trend from changing our nation into a totalitarian nightmare along the lines of *1984* and *Minority Report*, we must work politically to strike such preventive detention laws, and to clearly amend the Constitution to confirm that such laws *must not stand.*

Nor is this merely a 'fringe' alarmist view. No less a personage than Eric S. Janus, Vice-Dean of William Mitchell College of Law (St. Paul, MN), in his provocative yet rigorously analytical book, *Failure To Protect: America's Sexual Predator Laws And The Rise Of The Preventive State*[2], expands upon this very real prospect thus:

> "... [Sexual predator] laws allow the establishment of an expansive alternate system of justice, in which radical prevention prevails at the expense of liberty. Sexual predator laws do this by reintroducing and relegitimizing the concept of the degraded other. Membership in this outsider group is then used to rationalize a diminished system of justice, in which the normal protections of the Constitution do not apply.
>
> "Here is the cause for alarm: the predator laws ... may jump from the relatively narrow realm of sexual violence to the radically broader universe of providing protection from the risk of crime — and terrorism — in general.[3]
>
> "... The preventive state claims the right to deprive people of liberty before criminal action is afoot. Under this approach, it is enough that there is a potential for harm, that the individual's psychological makeup — or political inclinations — poses a grave risk. This attitude rips a large hole in the fabric of our American concept of justice ...

1 *Emphases supplied.*

2 *Cornell Univ. Press, 2006.*

3 *Ibid, pp. 94–95.*

> "If the government can lock up sexual predators in advance of their [predicted] crimes, why not other criminals? Why not terrorists? Why not political subversives? What is to stop the state from assessing all of us for 'risk' and locking up prophylactically those whose RQ — risk quotient — is assessed above an arbitrary threshold?"[1]

Judges have declined to halt this slide into this tyranny of fear. Therefore, only we, the people, can stop it.

And stop it we must.

1 *Ibid., pp. 4–5.*

Appendices

Appendix 1

Glossary of Legal, Technical and Obscure Terms

Ad hominem

An argument appealing to the emotions of the listener or reader based on asserted personal, detractive attributes, rather than to the merits of a logical position.

Anti-sexuality

Opposition to acknowledgement of the sexual nature of humanity, to recognition or emphasis of sexual matters, and to involvement of anyone in any form of sexual activity with anyone, with the possible exception of vaginal coitus for the sole reason of attempted procreation; an emotional revulsion from sexual activity or any thought thereof.

Antisocial personality disorder

A personality disorder characterized by chronic antisocial behavior and violation of the law and the rights of others.

APD

(See: Antisocial personality disorder)

Actuarial risk assessment. See text.

Clinical risk assessment. See text.

Base rates

As applicable herein, historically derived percentages of recidivism in a large-scale statistical cohort of sex offenders in general, as a starting point from which to calculate the asserted impacts of various factors in a given RAI as to elevation of predicted probability-percentages of recidivism likelihood as to a given sex offender.

Bill of Attainder

A legislative act pronouncing a person or group subject to punishment by sheer definition, rather than for future commission of a crime or other future violation of law (unconstitutional in the U.S.).

Bona fides

Good faith; the absence of fraud or deceit; the state of being exactly as claims or appearances indicate.

Boondoggle

An unnecessary, wasteful project or undertaking.

Bootstrapping

As applied to logical and legal argumentation, the practice of first proving one point and then using that first proven point as a premise to prove a second point. It is also applied derisively to invalid argumentation where the first point is not proven, but established only by fiat or ipsedixitism, rendering the second point merely a product of such sheer declaration, rather than by logically valid conclusion.

Burden of persuasion

The burden of convincing the jury or the court, as the trier of the issue or issues of fact; the ultimate burden of proof.

Burden of production of evidence

The burden of initial production of evidence to show the merit of the plaintiff/moving party's case to a threshold requirement before being allowed to proceed further.

Burden of proof

A general term reflecting the duty of establishing, either at some preliminary point in an adversarial proceeding or at trial the truth of a given proposition or issue by the standard of proof required at the respective stage and considering the type of case in which the issue arises.

Calumny

A false statement made maliciously to injure another's reputation.

Coding rules

In use of a risk assessment instrument, the accompanying set of rules specific to that particular RAI which dictate whether and under what circumstances a point or points are to be assessed in a given "factor" of the RAI as to the assessed sex offender and how assessed points for different factors are to be cumulated to an overall raw score for translation to a reoffense probability-percentage prediction.

Collateral estoppel

A form of the doctrine of estoppel by judgment broader that the limits of res judicata based upon the equitable principles of finality and previous passed up opportunity to litigate an issue at a time when fairness dictates it should have been litigated, if at all.

Complexity theory

The study of how, and the extent to which order, structure, and pattern may arise or be discerned from extremely complicated, apparently chaotic systems.

Confidence interval

A statistical range with a specified probability that a given parameter lies within the range.

Criminogenic needs

Volitions or desires producing a crime.

Cross-validation

The ARA research technique of applying the factor-coding, scoring, and reoffense percentages derived from the overall sampling used to construct a given RAI to a different large-scale sample, with an eye to determine whether the individual factors and combinations of factor found to yield percentage elevations in the RAI' s "construction sample" also yield the same percentage elevations in the other large-scale sample.

De facto

In fact; as things are, regardless of and as distinguished from "de jure," by right.

Discovery, pre-trial

The compulsory disclosure before trial of certain facts and/or documents to the opposing party in a judicial case.

Disorder

. Any of a large array of conditions (not "mental illnesses") set forth has a separate category by the Diagnostic and Statistical Manual, 5th edition ("DSM-V) of the American Psychiatric Association simply from the collective impressions of a panel of psychiatrists. Each of these "disorders" employ vague, ambiguous, and multiple-alternative elements of potentially endless applicability with no true basis in science. Most of these have been criticized as politically prompted, not for facilitation of treatment, but to justify harsher criminal sentencing outcomes and to create an otherwise nonexistent basis for commitment.

Double jeopardy

Putting one already tried and acquitted of a crime on trial a second time for the same crime or punishing one a second time for a crime as to which the person was already punished.

Dynamic risk factors

Including both risk-increasing and "protective" factors which are subject to change over time, either in response to changed external circumstances or internal mental/emotional factors, or simply as the natural progression of human life and aging, these non-static factors are thought to significantly alter every individual sex offender's prospect for reoffense. However, in any given sex offender's personal instance, unknown factors, factors of unknown or immeasurable significance, and different qualitative and quantitative impacts of generally recognized factors, all greatly confound efforts to estimate effects of recognized dynamic risk factors, as well as of static factors.

Dysfunction

An invention of the DSM-V allowing a "diagnosis" of the effective equivalent of a "disorder," even when one or more of the required elements of a given disorder are absent.

Ex post facto

Enacted or operating retroactively.

Expert testimony

The opinion of an expert witness; the testimony of persons who are particularly skilled, learned, or experienced in a particular art, science, trade, business, profession, or vocation a thorough knowledge of which is not possessed by men in general, in regard to matters connected therewith.

Extropunitivity

The urge to act in a harsh, punitive manner against those considered to be revolting, including to one's sense of sexual comfort. This emotionally based reaction has a definite footing in the need to deny in oneself the sexual motivations projected onto the victims of extropunitive actions, and provides a rationalization for dehumanization of such victims.

Falsus in uno (Falsus in uno, falsus in omnibus)

(Literally: False in one thing, false in everything) The general principle of law that where a witness has testified falsely to some material matter in a cause, the jury may choose to disregard all of his testimony in other respects, unless it is corroborated by other proof.

Generalizability

Generally, the ability to derive a general principle from particular facts or observations applicable generally to all other circumstances deemed materially similar; as to statistical derivation of recidivism probability predictions in sex offender actuarial risk assessment, the generally applicable validity of such calculated probabilities to those individuals and groups of individuals not within the construction sample.

Ibid

Latin term for 'in the same place'.

Indicia

Indications of a given trait, state, or quality.

Intensive Supervised Release

As employed in the Minnesota Department of Corrections, this may be thought of as 'super-parole.' Lengthy lists of prohibitions and requirements are included, as well as provision for close monitoring and surveillance of the prison releasee. See description at text, pages 100, 103-104, 186-187, and 193-194.

Inter alia

Latin for 'among others'. A term used in legal pleading to indicate that a particular statute set out therein is only a part of the statute that is relevant to the facts of the lawsuit and not the entire statute.

Ipsedixitism

The practice of making assertions without proof that may be baseless in fact, but which are to be accepted as true without question or challenge purely on the asserted authority of the asserting person.

Ipso facto

Latin for 'by the fact itself', meaning without need for proof or logical process.

Judicial notice

Facts which a judge may properly take notice of without proof because they are already known to him and are beyond any reasonable dispute.

Junk-science

Proclaimed conclusions from purported application of scientific principles in derivation of which either: (a) the asserted principle(s) is/ are nonexistent, false, or inapplicable to the instance at hand; (b) the method of application thereof is incorrect for any reason; (c) the facts to which such principles is/are applied are not correct or are significantly inaccurate; (d) proper scientific method has not been followed in any other way; or (e) representation, exaggerations, errors, misperceptions, unjustified characterizations, overgeneralization, or any other kind of unscientific or anti-scientific method or deductive or inferential process has deprived the proclaimed conclusion of its scientific validity.

Monahan factors

These factors, merely intuited by Monahan, were designed to estimate, purely as a means of 'guided clinical risk assessment, a person's tendency toward recidivating a violent (not sexual) act. Subsequently, these factors were applied sua sponte by the Minnesota Supreme Court to sex offender commitment case despite their baseless applicability to sex-crime recidivism.

Necessary and proper (Clause U.S. Constitution, Article I, Section 8, Clause 18)

Relied upon by the U.S. Supreme Court in the Comstock case (2010), this clause generally authorizes Congress to pass all laws "necessary and proper" to carry out enumerated powers of the federal government. In Comstock, the federal sex offender commitment law (applicable to federal prisoners) was held authorized as "necessary and proper" to the power to punish (as opposed to treat).

Non-routine sample

As to a specific RAI (notably, the Static-series RAIs), the unscientific, anti-actuarial rater option of using, in place of the general statistical cohort of sex offenders, the far-higher base rate of a unique sample of sex offenders selected for attributes deemed to make them more likely sex crime recidivists. Because such non-routine attributes reprise to some degree the "factors" which are then used to elevate a rated sex offender's reoffense probability, a duplication of such risk-elevation thereby occurs, drastically overstating the rated offender's probability of reoffense.

Nonsequitur

An inference or conclusion that does not logically follow from the premises or evidence.

Pedophilia / Paedophilia

The act or fantasy on the part of an adult of sexual activity with a child; also, an asserted type of "sexual disorder," according to the Diagnostic and Statistical Manual, version 5, of the American Psychiatric Association.

Pedosexual

A person whose main sexual attraction is toward either male or female children or both at or below the age of puberty.

Pedosexuality

A primary sexual interest or attraction toward either male or female children or both at or below the age of puberty.

Peer review

The process of critical intensive examination by other academicians and/or professionals of the relevant academic discipline unaffiliated with the submitting researcher of the data and methodology used by that researcher and of the integrity and accuracy of the conclusions reached by that researcher culminating from data research and statistical analysis employed.

Plethysmography

Use of an instrument that measures variations in size/turgidity of the human penis on the basis of the amount of blood present within it as a means of determining the existence and extent of sexual arousal in response to a given stimulus, typically visual, audio, or audiovisual.

Preventive detention

The practice of detaining/confining/incarcerating individuals other than as sentencing for criminal conviction(s), due to their suspected tendency/predisposition to commit crimes in order to prevent such commission.

Probable cause hearing

A preliminary judicial inquiry to determine whether there is sufficient "probable cause" in the facts to justify holding a defendant either accused of crime or petitioned for sex offender commitment for trial.

Psychopathy

A mental disorder manifested by amoral, aggressive or violent behavior without empathy or remorse.

RAI

A risk assessment instrument used in actuarial risk assessment.

Reasonable doubt

The required standard of proof for criminal conviction, demanding prosecution proof of guilt "beyond a reasonable doubt." Most states with sex offender commitment laws (but not Minnesota) also apply this standard of proof to such commitment trials.

Recidivate

To return to a previous pattern of criminal offense.

Recidivism

A tendency to recidivate.

Refuseniks

Those MSOP detainees who, for any reason, but typically including disillusionment with treatment as a means to achieve release, decline to participate in, or end their participation in treatment in MSOP.

Relapse prevention

A mode of cognitive-behavioral-type therapy originally designed for treatment of chemically dependent individuals, later applied to committed sex offenders on the inherently incorrect assumption that recidivism by sex offenders typically is a purported process of irresistible impulse, falsely likened to the urges of alcohol or drug addiction.

Res judicata

The principle that an existing final judgment rendered upon the merits, without fraud or collusion, by a court of competent jurisdiction, is conclusive of rights, questions, and facts in issue, as to the parties and all others whose rights stem from those parties, in all other actions in the same or any other judicial tribunal of concurrent jurisdiction

Re-weighting

As to the Static-99R and Static-2002R RAIs, the unscientific and anti-actuarial practice suggested by the test authors to raters of adjusting the predicted probability percentages based on rater impressions.

Scientific method

A method for obtaining knowledge, that requires repeated, systematic, and controlled observation (repeatable by independent observers), as opposed to information obtained from arbitrary authority.

Sexual disorder

A sub-category of the DSM-V category of disorders that includes just about every sexual minority in existence, save homosexuality (and would have, but for political infighting within the APA). Pedosexuality (denominated "pedophilia") is included, as well as fetishism of any imaginable description ('paraphilias').

Sexual predator

An unscientific, politically invented term meant to terrify and anger the populace about a conjured image of plotting, lurking rapists of random women and/or children. In the case of some of the states with sex offender commitment laws, original versions of such laws restricted their applicability to those who had used violence to perpetrate a sex crime, or who had sexually assaulted unknown women or unknown children, lending some credibility to use of that term. Recent revisions to such laws, however, have struck such limitations and indeed, have vastly expanded the crimes and the circumstances upon which commitment may be based.

Sexually dangerous person

(See elements at text, page 94) This tandem law, created in Minnesota's 1994 two-category sex offender commitment legislation, is known for its virtually limitless elements applicable to most sex offenders.

Sexually psychopathic personality

(See elements at text, page 89) This law was rewritten as part of Minnesota's two-category sex offense commitment legislation of 1994. Its elements, though vague, are regarded as more difficult to satisfy than the virtually boundless elements of its tandem, "Sexually Dangerous Persons" law. **Slander**

Oral communication of false statements injurious to a person's reputation.

Statistical cohort

A group of people defined for statistical purposes.

Supra

Latin word for 'above'. A legal term indicating that the matter under current consideration has appeared in the preceding pages of the text in which the reference is made.

Vituperation

An instance of harshly abusive, sustained censure; invective; denunciation.

Zero-percent public safety guarantee

Conceptually, an asserted assurance of public safety from crime victimization by achievement of a certainty of non-recidivism by one who has previously committed a crime, i.e., an unattainable 'zero percent' probability of reoffense by that offender.

Appendix 2

Index